Books by Robert Scheer

America After Nixon: The Age of the Multinationals
How the U.S. Got Involved in Vietnam

Co-author with Maurice Zeitlin

Cuba: Tragedy in Our Hemisphere

WITH ENOUGH SHOVELS

WITH ENOUGH SHOVELS

Reagan, Bush and Nuclear War

ROBERT SCHEER

with the assistance of Narda Zacchino
and Constance Matthiessen

RANDOM HOUSE · NEW YORK

Library of Congress Cataloging in Publication Data

Scheer, Robert.
With enough shovels.
1. Atomic warfare. 2. United States—Military policy.
3. United States—Politics and government—1981–
I. Title.
UF767.S2364 1982   355'.0217   82-40123
ISBN 0-394-41482-9

Manufactured in the United States of America
98765432
First Edition

Grateful acknowledgment is made to the following for permission to reprint previously published material:

Ambio: Excerpt from *Ambio*, the international journal of the human environment published by the Royal Swedish Academy of Sciences in Stockholm, Vol. 11, No. 2–3, 1982.

The Associated Press: "Arms Control Head: U.S. Nuclear Attack Possible" is reprinted by permission of The Associated Press.

The Bulletin of the Atomic Scientists: Excerpts from a speech by Jerry Hough at the conference on "Internal Security and Arms Control," April 1982; from "Running in Circles with the MX" by Christopher Paine; and from "Extreme Wrong on the Extreme Right" by Kosta Tsipis. Copyright © 1981, 1982 by the Educational Foundation for Nuclear Science, Chicago, IL 60637. Reprinted by permission of *The Bulletin of the Atomic Scientists*, a magazine of science and public affairs.

Commentary: Excerpts from "Why the Soviet Union Thinks It Could Fight and Win a Nuclear War" and "Soviet Global Strategy" by Richard Pipes, *Commentary*, July 1977 and April 1980. Copyright © 1977, 1980 by Richard Pipes. Excerpts from "The Case Against SALT II" by Eugene V. Rostow, *Commentary*, February 1979. Excerpts from "Making the World Safe for Communism" by Norman Podhoretz, *Commentary*, April 1976. Reprinted by permission; all rights reserved.

The Congressional Quarterly: Excerpt from the Republican Party Platform reprinted with the permission of Congressional Quarterly, Inc.

Daedalus: Excerpts from "The Relevance of Arms Control in the 1980s" by Richard Burt, Winter 1981. Reprinted by permission of *Daedalus*, Journal of the American Academy of Arts & Sciences, Cambridge, MA.

Dow Jones & Company, Inc.: Excerpt from "Fighting a Treaty, Nitze, Long a Backer of Arms

Studies, the Brookings Institution, and Edward A. Hewett, Senior Fellow in Foreign Policy Studies, the Brookings Institution.

The Stockholm International Peace Research Institute: Excerpt from *World Armaments and Disarmament Yearbook*, 1982. Copyright © 1982 by SIPRI, Bergshamra, S-171 73 Solna, Sweden.

United Press International: Specified excerpts reprinted courtesy of United Press International.

The Washington Post: Specified excerpts reprinted by permission; Copyright © 1977, 1979, 1981 by The Washington Post.

To my sons,
Christopher, Joshua and Peter

Don't put a loaded rifle on the stage unless someone intends to fire it.
   —Chekhov

HARVARD STUDENT: Do you believe the world is going to end, and, if you do, do you think it will be by an act of God or an act of man?

SECRETARY OF DEFENSE CASPAR W. WEINBERGER: I have read the Book of Revelation and, yes, I believe the world is going to end—by an act of God, I hope—but every day I think that time is running out.

HARVARD STUDENT: Are you scared?

WEINBERGER: I worry that we will not have enough time to get strong enough to prevent nuclear war. I think of World War II and how long it took to prepare for it, to convince people that rearmament for war was needed. I fear we will not be ready. I think time is running out . . . but I have faith.
   —"Washington Talk," August 23, 1982

Acknowledgments

I came upon the subject of this book as it emerged bit by bit in the words of the men who formed the Reagan Administration while I interviewed them on assignment for the *Los Angeles Times*. The book itself is an amplification of the work that I did for the paper, and I am grateful for the freedom and access which the *Times* granted me as I became increasingly concerned with the subject of the superpowers' drift toward nuclear war.

Six years ago two editors at the *Los Angeles Times*, William Thomas and Mark Murphy, hired me out of the rough-and-tumble world of magazine investigative journalism and introduced me to what remains a very sober and conservative publication. These *Times* editors laid down some good rules of the game as they wanted it played, and my grudging acceptance of the value of their approach marks something of a journalistic rite of passage.

But most importantly, it is through the *Times* that I met my wife, Narda Zacchino, who is the *Times* Bureau Chief in Sacramento and who provided critical direction to this book through each stage of the writing and editing, sacrificing months of evenings and weekends except when the legislature was in session or she was in labor with one of our newborns. Television writer and friend Lois Peyser has said that Narda is a cross between Mother Courage and Brenda Starr, and I would say more about Narda's contribution, but she is, after all, mentioned on the title page (although she tells me the typeface should have been bigger).

And then there is the big editor back in New York City who harassed me for years until he finally got a book out of it. This book is very much the product of the goading, lecturing, support, intimidation and above all education that I received from Random House editor Jason Epstein. I have never worked with anyone quite like Jason, whose brilliance and range of knowledge can be devastating when necessary as well as illuminating. Thanks to my word processor I found it easier to absorb Jason's seemingly endless requests and suggestions for clarification of ideas, improvement of style and introduction of common sense, all of which made this a far clearer and more readable book. At the risk of courting articles in the *Village Voice* about who actually wrote this book, I do want to confess that between Jason and Narda Zacchino it ended up a far better work than I alone would have been capable of. Jason and I were ably assisted at Random House by Laurie Stearns, who has been an excellent and very patient copy editor, and Beverly Haviland, who diligently checked the manuscript along with Laura Schultz.

Barry Golson, my editor at *Playboy*, once again provided his considerable editing talents and condensed the manuscript for publication in *Playboy*. My agent, Erica Spellman, as usual, brought her enthusiasm and expertise to this project.

Let me also acknowledge my indebtedness to Ronald Reagan for having, as a presidential candidate, been generous enough to spend many hours "putting up," as a far less gracious George Bush once complained to my editors, "with Scheer's vicious questions." Reagan is a man of strong convictions and a sense of humor, confident that his ideas can withstand challenge. At the beginning of one of our grueling sessions he leaned over to me and said in a stage whisper, "You know we'll have to stop meeting like this." I also want to thank Reagan's associates, Edwin Meese III, Michael Deaver, Richard Wirthlin, Vern Orr, Stu Spencer, William Casey, Jim Lake, Peter Hannaford and Maureen Reagan for their insights into Reagan's thought processes.

My original goal was to write about the Reagan phenomenon generally, but the Reaganites' attitudes toward the Soviets and nuclear war came early on to shout out for further investigation. I did not begin this task as an expert on nuclear war, and I am indebted to scores of those who are truly expert in the field. In particular I want to thank Hans Bethe, Roger Molander, Desmond Ball, Jerome Wiesner, Laurie Esposito, Dan Caldwell, Spurgeon Keeny, Herbert York, McGeorge Bundy, James Fallows, Jack Ruina, Christopher Payne and the Federation of American Scientists, Howard Hiatt, John Markoff, Cyrus Vance, Rusty Schweickart, Fred Kaplan, Andrew and Leslie Cockburn, Stan Norris and the Center for Defense Information, Gerald Warburg, Stanley Sheinbaum, Robert Shrum and Gordon Adams.

Connie Matthiessen, whom I stole from her job as a researcher for Governor Edmund G. Brown, was indispensable for everything except typing and spelling. For those last two tasks I have once again to thank the IBM display writer system 6360 which Marge Wilson at Security Pacific and Steve Millner at Wells Fargo helped finance and Nancy Krage of IBM made work. Connie Matthiessen compiled the notes and interviews at the back of this book, came up with many of the ideas and references and was in all sorts of intellectual and non-clerical ways an invaluable researcher. *Times* researcher Nina Green provided me with the source material that made the *Times* interviews reprinted in the book possible. We also benefited from the diligent research of Mary Zion at *Playboy*.

Less specifically, there is the journalist group of Amnesty International in Los Angeles, which has been my political nest these past few years and which includes Henry Weinstein and Laurie Becklund, two *L.A. Times* pros who kept me straight. There are too many people at the *Times* who helped me at one point or another in this work to mention all, but I must name Claudia Luther, Sharon Rosenhause, Tim Rutten, Bob Magnuson, David Shaw, Bill

Boyarsky, and John Dreyfuss as well as other friends Linda Douglass, John Phillips, Thea Golson, Maurice Zeitlin, Ann Weills, Dan Siegel, Betty Sheinbaum, Helen Zacchino, W. W. "Buzz" Wilms, Ann Dowie, Barry Weiss, Rachel Nitzberg, Jack and Kathy Schneider, Richard Fine and Linda Morse.

Times National Editor Dennis Britton and Assistant National Editors Linda Mathews and Stan Burroway were directly involved with all of the stories and interviews I did for the *Times* cited in this book, and made them better. They also supported my pursuit of this issue at the expense of other assignments.

Finally there is my mother, the garment worker, who at the age of eighty-two still reads far more than I and most of my friends do and who constantly undermines my efforts to become comfortably and conservatively middle-aged. She is allied with my ever-sharp and wonderful fifteen-year-old son, Christopher, in denying to me the joys of pomposity and arrogance that I might otherwise more fully embrace.

Contents

With
Enough
Shovels

1

Nuke War—and Birds

PRESIDENT Ronald Reagan had been in office less than a year when he approved a secret plan for the United States to prevail in a protracted nuclear war. This secret plan, outlined in a so-called National Security Decision Document, committed the United States for the first time to the idea that a global nuclear war can be won.

This book is about how our leaders during the time of Ronald Reagan have come to plan for waging and winning a nuclear war with the Soviet Union, and how they are obsessed with a strategy of confrontation—including nuclear brinksmanship—which aims to force the Soviets to shrink their empire and fundamentally alter their society.

"Nuke war," as Louis O. Giuffrida, whom Reagan named head of the Federal Emergency Management Agency, calls it, has come in the Reagan years to be discussed not only as a war that can be won, but as a war consistent with the preservation of civilization. "It would be a terrible mess, but it wouldn't be unmanageable," Giuffrida told ABC News. Or as Giuffrida's assistant in charge of the civil defense program, William Chipman, put it when I asked him if democracy and other American institutions would survive all-out nuclear war with the Soviet Union: "I think they would eventually, yeah. As I say, the ants eventually build another anthill."[1]

The idea that "nuke war" is survivable begins with the assertion that an effective civil defense is possible. Proponents of this view in the

Reagan Administration claim that civil defense can protect the Russian population, and, therefore, that Soviet military planners think they can survive and win a nuclear war. According to Reagan and his people, this confidence is one important reason for the Soviet military buildup and for our own urgent need to close the window of vulnerability—Reagan's phrase to describe the presumed vulnerability of the United States to a Soviet first strike. Ergo the renewed interest in America's civil defense, massive military spending and new Pentagon plans for waging a protracted nuclear war, what Reagan calls "the rearming of America."

This attitude results in part from the growing sophistication of nuclear weapons in the arsenals of both superpowers: weapons that can do more than destroy large populated areas; weapons whose accuracy and control are theoretically so refined that they tempt their makers to think they can be detonated not only as weapons of genocide or counter-genocide but as if they were conventional weapons, to take out selected enemy targets in a war that would be fought on a limited or at least less than catastrophic basis. In other words, a war with winners as well as losers.

Combined with this view is the idea that détente has not served us well, that the Soviets have not accepted its terms but instead have gained nuclear superiority. This argument was advanced by President Reagan, despite substantial disagreement among experienced people who have studied the question, as one justification for his $1.6 trillion five-year military program.[2]

Détente lost credit partly because it had been oversold from the beginning by its prime architects, former Secretary of State Henry A. Kissinger and former President Richard M. Nixon. While both the United States and the Soviet Union acknowledged that a nuclear arms control agreement could not be dependent upon the behavior of either superpower in unrelated areas, the hope nonetheless persisted that after an arms control agreement, the Soviet Union would moderate its other actions. The Soviet invasion of Afghanistan was taken by many as a betrayal of the spirit, if not the letter, of détente. That event, coming on the heels of apparent U.S. helplessness in the Iranian hostage crisis, added credibility to presidential candidate Reagan's attacks on détente and weakened President Jimmy Carter's defense of it.

Whatever its inherent defects, as long as we lived in the era of détente, with its seemingly endless arms control negotiations and other complex dealings between the superpowers, most Americans found it relatively easy to avoid thinking about nuclear annihilation. There was comfort in the knowledge that somewhere in the midst of all the interminable SALT talks, our respective leaders were trying to cut whatever deal was possible in the interest of their, and our, survival. One assumption of the détente period was that no matter how awful the other fellow might be, he still didn't want to commit nuclear suicide; that the instinct for self-preservation would win out over nationalist and ideological obsessions.

The notion that nuclear war means mutual suicide had for years been a basis of détente and arms control negotiations. It became obvious, however, as Reagan installed his people in high places, that all this had changed as many highly vociferous critics of détente and arms control moved into positions of authority in Washington, and attempts to live with the Soviets became more scorned than honored.

As we shall see, a Cold War cabal of unreconstructed hawks and neo-hawks who had never been at ease with the arms control efforts of the Nixon, Ford and Carter Administrations suddenly came into its own. The members of this group categorically reject peaceful coexistence with the Soviet Union as that country is now constituted. They seek instead through confrontation, through the use of political and economic pressure and the threat of military weapons, to radically alter the nature of Soviet society. They assume, as Reagan has stated, that "the Soviet Union underlies all the unrest that is going on. If they weren't engaged in this game of dominoes, there wouldn't be any hot spots in the world."[3] Convinced that the nuclear arms race is dangerous not in itself but only if the Soviets gain "superiority," they have shifted the emphasis of American foreign policy from the avoidance of nuclear war to the preparation for its possible outbreak.

As Eugene Rostow, the man Reagan put in charge of disarmament, had written before being selected for this important post: "We are living in a pre-war and not a post-war world. . . ."[4] Unfortunately, to use such a phrase as "pre-war" in reference to World War III is to invoke the specter of nuclear-war-fighting, as high officials of the Reagan government have repeatedly confirmed.

For example, we are now committed to what Deputy Defense Secretary Frank Carlucci III, in his Senate confirmation hearing, called a "nuclear-war-fighting capability,"[5] a position that presupposes that nuclear war can be kept limited, survivable and winnable.

In 1981, Defense Secretary Caspar Weinberger told the House Budget Committee that the Reagan Administration would expand the

U.S. capability "for deterring *or prosecuting* [italics mine] a global war with the Soviet Union."[6]

Halfway through Reagan's first year in office, Weinberger presented the President with a defense spending plan by which the United States could gain nuclear superiority over the Soviet Union within this decade. The goal, according to senior Pentagon officials, was to build a capacity to fight nuclear wars that range from a limited strike to an all-out exchange.[7]

One of those who helped provide Reagan the basis for his war-fighting views was former Harvard historian Richard Pipes. In 1978, before he was appointed the senior Soviet specialist on Reagan's National Security Council staff, Pipes criticized the nuclear war plans of previous Administrations, both Republican and Democratic, because "deeply imbedded in all our plans is the notion of punishing the aggressor rather than defeating him."[8] Or as Energy Secretary James B. Edwards put it, in a nuclear war, "I want to come out of it number one, not number two."

In a telephone interview with me in the fall of 1981, Charles Kupperman, a Reagan appointee to the Arms Control and Disarmament Agency, said that "it is possible for any society to survive" a nuclear war. He added that "nuclear war is a destructive thing, but still in large part a physics problem."[9]

Reagan's first year was continuously marked by such comments about waging nuclear war in some form or other. The President himself claimed that it would be possible to keep a nuclear war on the European continent limited to a tactical exchange, thereby making Western Europeans more nervous than they had been in some time.[10]

When word of the Administration's stance toward nuclear war began to spread, the result was a powerful sense of alarm among the general public, both in this country and abroad. By the end of Reagan's first year, public opinion polls were showing that proposals for a bilateral freeze on additional nuclear weapons were being approved by two-to-one margins. Massive demonstrations took place in Europe and the United States involving hundreds of thousands of people protesting the nuclear arms race. Whatever else Reagan and his aides may have accomplished, they greatly stimulated the dormant peace movement in the free world and gave the Russians a fine opportunity to trumpet far and wide that the United States was the more bellicose of the two superpowers, the greater threat to human survival.

By the spring of 1982, the Administration realized that it had got itself into deep trouble on this issue and began to alter its public posture. Reagan's pollster Richard Wirthlin told me in March 1982 that peace would be the big issue of the 1982 elections if the economy started performing well. In the spring of 1982 Wirthlin's polls, like everyone else's, showed strong support for a nuclear freeze. It was then that Reagan floated his so-called START proposal. START stands for Strategic Arms Reduction Talks and represented a replay of Reagan's successful ploy in his preelection debate with Carter, when he called for bilateral arms reductions in an effort to counter Carter's portrayal of Reagan as a warmonger.

Reagan's call for deep reductions in nuclear weapons during the campaign and in his START proposal may have been meant once again to divert attention from the demise of a SALT II treaty that Reagan had opposed, that had taken six years to negotiate and that put real limits on the number and characteristics of Soviet ICBM launchers, presumably the very ICBMs that are the source of our fears.

The Soviets were not likely to accept Reagan's START proposal because it takes from them half of their ICBM force while leaving ours relatively undisturbed. Former Secretary of State Edmund S. Muskie in fact suggested that START "may be a secret agenda for sidetracking *disarmament* while the United States gets on with *rearmament*—in a hopeless quest for superiority in these things."[11] Even so, the proposal made for good public relations.

With the START announcement, the Administration showed it had learned its lesson and thereafter would try not to alarm the public as it pursued its strategic arms buildup. From then on, there would be little public talk about nuclear-war-fighting. The interviews that other journalists and I had conducted with top Administration officials on nuclear-war-fighting and survival would be harder to come by. At least that was the plan, but such profound changes in U.S. defense strategy as were even then being conceived in the Defense Department and the White House were bound to leak out and would raise serious questions about the Administration's intent in the START talks.

In May 1982, a United Press International report by Helen Thomas stated:

A senior White House official said Reagan approved an eight-page national security document that "undertakes a campaign aimed at internal reform in the Soviet Union and shrinkage of the Soviet empire." He affirmed that it could be called "a full-court press" against the Soviet Union.[12]

(A full-court press is a basketball expression that describes an attempt to wrest the ball away from one's opponent in his own territory.)

This remarkable statement reflects the views of Reagan's Soviet expert Pipes, who had said in early 1981 that "Soviet leaders would have to choose between peacefully changing their Communist system . . . or going to war."[13] At the time, the Administration had sought to downplay Pipes's statement, but by the spring of 1982, this view seemed to have become official policy.

On May 30, 1982, a week after that UPI story, *New York Times* Pentagon correspondent Richard Halloran broke the story of the 1982 five-year Defense Guidance Plan. His article began with the following statement:

> Defense Department policy-makers, in a new five-year defense plan, have accepted the premise that nuclear conflict with the Soviet Union could be protracted and have drawn up their first strategy for fighting such a war.[14]

The document was signed by Defense Secretary Weinberger. It outlined the detailed strategy to be pursued by the Pentagon for the next five years but was intended as a general guide for the next decade as well.

It would be difficult to exaggerate the implications of this strategy document, for it resolves a debate in the highest councils of government and places the United States for the first time squarely on the side of those extremists in this country and in the Soviet Union who believe in the possibilities of fighting and winning a protracted nuclear war. As the *Times* put it:

> The nature of nuclear war has been a subject of intense debate among political leaders, defense specialists and military officers. Some assert that there would be only one all-out mutually destructive exchange. Others argue that a nuclear war with many exchanges could be fought over days and weeks.
>
> The outcome of the debate will shape the weapons, communications and strategy for nuclear forces. The civilian and military planners, having decided that protracted nuclear war is possible, say that American nuclear forces "must prevail and be able to force the Soviet Union to seek earliest termination of hostilities on terms favorable to the United States."

The nuclear war strategy outlined in the document aims at the "decapitation" of the Soviet political leadership as well as preventing communication between the leadership and forces in the field. It specifies further that the Chinese would be granted military assistance to keep Soviet forces pinned down on their eastern border. In addition, psychological warfare, sabotage and guerrilla warfare operations would be improved. All of this presumably has to do with the full-court press on the Soviet empire.

According to the *Times,* the document specified that "space would have to be exploited for American military needs."[15]

Halloran underscored the significance of this Administration's departure from the attitudes of its predecessors on the matter of nuclear-war-fighting when he wrote:

In many parts of this document, the Reagan military planners started with a blank sheet of paper. Their views on the possibility of protracted nuclear war differ from those of the Carter administration's military thinkers, as do their views on global conventional war and particularly on putting economic pressure on the Soviet Union.

The Defense Department's plan disturbed such experts as Nobel physicist Hans Bethe, who headed the Theoretical Physics Division of Los Alamos Scientific Laboratory during the Manhattan Project in World War II. Bethe and physicist Kurt Gottfried wrote that the plan "comes close to a declaration of war on the Soviet Union and contradicts and may destroy President Reagan's initiatives toward nuclear arms control."[16]

Nor did the professional military unanimously applaud these ideologically derived war-fighting plans. For example, the *Washington Post* reported on June 19, 1982, that General David C. Jones, who had retired as Chairman of the Joint Chiefs of Staff, "left office yesterday with the warning that it would be throwing money in a 'bottomless pit' to try to prepare the United States for a long nuclear war with the Soviet Union."[17] The newspaper said General Jones doubted that any nuclear exchange between the Soviets and the United States could be contained, but would escalate into an all-out war. According to the article: " 'I don't see much of a chance of nuclear war being limited or protracted,' said Jones, who has pondered various doomsday scenarios.... 'I see great difficulty' in keeping any kind of nuclear exchange between the United States and the Soviet Union from escalating."

Despite the reservations of the general and others in and out of the military, the Reagan Administration almost immediately reaffirmed its commitment to plans and programs in support of protracted nuclear war. In the summer of 1982, a Pentagon master plan to implement Reagan's strategic policy was drafted. It lays out specific military hardware requirements and nuclear targeting adjustments necessary to wage a protracted war. Unlike the Defense Guidance Plan described by Halloran in the *New York Times,* which is an internal Pentagon document, the new master plan, as I reported in the *Los Angeles Times,* was drawn up in response to a secret White House directive, called a National Security Decision Document—which mandated that the Defense Department provide a program for implementing Reagan's nuclear war policy. Reagan's NSDD is the first declaratory policy statement of a U.S. Administration to proclaim that U.S. strategic forces must be able to win a protracted nuclear war. This goes considerably beyond earlier tendencies toward nuclear-war-fighting strategies.

It is true that nuclear war game-playing has been a favorite pastime of some of the most prestigious strategic and military thinkers on both sides of the Cold War ever since the bomb was born. A growing and ominous interest in theories of nuclear-war-fighting preceded Reagan, although his Administration was the first to embrace the doctrine so enthusiastically. There have always been theoretical discussions of limited nuclear war, and military strategists on both sides have increasingly toyed with such a possibility as they planned their hypothetical strikes against enemy targets. Though both the Soviets and the Americans continued to declare in public that nuclear war for any worthwhile goal was unthinkable, planning for such a war by the military staffs of the two superpowers continued nonetheless, as we know from admissions by former members of the U.S. government and from Soviet military manuals that have found their way to the West.

In the 1940s and 1950s, when the United States enjoyed nuclear superiority, there was much support and planning within the U.S. government for a first-strike option. Marcus Raskin and Daniel Ellsberg, both of whom worked on strategic policy in the Kennedy government, claim that a first strike was actively considered during Kennedy's first year in office. Indeed, as late as 1962, a month after the Cuban missile crisis, as then-Defense Secretary Robert McNamara told me in a recent interview, the Air Force was urging President Kennedy to allocate resources for such a capability, which the President and his Defense Secretary rejected.[18] McNamara opposed the first-strike option, but he endorsed the policy of providing a nuclear shield for Europe, a policy he has since disavowed.

A decade later, in the Ford Administration, another Secretary of Defense, James Schlesinger, would go considerably further and recommend the capacity to carry out surgical—meaning limited and accurate —nuclear strikes against the enemy. Schlesinger was much criticized for these views, but later in the Carter Administration, a similar idea emerged in the form of Presidential Directive 59, a still-secret proposal which some claim contained options for limited nuclear strikes on military targets on the assumption that civilian fatalities could be kept within acceptable limits, as in conventional warfare.

Some Carter insiders claim that PD 59 was drawn up merely so that Carter could appear tough in the 1980 election rather than as a serious change in military doctrine. Others take an even more benign view of its contents. Cyrus Vance, Secretary of State during the Carter Administration, told me:

> What PD 59 was talking about was providing a range of options to the President so he had some element of choice and making sure that the only response need not be a total spasmodic launching of everything we've got. And that has been developing over a period of years. By "that" I mean providing a range of options to the President. Taking that step did not mean, in my judgment, that anybody believed you could fight a sustained nuclear war along the lines that some of the people in the new Administration are talking about. That . . . is fallacious, and totally unrealistic.[19]

However, Roger Molander, who was on Zbigniew Brzezinski's National Security Council staff under Carter, believes that National Security Advisor Brzezinski and his military aide William Odom actually did intend PD 59, which they wrote without the knowledge of the State Department or the CIA, to commit the Carter Administration to a nuclear-war-fighting stance. But he added that despite Brzezinski's intention, Carter and Secretary of State Muskie, as well as Secretary of Defense Harold Brown, softened its meaning in subsequent public renditions.

For example, Harold Brown explained PD 59 at the Naval War College by saying, "Nothing in the policy contemplates that nuclear war can be a deliberate instrument of achieving our national security goals, because it cannot be. But we cannot afford the risk that the Soviet leadership might entertain the illusion that nuclear war could be an option—or its threat a means of coercion—for *them.*" Brown added that "we have no illusions about what a nuclear war would mean for mankind. It would be an unimaginable catastrophe." As for limited nuclear war, Brown stated, "We know that what might start as a supposedly controlled, limited strike could well—in my view would very likely—escalate to a full-scale nuclear war."[20] Brown has also stated that nuclear superiority, no matter how it is defined, would be meaningless "if both nations had been reduced to radioactive rubble in the meantime."

Whatever the Carter Administration may actually have intended by PD 59, it no doubt planted the seed of nuclear-war-fighting at the highest level; the Reagan government has built the hothouse. The Reagan Administration's NSDD 13, which superseded PD 59, went further than the Carter document in specifically proclaiming that the goal of U.S. policy is to *prevail* in a protracted nuclear war. Carter's PD 59 stopped short of a declaration that nuclear war could be won.

The difference between Carter's position and what was to become the position of the Reagan Administration was acknowledged by Colin Gray, a leading advocate of the nuclear-war-fighting school and oddly now a top arms control adviser to the Reagan government. In 1980, at the time of the shift in Carter's policy, Gray wrote:

> To advocate . . . targeting flexibility and selectivity is not the same as to advocate a war-fighting, war-survival strategy . . . victory or defeat in nuclear war is possible, and such a war may have to be waged to that point; and, the clearer the vision of successful war termination, the more likely war can be waged intelligently at earlier stages.[21]

In this *Foreign Policy* article, Gray and his co-author Keith Payne complained that "many commentators and senior U.S. government officials consider it [nuclear war] a non-survivable event." Instead, Gray presented the nuclear-war-fighters' alternative vision:

> The United States should plan to defeat the Soviet Union and to do so at a cost that would not prohibit U.S. recovery. Washington should identify war aims that in the last resort would contemplate the destruction of Soviet political authority and the emergence of a postwar world order compatible with Western values.

Gray proposed that "a combination of counterforce offensive targeting, civil defense, and ballistic missile and air defense should hold U.S. casualties down to a level compatible with national survival and recovery." The "compatible" level he had in mind would leave twenty million dead.

While notions of nuclear-war-fighting had been advocated in previous Administrations, within the Reagan government the nuclear-war-fighters are apparently unchallenged. The policies and budget priorities of the new Administration proclaim that the unthinkable can now be planned without hesitation. This development has alarmed many of the key architects of America's strategic defense policy. One of these is Dr. Herbert York, a veteran of the Manhattan Project, which created the first atomic bomb, who was formerly director of California's Lawrence Livermore Laboratory, one of the nation's main developers of nuclear weapons. York, who was the director of Defense Research and Engineering under President Kennedy, told me in an interview in April 1982:

> What's going on right now is that the crazier analysts have risen to higher positions than is normally the case. They are able to carry their ideas further and higher because the people at the top are simply less well-informed than is normally the case. Neither the current President nor his immediate backers in the White House nor the current Secretary of Defense have any experience with these things, so when the ideologues come in with their fancy stories and with their selected intelligence data, the President and the Secretary of Defense believe the last glib person who talked to them.

An alternative view, dominant in the Reagan Administration, was offered by Richard Perle, Assistant Secretary of Defense for International Security Policy and a major architect of the Pentagon's five-year war-fighting plan, who told me:

> I've always worried less about what would happen in an actual nuclear exchange than the effect that the nuclear balance has on our willingness to take risks in local situations. It is not that I am worried about the Soviets attacking the United States with nuclear weapons confident that they will win that nuclear war. It is that I worry about an American President feeling he cannot afford to take action in a crisis because Soviet nuclear forces are such that, if escalation took place, they are better poised than we are to move up the escalation ladder.[22]

Perle strongly believes that we can stockpile nuclear weapons and threaten to use them without increasing the risks of nuclear war. When I asked him about the fear of the nuclear arms race expressed by such groups as Physicians for Social Responsibility, he replied:

> I am as aware as they [anti-nuclear weapons advocates] are of the presence
> of nuclear weapons in the world. I'm more confident about our ability to
> deter war, nevertheless, than they are, and that is based partly on some
> judgments about history . . .

Perle's "judgments about history" begin with the assumption, as he
told me, that the Soviet Union is much like Hitler's Germany, inexorably bent on world conquest unless an aroused West intervenes. Like
many others in the Administration, he fears that the danger of appeasement far exceeds that of nuclear escalation.

Reagan's director of the Arms Control and Disarmament Agency,
Eugene V. Rostow, echoed Perle's fear that we are up against another
Hitler. In 1976 Rostow wrote: "Our posture today is comparable to
that of Britain, France and the United States during the Thirties.
Whether we are at the Rhineland or the Munich watershed remains
to be seen."[23] When I interviewed Rostow in 1981 he told me, "I do
not think the real danger of the situation is nuclear war and mass
destruction, I think the danger is political coercion, based on the threat
of mass destruction . . . And that is very real. You can smell it."[24]

What Rostow, Perle and others who insist on this analogy ignore,
among other things, is that neither the Allies nor Germany possessed
nuclear weapons at the time of Munich. Would even a madman like
Hitler have attempted world conquest—would his generals have allowed him to—if French and British missiles had been holding Berlin
hostage? Nor would Perle find much support outside his own tight
cabal of anti-Soviet hard-liners for the idea that Soviet leadership is
driven by the same furies that possessed Hitler. As for the Soviets
themselves, who have their own memories of Hitler, the analogy can
only be enraging.

There are two possible inferences to be drawn from this recent
intensification of American rhetoric. Either the Reagan Administration, while believing that nuclear war is catastrophic, has chosen to play
nuclear chicken with the Soviets with the intention of changing their
political system and challenging their empire, or the United States
really has abandoned the view that nuclear war is inevitably cataclysmic
and believes that nuclear weapons can be detonated as viable instruments of policy.

The implications of either position are disturbing. As the Australian

Desmond Ball, a leading authority on strategic policy and research associate at the International Institute for Strategic Studies in 1979–80, said when I asked him about Reagan's shift toward a nuclear-war-fighting policy:

> It is coming closer to reality, but more than likely it won't become a reality because you can't do it. What is dangerous is that these characters will think that they can do it . . . that they do have the capabilities for controlling a nuclear war. And they don't. They are deluding themselves. They are deluding themselves in strategic terms because the U.S. has now put itself in a position where in places, most specifically in Europe but also in other places, where if push comes to shove, they rely on the ability to deter the Russians by threatening to have a limited nuclear attack.[25]

I conducted this interview with Ball soon after he published his much acclaimed study "Can Nuclear War Be Controlled?" which showed, at painstaking length, that it cannot be, and underscored the incalculable horror that is nuclear war.[26] It was a needed reminder—for the reality of nuclear war is often ignored in the nuclear-war-fighting debate.

Although I have spent much of the past three years reporting for the *Los Angeles Times* on our drift toward nuclear war, there are times when I still lose my sense of the utter devastation that lies behind the sterile acronyms by which these modern weapons are described. The words have grown stale after nearly four decades of so-called "strategic" development. We hear about SLCMs and MIRVs, or of that weird hodgepodge of nuclear-war-fighting strategies—the window of vulnerability, the first-strike scenarios, the city-strips—and after a while the mind doesn't react with the appropriate horror.

The question of universal death grows stale partly because the arguments are often unnecessarily complex, rely on an insider's lingo and use terms that pointedly mute just what it is these bombs will do, which is, to start with, to kill the people one loves and nearly everyone else as well.

I came to appreciate this fully only during a conversation with a former CIA analyst who had been responsible for evaluating Soviet strategic nuclear forces. He has spent much of his adult life concerned with the question of nuclear war and has heard all the arguments about nuclear-war-fighting and survival. But an experience from his youth, he told me, remains in his mind, and he admits it may yet color his view.

This man had conducted some of the most important CIA studies on the Soviets and nuclear war. Now in his middle years, still youthful in manner, clean-cut and obviously patriotic, the father of a Marine on active duty, he recently left the CIA to join a company that works for that agency, and so I cannot use his name.

He told me about this experience of his youth because he was frightened by the Reagan Administration's casual talk about waging and winning a nuclear war. He thought the Reagan people did not really comprehend what kind of weapon the bomb was, and so as an illustration he told me about his own earlier experience with the bomb when he had been a lieutenant in the Navy and had seen a bomb go off near Christmas Island in the Pacific. Years later at the CIA he had worked with computer models that detail the number of fatalities likely to result from various nuclear war targeting scenarios. But to bring a measure of reality to these computer projections, he would return in his mind as he did now to that time in the Pacific.

The birds were the things we could see all the time. They were superb specimens of life . . . really quite exquisite . . . phenomenal creatures. Albatrosses will fly for days, skimming a few inches above the surface of the water. These birds have tremendously long wings and tails, and beaks that are as if fashioned for another purpose. You don't see what these birds are about from their design, they are just beautiful creatures. Watching them is a wonder. That is what I didn't expect . . .

We were standing around waiting for this bomb to go off, which we had been told was a very small one, so no one was particularly upset. Even though I'd never seen one, I figured, well, these guys know what is going to happen. They know what the dangers are and we've been adequately briefed and we all have our radiation meters on . . . No worry. [27]

The former CIA analyst paused to observe that the size of the bomb to be exploded was ten k, or ten kilotons, the equivalent explosive power of ten thousand tons of TNT. The two bombs dropped at Hiroshima and Nagasaki were thirteen kt. and twenty-three kt. respectively. Now such bombs are mere tactical or battlefield weapons. Many of the bombs to be used in any U.S.–Soviet nuclear war are measured in megatons, millions of tons of TNT.

He went on with his account:

I didn't want to see a little one. A little one? Ten k? I mean come on, let's get serious. I was a kid. Anyway, we were standing around, and the count-

*down comes in over the radio. And we knew roughly where the designated
ground zero would be and about how high.*

*And suddenly I could see all these birds, I could see the birds that I'd been
watching for days before. They were now suddenly visible through the opaque
visor of my helmet. And they were smoking. Their feathers were on fire. And
they were doing cartwheels. And the light persisted for some time. It was
instantaneously bright but wasn't instantaneous, because it stayed and it
changed its composition slightly. Several seconds, it seemed like, long
enough for me to see birds crash into the water. They were sizzling, smoking.
They weren't vaporized, it's just that they were absorbing such intense radiation that they were being consumed by the heat. Their feathers were on fire.
They were blinded. And so far there had been no shock, none of the blast
damage we talk about when we discuss the effects of nuclear weapons. Instead
there were just these smoking, twisting, hideously contorted birds crashing
into things. And then I could see vapor rising from the inner lagoon as the
surface of the water was heated by this intense flash.*

*Now this isn't a primary effect of the weapon, it is an initial kind of effect
that precedes other things, although it is talked about and you can see
evidence of it in the Hiroshima blast and in Nagasaki—outlines of people
on bridges where they stood when the bomb dropped. But that initial thermal
radiation is a phenomenon that is unlike any other weapon I've seen. I've
never seen anything like that.*

The men who now dominate the Reagan Administration and who
hold that nuclear war is survivable would surely wonder what these
reflections have to do with the struggle against the Soviet Union. But
what my CIA friend was telling me is that these birds are us and they
never had a chance.

2

"It's the Dirt That Does It"

VERY late one autumn night in 1981, Thomas K. Jones, the man Ronald Reagan had appointed Deputy Under Secretary of Defense for Research and Engineering, Strategic and Theater Nuclear Forces, told me that the United States could fully recover from an all-out nuclear war with the Soviet Union in just two to four years. T.K., as he prefers to be known, added that nuclear war was not nearly as devastating as we had been led to believe. He said, "If there are enough shovels to go around, everybody's going to make it."[1] The shovels were for digging holes in the ground, which would be covered somehow or other with a couple of doors and with three feet of dirt thrown on top, thereby providing adequate fallout shelters for the millions who had been evacuated from America's cities to the countryside. "It's the dirt that does it," he said.

What is truly astounding about my conversation with T.K. is not simply that one highly placed official in the Reagan Administration is so horribly innocent of the effects of nuclear war. More frightening is that T. K. Jones's views are all too typical of the thinking of those at the core of the Reagan Administration, as I have discovered through hundreds of hours of interviews with the men who are now running our government. The only difference is that T.K. was more outspoken than the others.

After parts of my interview with T. K. Jones ran in the *Los Angeles*

Times,[2] a subcommittee of the Senate Foreign Relations Committee demanded that Jones present himself to defend the views that Senator Alan Cranston said went "far beyond the bounds of reasonable, rational, responsible thinking."[3] Meanwhile Senator Charles Percy, the Republican chairman of the Foreign Relations Committee, had confronted Jones at a town meeting in the senator's home state of Illinois and was sufficiently troubled by the Deputy Under Secretary's relatively complacent views of nuclear war to pressure the Pentagon for an accounting.

But by now the Administration had muzzled Jones, and he missed his first three scheduled appearances before the Senate subcommittee. It was at this point that a *New York Times* editorial asked: "Who is the Thomas K. Jones who is saying those funny things about civil defense?"[4] Elsewhere Jones's espousal of primitive fallout shelters was dismissed easily and properly by editorial writers and cartoonists as a preposterous response to what nuclear war was all about. However, what these dismissals ignored was that Jones's notions of civil defense, odd as they may have seemed, are crucial to the entire Reagan strategic policy.

Reagan's nuclear arms buildup follows from the idea that the United States is vulnerable to Soviet nuclear weapons, an idea that rests in part on calculations made by this same T. K. Jones before he joined the government, when he worked for the Boeing Company. It was Jones's estimates of the efficacy of Soviet civil defense that provided much of the statistical justification for the view that the Soviets could reasonably expect to survive and win a nuclear war while we ourselves, without a comparable civil defense program, would necessarily lose.

And it was Jones's celebration of the shovel and primitive shelters as the means to nuclear salvation, once it was exposed to public debate, that helped to call into question the Reagan Administration's claim of American vulnerability. Jones had become fascinated with digging holes and with the powerful defensive possibilities of dirt only after he had read Soviet civil defense manuals that advocated similar procedures. In fact, it was from the Russians that he borrowed the idea of digging holes. If Jones's evacuation and sheltering plans were absurd on the face of it for the United States, how then could any observer take the Soviet civil defense program seriously? And if the Soviets are not capable of protecting their society and recovering from a nuclear war, how can anyone genuinely believe that they are planning to fight and win such a war?

Jones has been obsessed with the Russian threat ever since he served as a consultant for Nixon's SALT I negotiating team. An illustration of this obsession was offered by Roger Molander, a former staff member of the National Security Council under three Presidents. Molander, who left the government after the Carter Administration to found Ground Zero, the nuclear war education project, recalled that in 1973, he and Jones decided to accept an invitation to leave the SALT I talks in Geneva and visit the Paris Air Show, an elaborate event at which military contractors show their wares. As luck would have it, they ended up at a party sponsored by a U.S. defense contractor at a restaurant on the Eiffel Tower and met what Molander described as "an attractive American brunette and a beautiful Norwegian blonde."

"It's a June night in Paris," Molander told me,

> free champagne, hors d'oeuvres, the lights of Paris—not bad, right? I'm a very aggressive bachelor at the time, T.K. is too, and we meet a couple of young women. At eleven o'clock we all go out to dinner, T.K. and I and these two girls. We find a beautiful little bistro, I remember running up the steps of Montmartre, feeling the effects of the champagne and a June night in Paris. An hour into dinner I am deep in conversation with one of the girls about who knows and who cares? It is Saturday night in Paris, I'm sitting at Montmartre, I'm eating canard à l'orange, and the last thing I'm thinking about is nuclear war.
>
> Wafting across the table comes [the voice of] T. K. Jones, seriously talking to this Norwegian girl who is nodding, but who knows what is going through her mind? T. K. Jones is saying to her, ". . . and because the Soviet Union is threatening our ICBM force, we have to have mobile ICBM systems that would move around—" I'm thinking, "What? I've got an appointment back on planet Earth. Is this a human being? Does he understand why life is worth living?" We are in Paris on a Saturday night in Montmartre, off the Eiffel Tower with a couple of delightful young women. It is midnight, we don't have to be home until who knows what, and he is talking about mobile ICBM systems. I could not believe it! T.K. was still doing it when the evening ended.[5]

T.K. is nothing if not consistent. Since his days as manager of program and product evaluation at Boeing, after he returned from the SALT I talks in 1974, he has been a major proponent of the view that we are vulnerable to a Soviet first strike unless we emulate the Soviet civil defense program. At Boeing, Jones had led a team that conducted tests attempting to simulate the effects of a nuclear blast on persons huddling in civil defense shelters and on machinery buried in the ground. On the basis of those tests, he argued later, both persons and machinery would have emerged barely scratched, even if the explosive had been nuclear rather than TNT. His colleagues from the Boeing project have recently been awarded contracts by the Reagan Administration to determine how to fight and survive a protracted nuclear war. In his new job at the Pentagon, Jones himself is one of the key officials in charge of coordinating the planning and acquisition of equipment for such a protracted nuclear war.

I had first interviewed T.K. for about an hour one morning in the fall of 1981 at his Pentagon office. I was interested in his views because of his extensive past testimony before congressional committees and because of articles he had written on the need for civil defense and the possibilities for surviving nuclear war. The Reagan Administration's appointment of T. K. Jones to a high Pentagon post despite his extreme views, which were well known in defense circles at the time, was one of many clues that alerted me to the possibility that this Administration holds a fundamentally different view of nuclear war from that of its Democratic and Republican predecessors.[6]

The interview in his Pentagon office had centered around pictures of the atomic devastation of Japan. Jones, as in his barely reported congressional testimony five years earlier, was reassured by the familiar scenes of destruction and pointed to the few surviving structures in an otherwise barren wasteland of rubble to support his analysis that, indeed, there are defenses against nuclear war. He praised the resilience of the Japanese, noting, ". . . in about thirty days after the blast, there were people in there, salvaging the rubble, rebuilding their houses." Jones acknowledged during our morning interview that modern nuclear strategic weapons are hundreds of times more powerful than the devices exploded in Japan, and that a large U.S. city would receive not one but perhaps more than a dozen incoming warheads. Yet he insisted that the survival of more than 90 percent of our people was possible.

I cannot easily explain Jones's interest in prolonging our interview after the morning session. Perhaps he invited me home for the evening because he recognized that I was genuinely perplexed by his claim, made as we stood in the anteroom of his office, that nuclear war is survivable. He told me it was a matter of building primitive shelters: "Dig a hole, cover it with a couple of doors and then throw three feet of dirt on top." My questions must have suggested to him that I needed something more than the short course he had already given me that

morning on nuclear survival. The long course at his home that evening
was an effort to explain just how we could survive the carnage.

I listened with utter incredulity to Jones's monologue during our
interview that night, beginning when he, his woman friend and I sat
down to dinner at eight—the woman nodding her approval at what
seemed to me Jones's terrifying inanities—and ending at four in the
morning when I had run out of tape and Jones's friend was asleep on
the couch.

The evening began with one glass of white wine each with our
sautéed shrimp and onions and ended with an after-dinner drink that
my host concocted according to a treasured Seattle recipe, as he said
he does once each evening, of brandy, Kahlúa and whipped cream,
served with cookies. Throughout the evening, Jones was scrupulously,
indeed tediously, reasonable as he built his case that nuclear war was
something far less terrible than I had been led to believe: that it was
survivable, and not just by lonely bands of savages roaming a devastated
landscape. What Jones foresaw was the preservation and quick reassem-
bly of our advanced institutions, modes of production and normal ways
of life.

Do not misunderstand. There was nothing deranged or hysterical
about Jones's performance that night, nothing even intemperate.
Jones's manner is circumspect. His house reflects a Spartan personal
lifestyle—sparsely furnished, with just enough chairs for a few people,
despite his woodworking shop in the basement. His looks are clean-cut,
if plain, and he's trim for his forty-nine years. He seldom raises his voice
and tends to speak in a drone, sometimes inaudibly. This studied,
matter-of-fact style persisted even when he discussed the deaths of
hundreds of millions of people, as if he were attempting by the measured tone of his voice to deny the ultimate horror of it all. I have
listened many times to the tapes of this interview, and what startles me
most is how easily Jones seemed to make the subject of mass death
almost boring.

That evening Jones showed me pictures from Soviet civil defense
manuals of designs for primitive shelters that were little more than
holes in the ground covered with some thatching.

"This little primitive-looking thing in this picture is a Soviet-
designed shelter," he said. "In essence you dig a hole, take lumber,
small saplings or something like that, and build this thing and cover
it with dirt . . . that cuts the lethal area of that megaton weapon down
to about two square miles . . . [The] Russians have twenty to thirty

designs. The idea is you pick a design to match the material you have on hand."

Then he acknowledged a major obstacle to such a plan where the United States was concerned: "The problem is we've conditioned our people to believe that once the first nuclear bomb goes off, everybody's going to die. It's hard to get people to do anything if that's the conditioning they've been through." Nevertheless, Jones described what is required for survival: "Things you need [in the shelter], . . . first you need air, then water, then food, in that order . . . You have to take your food with you, a little bit of water . . . wait until there's no radiation . . . [you] can tell by the dust that comes down. If there's no dust, there's no radiation . . ."

He explained how to build a shelter with simple household materials: "You can make very good sheltering by taking the doors off your house, digging a trench, stacking the doors about two deep over that, covering it with plastic so that rain water or something doesn't screw up the glue in the door, then pile dirt over it. If your house is built on a slab, one very good blast and radiation protection is to dig a tunnel underneath the slab . . . Learn how to make a ventilation pump . . . how to deal with sanitation, supplies, this kind of thing. In the business of nuclear war, what you don't know can kill you . . ."

I asked Jones about the Administration's vision for civil defense for Los Angeles in the eighties. His answer and a portion of the interview follow:

JONES: Vision of that would be, in essence, learning what we can learn from the Russians . . . In Los Angeles the vision of the fifties was to put a shelter in your basement or something like that. Turns out these other shelters, which you dig in ten hours, give you better protection. For apartment dwellers, you'll want to move these people a little ways out, move them over the first ridge, get them into the San Bernardino–Riverside area, someplace like that, dig them in there. The second problem of the fifties was we fell into that argument of: If you've got a shelter and your neighbor's got a gun, how's this going to be handled? Turns out with the Russian approach, if there are enough shovels to go around, everybody's going to make it . . .

SCHEER: To dramatize it for the reader, the bomb has dropped [in Los Angeles]. Now, if he's within that two-mile area, he's finished, right? If he's not in the two-mile area, what has happened?

JONES: His house is gone, he's there, wherever he dug that hole

. . . You've got to be in a hole . . . The dirt really is the thing that
protects you from the blast as well as the radiation, if there's radiation.
It protects you from the heat. You know, dirt is just great stuff . . .

Stabbing at his living-room carpet with an imaginary spade, he
showed me how to dig a hole in even the hardest Siberian tundra so
that a man could crawl into it and protect himself from radiation by
placing doors over the hole and three feet of dirt on top of the doors.

Jones told me that he had been deeply impressed with what he
claimed was the Soviet plan to evacuate the cities and protect the urban
population in hastily constructed shelters in the countryside. He also
referred to his studies at Boeing to show that the Soviet method of
piling dirt around factory machines would permit their survival even
if nuclear bombs fell close by.

These studies, he explained, were not universally admired. Some
critics, for example, did not share his enthusiasm for the Soviet civil
defense program and scoffed at the prospect of millions of Soviet
citizens digging holes during the freezing winter in order to cover
themselves and their machinery. To these objections, he replied that
it is easier to dig up frozen dirt than warm, muddy dirt. Because I had
no direct experience one way or the other, I could hardly join Jones's
woman friend, who sat with us at the dinner table, in nodding agreement.

I asked him: If the Russians are really angry, they've wiped out our
civilization, we're wiping out theirs, they do ground blasts. How long
does radiation last?

JONES: For a high-density area like Los Angeles, shelter stay time
should be about a week. But then it's going to require some radiation
survey teams to mark out the least contaminated areas. You'll find in
an area like that you'll have some hot spots and not-so-hot spots and
once again, it's knowledge of what to do that's useful. Let's talk about
what you do. One is if you're lucky enough to have a rainstorm you'll
find a lot of radiation gets leached into the ground, which in essence
shields you, or you'll find that those river runoff basins get awfully hot,
that stuff is going to collect there.

Stay out of that area . . . go into another area where it's not so hot,
clean off the topsoil, scrape away the radioactive particles from the top
of the dirt, go into an area where there's some surviving housing or
something like that . . . Radioactive particles can attach to dust which

sits there on top of the ground. If you go in with a power shovel or hand shovel and clean off the top inch of dirt, mound it off somewhere out of the way, you've gotten rid of the radiation in that area . . .

After about the first day [in the shelter], you probably can go outside for sanitation reasons and get more water. If you have six to eight people in the shelter, take turns going out . . . you can afford a couple of hundred rads without getting sick . . . For trips out of shelter, you don't want to get more than twenty or thirty; keep your trips short. . . .

SCHEER: Aren't there long-term effects?

JONES: Yup.

SCHEER: What do you mean?

JONES: Let's put it this way. People in Nagasaki and Hiroshima had a higher incidence of leukemia than the Japanese population in general. On the other hand, their longevity has proven to be greater than the Japanese population in general, probably because of the increased standard of medical care they've received since then.

SCHEER: . . . How long would it take to get Los Angeles back to where it was?

JONES: Let me give you a more general answer: If we don't protect our society, we've not been able to calculate recovery time because we've lost so many people it's beyond calculation. It would take a couple of generations, probably more. You'd lose half the people in the country. With protection of people only, your recovery time to prewar GNP levels would probably be six or eight years. If we used the Russian methods for protecting both the people and the industrial means of production, recovery times could be two to four years.[7]

I know that I was sober that evening because as I waited with my right-turn blinker on for a seemingly endless red light to change, a Virginia state trooper in the car behind me got tired of waiting and put me through my paces before telling me it was okay to turn right on a red light in Virginia.

The next morning, after breakfast at the Jefferson Hotel in Washington, D.C., I noticed that Attorney General William French Smith, who had taken up residence there, was already stirring with his entourage. It was a reassuring sight—Smith and his colleagues all looked so solidly adult, sober, respectable. Surely this prosperous Attorney General, reeking of dignity and confidence, former personal attorney to Reagan, a major investor in land and, it was later revealed, controversial tax shelters, had too much going for him to accept complacently the prospect of giving it all up for a hole in the ground or even for one of the fancy but ultimately no more useful blast shelters that would be made available to him as a high official were he still in office when the bombs fell. And just as surely, Ronald Reagan and George Bush were themselves equally solid and responsible. Or were they? How much, I wondered, did the views of men like Jones really reflect the thinking of our new heads of state? Had they all gone mad in their obsessive fear of the Russians? Or was T. K. Jones an aberration, a solitary eccentric who had somehow found his way into the Pentagon?

3

Reagan and Bush

REFLECTING on T. K. Jones's startling remarks, as I sat in the tranquil flower-bedecked lobby of the Jefferson Hotel, I thought back to the time in January 1980 when I had interviewed presidential candidate George Bush aboard a small chartered plane en route from Houston to New Orleans.

In that interview, I was to stumble upon an emerging shift in thinking about nuclear war that would prove to be profoundly significant—that would in fact shape the war-fighting policy of the future Reagan government. What Bush told me aboard his campaign plane that day helps explain why T. K. Jones, despite his extraordinary opinions about the possibility of surviving a nuclear war, would be hired as Deputy Under Secretary of Defense for Research and Engineering, Strategic and Theater Nuclear Forces. My interview with Bush also helps explain much of the loose talk in the first year of the Reagan Administration about nuclear-war-fighting and limited nuclear war, talk that foreshadowed active planning for what has come to be called a nuclear-war-fighting capability.

I had first interviewed Bush early in the lengthy primary campaign, weeks before his surprising victory in the first contest in Iowa, when he still was not being taken very seriously. On the way to New Orleans, I was the only reporter on what was the first jet his campaign had chartered. Bush was excited that his campaign had become promising enough to warrant a chartered plane of its own. He was almost as excited by Houston Oilers coach Bum Phillips, who had given "one hell of a speech" the night before at the Houston Astrodome after his team had been defeated in the AFC playoffs. After emotional prayers had been said for the Iranian hostages, Phillips had threatened to avenge his team's defeat. "This year we knocked on the door," Phillips declared. "Next year we're going to kick the son of a bitch in."

That night in Houston, I had been caught in the drunken swirl of the crowd, and the next day I suggested to Bush that the results of the playoffs and the continuing hostage crisis were getting mixed up: some of the people on the streets that night may have thought Phillips meant he was going to knock down the Ayatollah Khomeini. Wasn't there some danger of jingoism, I asked, lurking in all this emotional outpouring over the fate of the Iranian hostages? Bush, ever upbeat, said, "No," and went on to add that what he gleaned from the Astrodome event was that the country was starting "to feel good about itself again." We both agreed on the obvious—that America's humiliation over the hostage crisis would set the mood of the upcoming election. It was not yet clear that it would also help spell the end of détente and arms control.

Between them, the taking of the hostages and the indefensible Soviet invasion of Afghanistan had encouraged militarist sentiment within the United States, sentiment that would end the prospects for Senate ratification of the SALT II treaty. But in January 1980 it still seemed reasonable to assume that this bellicosity was temporary and that after the election, SALT II would be ratified. After all, the SALT II treaty had been negotiated by both the Ford and Carter Administrations after the pioneering efforts of Richard Nixon, who certainly was not given to a benign view of the Soviet menace. Few experts on the subject doubted that the limits SALT II placed on Soviet strategic missile launchers would make our own less vulnerable. In fact, the controversial MX mobile missile-basing scheme that Carter had advocated made sense only if Soviet land-based missiles could be held to the level dictated by SALT II.

Surely, I assumed, the foreign policy establishment would resume its former cohesiveness and impose its sensible priorities once the election was out of the way. I had no doubt that the establishment would push SALT II through Senate ratification as it had the Panama Canal Treaty, despite the old right and its neo-conservative allies. Most commentators at the time agreed with me that even if Carter lost, his successor would be a Republican who, like Eisenhower, Nixon and

Ford, would continue the ever fitful, always chancy but gradual introduction of sanity into superpower relations—which is all anyone could reasonably expect. Bush was generally regarded as that sort of Republican alternative to Carter, and it was for this reason that what he told me that day on his campaign plane startled me so, although at first I barely caught its implications.

The small jet plane tossed in the wind with a ferocity that made it hard to hear, let alone care much what Bush was saying—except that this man who would be President, and who, it turned out, was the future Vice President of the United States, just at that moment was discussing the prospect of winning a nuclear war and was doing so with remarkable equanimity, as if he were talking about a football game.

The question that provoked Bush's reply derived from the conventional wisdom of the previous twenty years that there was a limit to how many nuclear weapons the superpowers should stockpile, because after a point, the two sides would simply wipe each other out, and any extra fire power represented overkill. This had been the assumption ever since former Defense Secretary Robert McNamara conceived the Mutual Assured Destruction policy. But Bush had faulted Carter for not being quick enough to build the MX missile and B-1 bomber, and I asked, "Don't you reach a point with these strategic weapons where we can wipe each other out so many times and no one wants to use them or be willing to use them, that it really doesn't matter whether you're ten percent or two percent lower or higher?"

Bush bristled a bit and replied, "Yes, if you believe there is no such thing as a winner in a nuclear exchange, that argument makes a little sense. I don't believe that."[1]

I then asked, "How do you win in a nuclear exchange?"

Bush seemed angry that I had challenged what to him was apparently an obvious truth. He replied, "You have a survivability of command and control, survivability of industrial potential, protection of a percentage of your citizens, and you have a capability that inflicts more damage on the opposition than it can inflict upon you. That's the way you can have a winner, and the Soviets' planning is based on the ugly concept of a winner in a nuclear exchange."

"Do you mean," I asked, "five percent would survive? Two percent?"

"More than that," Bush answered. "If everybody fired everything he had, you'd have more than that survive."

I have played that tape many times since then, mostly because when

I reported Bush's idea in the *Los Angeles Times* that a nuclear war was winnable, his remarks created a flap. Each time the subject surfaced on the campaign circuit Bush or his aides would offer a disclaimer of sorts, until they were challenged, and then they backed off. When he came under heavy criticism in the press for his comments, he would point to that one sentence, ". . . the Soviets' planning is based on the ugly concept of a winner in a nuclear exchange," and insist that he himself did not believe anyone could win a nuclear war: that in his remarks to me, he had been referring only to what the Soviets believed to be true.

But Bush clearly had begun the exchange by telling me he did not believe "there is no such thing as a winner in a nuclear exchange."

I wasn't sure at the time whether Bush really believed that we could survive a nuclear war or whether he was merely trying out a line that might prove useful in the Republican primaries, where he was worried that he had been unfairly labeled a moderate. To confuse matters further, he then went on to say that we should push ahead toward arms reduction but only after we had reversed the trend toward Soviet superiority and once we could be certain of verifying Soviet compliance.

The confident style with which Bush delivered these statements was in part that of someone who claims to have been briefed by intelligence agencies. The tone of his bald assertion that we could survive and win a nuclear war implied that this former CIA chief had knowledge of secret data that would convince the skeptic if only he could be trusted with access to it but, for obvious reasons, could not be.

Bush is one of those well-turned-out Yale men of a bygone era who seem to thrive on subtle distinctions of class and status and who appear fully confident that style alone will transport them through vast areas of personal ignorance. Perhaps this is why Bush could, without the slightest alarm or doubt, express the extraordinary idea that even after enormous casualties, there can be something called victory in a nuclear war.

The interview that Bush gave me on his campaign plane seemed internally inconsistent at the time. But later, when I came to learn about an organization that called itself the Committee on the Present Danger and of which we shall hear more in the next chapter, I discovered the source of this dangerous if muddled line of thought. The key organizers of the Committee had formed the center of opposition to détente. They had introduced the idea that the Soviets are bent on nuclear superiority and believe they can be victorious in a nuclear war.

As I would learn, these men were influential not only with Bush but even more so with his campaign opponent, Ronald Reagan.

A month after I interviewed Bush, I was in another airplane and the man beside me was saying, "We have a different regard for human life than those monsters do." He was referring to what he said was the Soviets' belief in winning nuclear war despite casualties that we would find unacceptable. And he added that they are "godless" monsters. It is this theological defect "that gives them less regard for humanity or human beings."[2]

The man telling me all this was Ronald Reagan, as I interviewed him on a flight from Birmingham to Orlando, where he was headed to pick up some votes in the upcoming 1980 Florida Republican primary. By mentioning the Soviets' low regard for human life, Reagan meant to validate the view that he confided to me later—that the Russians for some time have been preparing a preemptive nuclear war. His words echoed the sentiments I had heard earlier from Bush, who at that moment was still Reagan's rival for the Republican nomination. But despite their rivalry, both men seemed comfortable with the language of nuclear-war-fighting, a language that rejected the deterrence policies of prior Administrations.

Reagan told me:

> We've still been following the Mutual Assured Destruction plan that was given birth by McNamara, and it was a ridiculous plan, and it was based on the idea that the two countries would hold each other's population hostage, that we would not protect or defend our people against a nuclear attack. They in turn would not do the same. Therefore, if both of us knew that we could wipe each other out, neither one would dare push the button. The difficulty with that was that the Soviet Union decided some time ago that a nuclear war was possible and was winnable, and they have proceeded with an elaborate and extensive civil protection program. We do not have anything of that kind because we went along with what the policy was supposed to be.[3]

As President, Reagan set out to get something "of that kind." The goal of the Reagan/Bush Administration has been to emulate what Reagan claimed is the Soviet program by developing the ingredients of a nuclear-war-fighting capability. And the key ingredient, even more than the number and power of the nuclear weapons themselves, is the ability of a country's leadership to control the war in the midst of massive nuclear explosions. This is what Bush had in mind when he told me that nuclear war is winnable by having "survivability of command and control." In military jargon, this ability to maintain communication between leadership and forces is known as "command, control and communications," or "C^3."

Those who believe that it is impossible to successfully wage a limited nuclear war argue that the leadership would not be able for long to maintain contact with its forces. The devices that permit communication—ranging from land-based antennas to space satellites—are inherently highly vulnerable to attack. As noted in Chapter 1, the Reagan Administration's Defense Guidance Plan calls for the "decapitation" of the Soviet leadership in the event of war, which refers to knocking out the enemy's command centers. It is safe to assume that the Soviets have similar plans.

But the Reagan Administration believes that the United States has the capacity to develop a C^3 that would endure through the ravages of nuclear war. The survivability of command and control is central to the Administration's strategy to fight and win a protracted nuclear war. When President Reagan in the fall of 1981 announced his strategic package, he singled out an $18 billion program for enduring command and control as the most important element in his program.[4]

T. K. Jones's boss at the Pentagon, Richard D. DeLauer, Under Secretary of Defense for Research and Engineering, emphasized at an Air Force conference that C^3 was the key to Reagan's strategic program, and that the combination of an enduring C^3 plus the Navy's new ballistic missile would give the United States the very sort of offensive weapon we claim to fear in the hands of the Soviets. As *Aviation Week* reported: "The improved accuracy expected with development of the Trident II or Lockheed D-5 submarine-launched ballistic missile, DeLauer said, will provide a counterforce capability enabling destruction of hardened Soviet targets and could even provide the capability for pre-emptive strike."[5]

A preemptive strike means that you launch your nuclear weapons before they do. DeLauer was projecting a window of vulnerability, only this time the Russians were, theoretically, on the receiving end of an attack.

What Reagan's C^3 provides is not simply better communications with one's forces, which should enjoy wide support if for no other reason than to avoid accidental launchings of nuclear weapons. Enduring C^3 as outlined in the Reagan program goes far beyond this, for its aim is to give our leaders the means to direct American submarines, airplanes and land-missile crews for an extended period of war-fighting. Its aim is to make nuclear weapons usable in a war like any other war. As Colin Gray told me when I interviewed him in May 1982, "The C^3 modernization story doesn't make any sense if you're not thinking along these lines [of protracted nuclear war] . . . If you only need your forces to go bang on day one, who cares about survivability of the satellites?"

The distinction was summarized by former Secretary of State Cyrus Vance in an interview in March 1982 when I asked him what he thought of the Reagan Administration's plans to improve C^3 in order to attain a nuclear-war-fighting capability. "I think it is sound and proper," Vance said,

> to have a command and control which could hopefully survive a nuclear attack. However, to take the next leap, that it is important to have a command and control that is survivable so that you can fight a nuclear war, is a wholly different situation . . . I happen to be one of those who believe it is madness to talk about trying to fight a continuing nuclear war as though it were like fighting a conventional war, and that one could control the outcome with the kinds of precision that is sometimes possible in a conventional war situation. It is a totally different world, a world that is hard for any of us to conceive, because none of us knows what a nuclear war is like. But by extrapolation, we can have some idea of the incredible devastation that would come from it and the almost unimaginable consequences that would flow from it.[6]

That the Reagan Administration had begun moving in a direction that Vance called "madness" was made abundantly clear by another speaker at that same Air Force conference which DeLauer addressed and which was reported in *Aviation Week*. Lieutenant General James W. Stansberry, commander of the Electronics Systems Division of the Air Force, which would run much of the C^3 program, said:

> In previous years the concept for C^3 was that it only had to be able to get off a launch of U.S. strategic weapons in response to a first strike before damage was unacceptable. The idea that there was no way to win a nuclear war exchange sort of invalidated the need for anything survivable. There is a shift now in nuclear weapons planning, and a proper element in nuclear deterrence is that we be able to keep on fighting.

As *Aviation Week* reported, enduring C^3 makes sense only for prolonged nuclear-war-fighting:

> Stansberry said there is now a shift in strategic warfare philosophy in the U.S. and that the country must be prepared to fight and to keep on fighting, and that an eight-hour nuclear war is no longer an acceptable concept.

The main reason that an eight-hour war is no longer acceptable is that the Reagan Administration has adopted the view, once held by only a fringe group of strategic analysts, that the Soviet Union is bent on acquiring nuclear superiority so as to win a nuclear war, as Bush had said in his interview with me.

This was the point of Colin Gray's controversial article on nuclear war, "Victory is Possible," which he wrote in collaboration with Keith Payne, referred to in Chapter 1. Gray argued not only that nuclear war is winnable but also that the United States should be prepared to initiate nuclear war against the Soviet Union.[7]

Two years later, Gray was appointed by the Reagan Administration as a consultant to the Arms Control and Disarmament Agency. He was also named a member of the General Advisory Committee to the Arms Control and Disarmament Agency and a consultant to the State Department.

Central to the arguments of Gray and other nuclear-war-fighters is that they are not talking simply about deterring a Soviet first strike or responding to one after it has occurred. They want the capacity that the United States had during its decades of nuclear superiority to move up the so-called "escalation ladder." It is only by adding "threat escalation" to one's deterrent paraphernalia that the nuclear-war-fighters believe they can stop conventional as well as strategic Soviet moves. Nuclear-war-fighting makes sense only as part of a plan to threaten or actually to initiate an attack—"counterforce offensive targeting," as it is called—that seriously limits the enemy's ability to retaliate.

"Initiating" a nuclear attack is precisely what Gray advocated when he wrote:

> American strategic forces do not exist solely for the purpose of deterring a Soviet nuclear threat or attack against the United States itself. Instead, they are intended to support U.S. foreign policy, as reflected, for example, in the commitment to preserve Western Europe against aggression. Such a function requires American strategic forces that would enable a president to

initiate [italics mine] strategic nuclear use for coercive, though politically defensive, purposes.[8]

When the Gray/Payne article first appeared in *Foreign Policy,* it was greeted largely with derision. But when Reagan moved into the White House all that changed. As Lee Bruce, one of the magazine's editors, told me:

In Washington now it's not as fringe a view as it was just a couple of years ago. Colin Gray is at the extreme of that view; however, that extreme is very politically powerful, there are a certain number of representatives of that view in this Administration, obviously. I think Richard Pipes has made no bones about it—he had a piece in the *Washington Post* a few weeks ago in the Outlook section that basically said why he didn't fear the bomb and why nuclear war was winnable. People like him, people like Richard Perle in the Defense Department, there's a number of people who believe in this stuff and they have a fair amount of influence.[9]

If the Russians had appointed a man with Gray's views to a significant and visible government post, our own hawks would surely say "we told you so," and demand vast new categories of armaments. Nor did Reagan appoint men like Gray and T. K. Jones inadvertently. Their views and those of the other hard-liners, which I shall explore further in the next chapter, were well known to the Reagan people who selected them, and they were compatible with the strategic policy pursued by the Administration. For the views of these hard-liners, in fact, permeate the new Administration. These are views that had been espoused for years by men languishing in the wings of power, waiting for one of their own to move to center stage. With Reagan, their time had come.

4

*The Committee
on the Present Danger*

I T was the fall of Reagan's first year in office, and Charles Tyroler II, the director of the Committee on the Present Danger, was boasting a little. Five years ago he and a small band of cold warriors had set out to reshape American foreign policy, which they felt was too soft on the Russians, and suddenly they had succeeded beyond their wildest dreams. One member of their group was now the President of the United States, and he had recruited heavily from the Committee's ranks for his top foreign policy officials.[1]

Committee members were now ensconced as heads of the CIA and the Arms Control and Disarmament Agency, and in top State and Defense Department and White House positions. Paul Green, the Committee's public relations director, told me that Eugene Rostow, founding member of the Committee and the new head of the Arms Control and Disarmament Agency, had just that week written part of the President's speech on arms control. It was in that speech that Reagan for the first time had referred to START as the alternative to SALT. Green was proud that it had been Rostow who first came up with the acronym START, and both Green and Tyroler were obviously pleased that SALT II, which had taken three Presidents and six years to negotiate and which the Committee had strenuously opposed, now seemed securely buried.

The work had gone well and now, high up in one of those glass-walled offices that successful Washington lobbyists prefer, Director Tyroler found himself able to relax and even gloat a bit as he detailed for me the extent of his group's conquest.

Tyroler looks like George Bush—lanky, thin, gray in suit and skin—and is waspish in personality. His body tends to unwind and then coil again as he talks, which makes for difficult listening, particularly since he speaks in short, rapid bursts, rather like hurried instructions to a subordinate. In this instance, I could have been taking dictation from Director Tyroler on what he clearly believed to be his committee's seizure of state power:

"The leaders of the government, the Secretary of Defense, the President of the United States, and the Secretary of State, the head of the Arms Control and Disarmament Agency, the National Security Adviser—when they give a speech, in general terms, it sounds like what we said in 1976. Yes. I think that is a fair statement." He then offered a self-satisfied laugh and added, "And why wouldn't that be? They use the same stuff—and they were all members back then."

The "same stuff," of course, was the Committee's persistent and shrill criticism of the SALT II treaty in particular and détente with the Soviets in general, criticism which the Committee had mounted since its inception in 1976 and which contributed to the demise of the treaty. As Carter's Secretary of State Cyrus Vance told me in March 1982:

> There is no doubt that the Committee on the Present Danger had a great deal to do with undermining SALT. No question. And to hear people talk about a hopelessly flawed agreement which this Administration continues to abide by—when you ask them what is wrong with this hopelessly flawed agreement, they cannot tell you what is wrong with it. It leads you to believe that it is ideological rather than based on fact or hard thought.

What emerges from the Committee's literature is the view encountered earlier in this book, that the Soviet Union is as unrelentingly aggressive as Nazi Germany was in the thirties—except that the Soviets now have nuclear weapons and are willing to use them. This is what the Committee says on the subject:

> The Soviet military buildup of all its armed forces over the past quarter century is, in part, reminiscent of Nazi Germany's rearmament in the 1930s. The Soviet buildup affects all branches of the military: the army, the air force and the navy. In addition, Soviet nuclear offensive and defensive

forces are designed to enable the USSR to fight, survive and win an all-out nuclear war should it occur.[2]

This last notion, later embraced by both candidates Bush and Reagan, originated with the men who founded the Committee and who have since become key players in the Reagan campaign and presidency. It is they who have given us the language and imagery of limited nuclear war and who claim that we can survive and even win such a conflict. It is they and their allies within the Administration who have pushed most strenuously for a rapid arms buildup. And it is they who are responsible, along with their Soviet counterparts, for dragging the world back into the darkness and danger of the Cold War.

The Committee's ideologues couldn't have done it alone. Their rhetoric fed on the continued Soviet military buildup and the wasteful civil defense program that accompanied it; to say nothing of the violent statements of various Soviet military leaders and the outrageous suppression of their own and their satellites' people, as well as the invasion of Afghanistan. Yet the Soviet buildup does not, as we shall see, justify the Committee's program or that of the Administration it now so profoundly influences. As Paul Warnke, Carter's arms control director, said, "If you figure you can't have arms control unless the Russians are nice guys, then it seems to me that you're being totally illogical. If the Russians could be trusted to be nice guys, you wouldn't need strategic arms control. And you wouldn't need strategic arms."[3]

But Soviet behavior did alienate much American opinion which might have favored arms control and thus provided the emotional context and minimum plausibility that were essential for the revival of a Cold War mood. The hawks on both sides of the superpower confrontation have a long history of feeding on each other's rhetorical and strategic excesses. In particular, both sides tend to exaggerate the technological success of the opposing side's defense program, meanwhile denying that the enemy can do anything else right.[4] The hawks of both sides, including the Committee on the Present Danger, are threat-inflaters who dourly predict every success for the forces of evil and nothing but trouble for the side of virtue unless this side, too, adopts the methods and programs of its opponents.

The founding members of the Committee included, among others, veterans of what came to be known as Team B, a group of hawks whom George Bush brought into the CIA from outside its ranks when he was that agency's director in 1975–76. The aim of Team B was to reevaluate the agency's own assessment of the Soviet menace, which Team B found too moderate. Team B's chairman was Richard Pipes, who went on to become Reagan's top Soviet expert on the National Security Council. And one of its most active members was former Secretary of the Navy Paul Nitze, who has since become Reagan's key negotiator on European strategic weapons. To no one's surprise, Team B concluded what it had originally hypothesized: that the CIA had seriously underestimated the Soviet threat. In November 1976, Nitze, along with Eugene Rostow, formed the Committee on the Present Danger and asked several hundred prominent individuals, including Pipes, to support them. I discuss the work of Team B in detail in the next chapter and mention it here only insofar as it was the catalyst for the formation of the Committee.

"So the Committee's philosophy is dominant," said Paul Green, who had joined Tyroler and me in the Committee's offices. Green is the Committee's genial public relations director, and his cherubic demeanor and pleasant smile promise something far less threatening than the group's dire warnings about the strategic balance. Yet what he was about to outline spelled the end for serious efforts at arms control during the Reagan Administration.

"So the Committee's philosophy," Green went on, "is dominant in the three major areas in which there is going to be U.S.–Soviet activity." He was referring to the various arms control negotiations which were then being resumed with the Soviets and which were directed by Committee members Reagan had appointed to his Administration, all of whom had been strident critics of SALT II. The implications of Reagan's victory not only for arms control but for relations in general with the Soviets became starkly clear as Tyroler continued his inventory of the powerful posts then held by members of his group:

We've got [Richard] Allen, Pipes, and Geoffrey Kemp over at NSC. We've got the people most intimately involved in the arms control negotiations for the Defense Department. [Fred] Iklé [Under Secretary of Defense for Policy], his deputy, [R. G.] Stillwell, and Dick Perle [Assistant Secretary of Defense for International Security Policy]. In the Arms Control and Disarmament Agency there is Rostow, the head of it, [Edward] Rowny, the SALT negotiator, and Nitze, the TNF [Theater Nuclear Forces] negotiator. And [William] Van Cleave on the General Advisory Committee. Well, that's the whole hierarchy.

Richard Allen was later forced to resign as the President's National Security Adviser over allegations, later dismissed, that he had improperly received money from Japanese journalists, and Van Cleave's nomination was withdrawn because his abrasive personality offended Caspar Weinberger. Edward Rowny, while sympathetic, was not actually a member of the Committee. But Tyroler could have added Committee member William Casey, who became head of the CIA; John F. Lehman, Secretary of the Navy; Jeane Kirkpatrick, Ambassador to the United Nations; Colin Gray, nominated to the Arms Control Agency advisory committee; as well as scores of other highly placed members of the Administration. Tyroler himself was appointed a member of the President's Intelligence Oversight Board.

It wasn't quite the whole hierarchy, as Tyroler claimed, but according to Tyroler and Green, it was only accidental that then-Secretary of State Alexander Haig and Defense Secretary Weinberger had not signed up with the Committee. When Secretary of State Alexander Haig resigned in June 1982, he was replaced by George Shultz, a founding member of the Committee on the Present Danger, who appointed another Committee member, W. Allen Wallis, as a top assistant. According to Green, Weinberger had not joined because he thought it would be hard to get to Washington from his job with Bechtel on the West Coast, but Green said Weinberger "is very sympathetic to our point of view." He added that "it would be hard to find an outspoken opponent of our point of view who is still in the government." Tyroler and Green reported somewhat gleefully that even Henry Kissinger, ever one to sniff the winds of change, had sent in a $100 contribution after Reagan won the election.

But as Tyroler went on with his account of the Committee, it seemed to me inevitable that members of his group should have come to play a dominating role in the Reagan Administration. As Tyroler boasted, this group of intellectual hawks, its leadership drawn mostly from the ranks of aging Truman and Johnson Democrats with several score young disciples, had been important to Reagan's 1980 campaign victory. Tyroler noted, "All of his top foreign and military advisers were members of the Committee."

According to Tyroler, Reagan had used the Committee's publications as the basis of many of his radio programs, in particular a five-part segment devoted to his opposition to the SALT II treaty, for which the Committee was credited on the air.[5] The future President did not attend board meetings of the organization, but he was briefed regularly by its members. Tyroler recalled a dinner at Paul Nitze's house in which he, Nitze and Rostow met with Reagan and they discussed the military balance and SALT for about five hours of what Tyroler called "very serious conversation." The subject was the same at another five-hour briefing session they held for Reagan in California later in the campaign. Tyroler was impressed with Reagan's seriousness during those and other briefings. As he recalls:

> Reagan spent an enormous amount of time in briefings. He is a very serious figure. That also surprised me. I've dealt with a lot of politicians in the last thirty or forty years, and this guy is very serious, for long periods of time. He'll just talk policy. And when he held those meetings that Allen set up for him, Allen would say, "You can speak for three minutes, no more than that. Don't give the Governor any political advice. All he wants to hear from you is what is the right thing to do, he'll make up his mind."

I asked Tyroler and Green whether an article I had written for the *Los Angeles Times*[6] that stressed the Committee's influence in the Reagan Administration had exaggerated the case, and they both said no. Tyroler said, "What we're talking about is [the Committee's founding statement]—is that the viewpoint of this Administration? The answer is yes. Reagan has said so time and time again."[7]

Special-interest groups tend to exaggerate their influence, but in this instance we have the word of Ronald Reagan himself to confirm the Committee's importance. After his election, he wrote in a letter to the Committee, "The statements and studies of the Committee have had a wide national impact, and I benefited greatly from them."[8] He added that "the work of the Committee on the Present Danger has certainly helped to shape the national debate on important problems."

Reagan, of course, did not need the Committee or anyone else to stimulate his anti-Soviet feelings. He had long shared rightist suspicions of détente and had strongly criticized the arms control agreements that were its most visible accomplishment. Nor did he need the Committee to tell him that the Soviets were up to no good. This perception had been his stock-in-trade since his tenure, thirty years earlier, as president of the Screen Actors Guild, when, in his eyes, he heroically battled the Hollywood Reds, who he felt certain were acting under direct orders from Moscow. As Reagan stated back in 1951: "The Russians sent their first team, their ace string, here to take us over . . . We were up against hard-core organizers."[9]

Of the scores of people I've interviewed who have been close to Reagan, none has denied the strong visceral antagonism the President feels toward the Soviets. Reagan's longtime actor friend, former California Senator George Murphy, told me it was he who first alerted Reagan to the "Red menace" after learning from J. Edgar Hoover, a close personal friend, that Franklin D. Roosevelt's New Deal was masking a plot to socialize America.[10]

In my own interview with Reagan during the campaign, he commenced a tirade on the subject of Communism. I had asked him why he attacked Communism as godless since it seemed to me that one could be a bad or good player on the international scene regardless of one's religious convictions. I gave as an example the Ayatollah Khomeini. Reagan conceded that there have been problems down through the ages with religious fanaticism, but then he embarked upon a long monologue that reveals his most deeply felt passions and past hurts on the subject of Russian Communism:

But the reason for the godlessness with regard to Communism—here is a direct teaching of the child from the beginning of its life that it is a human being whose only importance is its contribution to the state—that they are wards of the state—that they exist only for that purpose, and that there is no God, they are just an accident of nature. The result is, this is why they have no respect for human life, for the dignity of an individual. And I remember one night, a long time ago, in a rally in Los Angeles, sixteen thousand people in the auditorium, and this was at the time when the local Communists, the American Communist Party—and this is all well-documented—was actually trying, and had secured domination of several unions in the picture business, and was trying to take over the motion-picture industry, and all of the rewriting of history today and the stories that we have seen and screenplays and television plays, and so forth, about the persecution for political belief that took place in Hollywood, believe me, the persecutors were the Communists who had gotten into positions where they could destroy careers and did destroy them. There was no blacklist of Hollywood. The blacklist in Hollywood, if there was one, was provided by the Communists.[11]

In this interview Reagan, with no prompting from me, in what seems in fact to have been a compulsive non sequitur, had resurrected events that took place some thirty years earlier, his wounds still raw and his hatred of the enemy unyielding. Most curious of all is that his view of the Soviet menace today is so deeply colored by events that took place in Hollywood more than a generation ago, as if today's Soviet government were simply the Hollywood Communists projected on a larger screen.

As Jim Lake, who was Reagan's press secretary during the 1976 and much of the 1980 campaign, told me: "On the question of the Russians and Communism Ronald Reagan is a true believer, no doubt about it."[12]

Reagan came into office loaded for the Russian bear, and this would have been true with or without the Committee on the Present Danger. But while Reagan did not need the Committee to fuel his anti-Sovietism, the Committee nevertheless refined the future President's sentiments and his rhetoric. What the Committee did for Reagan was to apply a patina of intellectual respectability to what might otherwise have seemed to the voters no more than out-of-date and primitive anti-Communist ravings. What the Committee attempted with considerable success was to return the simplicities of 1950s Cold War thinking, clothed in new and sophisticated language, to the center of U.S. foreign policy decision-making.

For a while, before Reagan's victory, the Committee had been dismissed by most of the political and media establishment as extremist critics of détente and arms control and of the balance-of-power arrangements that the Committee's nemesis at the time, Henry Kissinger, had wrought. The Committee's core group, some of whom had labored long in government and business, seemed mostly to be cranky critics of the status quo. As founding Committee board member Norman Podhoretz wrote, "The issue boils down in the end, then, to the question of will. Have we lost the will to defend the free world—yes, the free world—against the spread of Communism? Contemplating the strength of isolationist sentiment in the United States today, one might easily conclude that we have."[13]

Some of the original members of the Committee eventually recognized this crankiness and resigned or became inactive when the group moved on from a generalized plea for a stronger military into specific opposition to SALT II. But the key members of the Committee— former Secretary of the Navy Paul Nitze, former Under Secretary of State and Yale law professor Eugene Rostow and Harvard Soviet expert Richard Pipes—had become identified with unrelenting opposition to Kissinger's détente initiatives and were commonly associated with the minority within the foreign policy establishment who continued to insist upon the Cold War positions of the Stalin era.

In a way, these unremitting cold warriors seem almost to miss the myths of the Stalinist era, those black and white years when the Soviet Union with its timetable for world conquest seemed to hold the unchallenged leadership of a monolithic international Communist movement arrayed against a united free world content within its own borders. They seem uncomfortable with events as they have evolved since then; the Sino-Soviet split, West Germany's increasingly close ties to Russia, and the Eurocommunist movement independent of Moscow seem to annoy them by having introduced troublesome complexity into this world view. For them Communism is evil, and that's all there is to it.

Thus, while our allies and many of our own industrialists more often than not were looking for trade opportunities with the Soviets, these hard-liners were doggedly decrying the present danger. While Nixon, Ford and Carter were pursuing détente, they were drawing analogies between the current leaders of the Soviet Union and Hitler. While friends of Richard Nixon went off to Moscow to sell the Bolsheviks Pepsi-Cola and Caterpillar tractors, the men who would later found the Committee and assume high office in the Reagan government were even then complaining about appeasement. Doggedly they warned that the Soviets would gain military superiority over the West while we negotiated the SALT II agreement and President Carter refused to fund the B-1 bomber.

The Carter years were a time to try the patience of these men, committed as they were to a world that, for almost everyone else, no longer existed, a world in which all evil resided in the bosom of one's enemy while all was virtuous at home.

Lest I be accused of exaggeration, I should report that when I interviewed Eugene Rostow, a founding member of the Committee, in the spring of 1981, just after he had been appointed director of the Arms Control and Disarmament Agency, and asked him if he believed that the Soviet Union had any legitimate grievances against the United States, he replied, "None whatever." The interview continued:

SCHEER: You don't think that they can correctly feel that, for instance, our policy toward China or the Vietnam War or the Korean War or towards Cuba violated the United Nations Charter?

ROSTOW: No. Impossible. It's impossible to take that position. Cuba is the closest case, but I would strongly defend what Kennedy did with Cuba, yes.

SCHEER: For instance, supporting efforts to assassinate Castro, which we have admitted to—is that not a violation of the U.N. Charter?

ROSTOW: There has been testimony to that effect. The government hasn't admitted it. No, I don't mean to say that if we ever undertook to assassinate another person, that wouldn't violate the U.N. Charter, and other things besides, the laws of the United States, for example. Those charges were made, but they were also denied . . .

SCHEER: When you look at the world, there is no sense that we could possibly have done anything similar in any of these areas? The Soviets claim they were invited into Afghanistan; we claim we were invited into Vietnam to save the legitimate government. You don't feel that there is any serious duplicity on the part of both major powers in some of these cases?

ROSTOW: No, I don't. And I think it is a great mistake to try to evade responsibility by taking that easy option.

In the special world of Rostow and the Committee on the Present Danger, the Cuban missile crisis of 1962, the high point of American nuclear superiority over the Soviets, represents the good old days. Because of this superiority in nuclear as well as conventional weapons at the scene, we were able to make the Soviets blink and take their missiles out of Cuba. But by the late sixties, despair over Vietnam had sapped the national will and led to the détente and disarmament of the seventies—the most dangerous of decades, in the Committee's view.

It is anything but clear, however, that the increase in Soviet nuclear weapons has led to an increase in Soviet geopolitical influence. In fact, the Soviets seem to have done better in the decade after the Cuban missile crisis, when they were still relatively weak in strategic power, and rather worse in the seventies, when they had gained parity.

In the early sixties, the Soviets had extended their influence to Egypt, where their advisers were well entrenched in the Egyptian army. In the seventies the Egyptians threw them out, a serious reversal given Egypt's critical importance to the politics of the Mideast. But in the special calculus of the Committee, what is geopolitically important is almost by definition whatever the Soviets have gained, while what they have lost is unimportant. By the Committee's reckoning, increased Soviet influence in Southern Yemen makes up for influence lost in Egypt. But this argument is absurd on the face of it. Egypt has the largest army in the Mideast and the eradication of Soviet influence there is a defeat that obviously dwarfs any other gains that they have made in the area.

More recently, Soviet support for the PLO and Syria collapsed in the face of the Israeli invasion of Lebanon, and again intercontinental missiles proved irrelevant to the military task at hand.

Nowhere is this gap between military power and geopolitical influence clearer than in the Sino-Soviet dispute. In 1949, the Soviets, it may be recalled, took over China, or so the folklore of the day had it, and they managed to do this even though the United States at that time still had a monopoly on nuclear weapons. During the fifties, when the strategic imbalance with the United States was still one-sided, the U.S.S.R. enjoyed good relations with her "satellite." But in the sixties, the Soviet grip on China loosened in almost direct proportion to Russia's increasing nuclear strength. And of course it was during the seventies, when the Soviets were said by the hawks to have caught up with and even surpassed us as a nuclear power, that the break with China became total and China became not a Soviet dependent but a Soviet enemy.

The example of China's defection might suggest that the possession of greater numbers of nuclear weapons may be irrelevant or even detrimental to the attainment of geopolitical power. Rostow has attempted to resolve this contradiction by rewriting history and postulating that the loss or gain of China is just not that important. When Rostow appeared before the Senate Foreign Relations Committee at his confirmation hearing to head the Arms Control and Disarmament Agency, he said, "I think the Soviet Union has a very intelligent and prudent government . . . I cannot imagine that the Soviets regard the Chinese army, the Chinese People's Republic Army, as a significant threat to their own forces."[14]

This would probably come as news to the Soviets, who, despite Rostow's assurances, keep 25 percent of their army on the 4000-mile border with China. Rostow's testimony before the Foreign Relations Committee also mocks the fiery debates held on this subject in the forties, for if China is as negligible in the calculations of world power as Rostow thinks, then it can hardly have mattered whether China had been lost or not.

But memories are short. A nation that once was whipsawed by arguments over "who lost China" and later fought in Vietnam in part to stop Chinese Communism now seems to gain scant security, according to Rostow, from a growing political and military alliance with that country of more than a billion people. Nor does this reversal on the part of one Communist giant give pause to those who think of Communist Russia as inherently and unbendingly hostile toward U.S. interests.

In July 1970, in a long interview in *The New Yorker* magazine, this same Rostow provided a rationale for the Vietnam War which rested almost exclusively on the need to check Chinese Communist expansion in Asia. In that interview, Rostow argued that if the United States pulled out of Vietnam, the result might be a Chinese-Japanese alliance to exclude the United States from Asia entirely. Rostow added that the Chinese were a threat as a growing military power, and, "You find the Chinese trying to foment revolution all over Africa, the Middle East, and Southeast Asia."[15]

In July 1981, when I asked him about this, Rostow observed that Chinese Communism was always "skin deep" and not expansionist, not even in the Maoist days. He told me in a long interview for the *Los Angeles Times* that he now finds it "a very plausible hypothesis" that the United States provoked the Chinese to enter the Korean War, and added that China had "an historical claim" to Tibet, which he termed "an ambiguous place, a Chinese suzerainty." He also denied that the U.S. decision to go into Vietnam had anything whatsoever to do with a fear of China, despite his own remarks eleven years earlier.

It is impossible to understand a hard-liner like Rostow without grasping the profound trauma that he and others like him experienced beginning with the Nazi-Soviet agreement of the thirties and continuing on through the endless "betrayals" of socialism that have followed ever since. Many so-called neo-conservatives share with Rostow a youthful commitment to idealistic socialism, a commitment they have long since repudiated but which they still recall with feelings of great bitterness. Rostow, for example, was not named Eugene Victor Debs Rostow by his father and mother—who, as he told me, met at a socialist rally in Brooklyn—because they wanted him to grow up to be a neo-conservative.

Others in the inner core of the Committee and the neo-conservative circles that surround it are disenchanted veterans of past liberal Democratic Administrations who feel that leftist zealots captured and distorted the Democratic party's agenda. The opposition to Johnson's Vietnam War policies which led to the repudiation of Hubert Humphrey and later to the nomination of George McGovern in 1972 seems to have been the watershed event in their rightward conversion.

The marriage of this generally sophisticated ex-left and ex-liberal ideology with the more purely primitive rightist views of Ronald Reagan and his advisers and aides-de-camp has many implications for American policy. One is that their earlier polemical experiences imbued these ex-leftists with great argumentative skills and the ability to make a sophisticated critique of liberal positions not often found among traditional rightists. That, combined with their own painfully remembered maltreatment at the hands of the sixties campus left as they doggedly defended the Vietnam War, has left many of them armed with self-righteous anger directed at those liberal intellectuals who they feel coddled an irrational left.

This sophisticated, vehement and articulate rage at the direction taken by post-Vietnam America may have been the most important contribution these intellectuals offered to the campaign and now the government of Ronald Reagan. They provided the strong ideological horses to pull Reagan's right-wing wagon out of its intellectual mud. It would not be an exaggeration to say that their contribution to Reagan's successful campaign was incalculably large, perhaps even critically important. For one thing, they succeeded in making opposition to SALT II and détente intellectually respectable.

The speeches of Reagan and Bush during the campaign were laced with statistics, anecdotes and analyses provided by the Committee. Tyroler told me that Richard Allen, Reagan's top foreign policy coordinator during the campaign, was the main conduit for this information. The Committee's main themes—that the Soviets were in the process of attaining superiority in nuclear and conventional weapons; that they were bent on world conquest; that the United States, misled by the spirit of détente, had disarmed during the seventies while the Soviets went barrelling ahead in the arms race; that nuclear deterrence and the assumption of Mutual Assured Destruction were no longer adequate; and that the Soviets were in fact preparing to fight and win a nuclear war—all showed up prominently in the major foreign policy pronouncements of candidates Reagan and Bush, right through their occupancy of the White House and its adjacent Executive Office Building.

The origins of Administration policy can be found in the Committee's founding statement:

The principal threat to our nation, to world peace, and to the cause of human freedom is the Soviet drive for dominance based upon an unparalleled military buildup . . . For more than a decade, the Soviet Union has been enlarging and improving both its strategic and its conventional military forces far more rapidly than the United States and its allies. Soviet military power and its rate of growth cannot be explained or justified by considerations of self-defense.[16]

Some notable experts disagree. When I interviewed former Secretary of Defense Robert S. McNamara, he suggested that the Soviet buildup could be seen as a reaction to the earlier U.S. military buildup and to rumors that the United States was seeking a first-strike capability. Those rumors may have stemmed from an Air Force proposal to develop such a capability, a plan to which McNamara referred in a November 21, 1962, memo he wrote to President Kennedy recommending that the proposal be rejected as a U.S. policy objective. "My God," McNamara told me,

if the Soviets thought that was our objective, how would you expect them to react? I think that explains . . . a lot of their actions. I gave a speech in San Francisco . . . I think it was in mid-'67, in which I said that "action and reaction," the internal dynamics of the nuclear race, explained a lot of what the Soviets were doing . . .[17]

McNamara added,

If I had been the Soviet secretary of defense, I'd have been worried as hell about the imbalance of force. And I would have been concerned that the United States was trying to build a first-strike capability. I would have been concerned simply because I would have had knowledge of what the nuclear strength was of the United States and I would have heard the rumors that the Air Force was recommending achievement of such a capability. You put those two things together: a known force disadvantage that is large enough in itself to at least appear to support the view that the United States was planning a first-strike capability and, secondly, talk among U.S. personnel that that was the objective—it would have just scared the hell out of me!

McNamara offered his memo to Kennedy as an example of the sort of U.S. military thinking about a first-strike that might have alarmed the Soviets. But he was quick to note that "I didn't believe, and President Kennedy didn't believe, we had a first-strike capability . . . We didn't have any intention of trying to attain a first-strike capability . . . If we had had any such intention, there is no way we could have done it, in my opinion."

Another critic of the Committee's perspective on the Soviet buildup was Oxford Professor Michael E. Howard, an internationally respected expert on nuclear strategic questions. In November 1980, Howard gave the Bernard Brodie Memorial Lecture at UCLA, in which he quoted the late Bernard Brodie, the dean of U.S. strategic thinkers and former Rand Corporation and UCLA scholar. Brodie had written:

Where the Committee on the Present Danger in one of its brochures speaks of "the brutal momentum of the massive Soviet strategic arms buildup— a buildup without precedent in history," it is speaking of something which no student of the American strategic arms buildup in the sixties could possibly consider unprecedented.[18]

To this Howard added:

In fact, one of the oldest "lessons of history" is that the armaments of an adversary always seem "brutal" and threatening, adjectives that appear tendentious and absurd when applied to our own. The sad conclusion of this debate is that no amount of argument or evidence to the contrary will convince a large number of sincere, well-informed, highly intelligent and, now, very influential people, that the Soviet Union is not an implacably aggressive power quite prepared to use nuclear weapons as an instrument of its policy.

But I would argue that the leadership of the Soviet Union, and any successors they may have within the immediately forseeable future, are cautious and rather fearful men, increasingly worried about their almost insoluble internal problems, increasingly aware of their isolation in a world in which the growth of Marxian socialism does little to enhance their political power . . . That complex web of interests, perceptions and ideals . . . thus gives them no clearer guidance as to how to use their armed forces than it does to us.[19]

Howard ended his lecture by warning of "the possibility that, in a lethal mixture of hubris and despair, we might one day feel ourselves compelled to initiate a nuclear war. Such a war might or might not achieve its objective, but I doubt whether the survivors on either side would very greatly care."

But whereas critics like Howard and McNamara tended to stress the danger of accidental nuclear war, Committee members were more preoccupied with the dangers of appeasement, further evidence of their obsession with the 1930s.

Ironically, Committee leaders who for decades had supported the U.S. nuclear weapons buildup offered the Soviet counterpart of their own hawkish position as proof that the two nations do not share a common perception and fear of nuclear war. Yet their own language is far closer to that of their counterpart Soviet hard-liners than they might want to acknowledge.

For example, if we substitute the United States for the Soviet Union in the following statement by the Committee, we can imagine that it was written by a comparable group of Soviet hawks:

> By its continuing strategic nuclear buildup, the Soviet Union [read United States] demonstrates that it does not subscribe to American [read Soviet] notions of nuclear sufficiency and mutually assured deterrence, which postulate that once a certain quantity and quality of strategic nuclear weapons is attained, both sides will understand that further accumulation or improvement becomes pointless, and act accordingly.[20]

Of course, it would be splendid news for everyone if the Soviet Union agreed to unilateral restraints in the arms race. Ever since their humiliation during the Cuban missile crisis, the Russians have piled missile upon missile, and who wouldn't cheer if they admitted "that further accumulation or improvement becomes pointless, and act accordingly"? However, the Committee wants the United States to pile weapons systems on weapons systems, and as long as this is so, the cheering will have to wait.[21] The Committee's leaders must be aware that the United States did not hesitate to develop each new weapons system it thought workable and useful as the Soviets were pursuing their own buildup in the seventies. Thus we have the Pershing II and cruise missiles, the Trident submarines and missiles and the technological basis for the MX missile, each of which exceeds Soviet development by a good five years, jeopardizing the expanding Soviet array of land-based missiles—the basket into which they have put most of their nuclear eggs.

How can such presumably informed people as the Committee members including Reagan on the one hand and McNamara and Professor Howard on the other have such wildly different estimates of what should be a clear factual situation? One reason is that the facts are anything but clear. Much of what we know, or think we know, about Soviet intentions and strength is based on estimates inferred from U.S. intelligence data, although during the SALT talks both sides did provide details of their strategic systems.

The Soviets do not reveal many details of their defense budget or force structure, and they alone seem to take seriously the relatively low annual defense budget figure that they publish. The Western countries, however, possess a great deal of highly accurate information on the specifics of the Soviet force make-up gleaned from constant and increasingly precise satellite surveillance, as well as from old-fashioned spying. But this vast amount of material has to be submitted to intelligence analysis before its meaning becomes clear. To do this, however, involves interpretation based on the skills and experience of U.S. intelligence agencies, particularly the CIA, which has traditionally attempted to evaluate Soviet strength in an objective manner.

One reason for the current confusion is that this objectivity was seriously compromised under the administration of CIA Director George Bush with the help of some key founders of the Committee on the Present Danger. These events occurred in 1976, and they were to have a profound effect on our evaluation of the Soviet threat and on the course of presidential politics. I am referring to the creation of Team B, the group of outside analysts whose leaders were permitted by Bush to reevaluate the CIA's own estimates of Soviet strength and intentions. The objective procedures by which the CIA formerly evaluated the scope and nature of the Soviet threat may thus have been the first casualty of the new Cold War.

5

Team B

Until 1976, the CIA did not believe that the Soviets were militarily superior to the United States or were aiming at nuclear superiority. Nor did agency analysts believe that the Soviet leadership expected to survive and win a nuclear war. Then George Bush became head of the CIA, and the professionals at the agency were told to think otherwise.

Bush was appointed CIA director during the last year of Gerald Ford's presidency and took the unprecedented step of allowing a hawkish group of outsiders to challenge the CIA's own intelligence estimates of Soviet strength. In a break with the agency's standards of secrecy, Bush granted this group access to the most sensitive data on Soviet military strength, data that had been culled from satellite photos and reports of agents in the field, defectors and current informants. Never before had outside critics of government policy been given such access to the data underlying that policy. Bush did not extend similar privileges to dovish critics of prevailing policy.

This intrusion into the objective process of CIA analysis greatly inflated the existing estimate of United States vulnerability to Russian forces and would eventually be used to justify an increased American arms buildup.

As the *New York Times* noted in a strongly worded editorial at the time:

For reasons that have yet to be explained, the CIA's leading analysts were persuaded to admit a hand-picked, unofficial panel of hard-line critics of recent arms control policy to sit at their elbows and to influence the estimates of future Soviet military capacities in a "somber" direction.[1]

The group that Bush appointed was called Team B, to distinguish it from Team A, the CIA professionals who were paid to evaluate Soviet strength in an unbiased fashion. Thanks to Bush, Team B was successful in getting the U.S. government to profoundly alter its estimates of Soviet strength and intentions, though critics charged that Team B seriously distorted the CIA's raw data to conform to the political prejudices of its members.

Those prejudices were described in a *New York Times* report as follows: "The conditions [for Team B members] were that the outsiders be mutually agreeable to the [Foreign Intelligence] advisory board and to Mr. Bush and that they hold more pessimistic views of Soviet plans than those entertained by the advocates of the rough parity thesis."[2]

The Team B report helped bolster and may even have been the source for both Bush's and Reagan's assertions in the 1980 campaign that the Soviets had betrayed the hopes of détente and were bent on attaining nuclear superiority. It was the Team B study that led to charges during the campaign that Carter had allowed the Soviets to gain nuclear superiority and that the United States must "rearm."

The *Times* account of what followed the introduction of Team B was based on non-attributable interviews which suggest a civil war within the intelligence community. One intelligence officer

spoke of "absolutely bloody discussions" during which the outsiders accused the CIA of dealing in faulty assumptions, faulty analysis, faulty use of intelligence and faulty exploitation of available intelligence. "It was an absolute disaster for the CIA," this official added in an authorized interview. Acknowledging that there were more points of difference than in most years, he said: "There was disagreement beyond the facts."

Another outspoken critic of Team B was Ray S. Cline, a former deputy director of intelligence of the CIA who, according to the *Washington Post,* is "a leading skeptic about Soviet intentions, and a long-time critic of [Secretary of State Henry] Kissinger." The article continued: "He [Cline] deplored the experiment. It means, Cline said, that the process of making national security estimates 'has been subverted,' by employing, 'a kangaroo court of outside critics all picked from one point of view.' "[3]

Team B was hand-picked by Bush, and as noted by the *New York Times,* a "pessimistic" view of the Soviets was a prerequisite for inclusion on the team.[4] The committee's chairman was Harvard Professor Richard Pipes, a Polish immigrant and a notorious anti-Soviet hardliner, the same Pipes who, in 1981, announced that the Soviets would have to choose between peacefully changing their system or going to war.

According to Jack Ruina, professor of electrical engineering at MIT and former senior consultant to the Office of Science and Technology Policy at the White House, "Pipes knows little about technology and about nuclear weapons. I know him personally. I like him. But I think on the subject of the Soviets, he is clearly obsessed with what he views as their aggressive intentions."[5]

Pipes is the intellectual godfather of the thesis that the Soviets reject nuclear parity and are bent on nuclear-war-fighting, a thesis later advanced by candidates Bush and Reagan and which now permeates the Reagan Administration in which Pipes serves as the top Soviet specialist.

Pipes clarified his position and that of Team B in a summary of the classified Team B report that he provided in an op-ed piece in the *New York Times.* This article criticized the view that each side had more than enough nuclear weapons and that the notion of nuclear superiority between the superpowers no longer made sense. Pipes wrote:

> More subtle and more pernicious is the argument, backed by the prestige of Henry A. Kissinger, that nuclear superiority is meaningless. This view was essential to Mr. Kissinger's détente policy, but it rests on flawed thinking. Underpinning it is the widely held notion that since there exists a certain quantitative level in the accumulation of nuclear weapons that, once attained, is sufficient to destroy mankind, superiority is irrelevant: There is no over-trumping total destruction.[6]

Pipe's alternative to Kissinger's view of strategic policy was the one embraced by Team B. His article continued:

> Unfortunately, in nuclear competition, numbers are not all. The contest between the superpowers is increasingly turning into a qualitative race whose outcome most certainly can yield meaningful superiority.

Five months after his piece in the *Times,* Pipes argued in a *Commentary* article that the Soviets do not agree that nuclear war is fundamentally different from conventional wars, a viewpoint which he himself seems to share as more realistic than the prevailing American idea that nuclear war would be suicidal. Pipes noted that the U.S. military at first held what he claims is actually the Soviet view, that "when it [comes] to horror, atomic bombs had nothing over conventional ones," a point he attempted to prove by reference to the devastation of Tokyo and Dresden by conventional weapons. Pipes argued that this sound thinking on the part of the military was "promptly silenced by a coalition of groups each of which it suited, for its own reasons, to depict the atomic bomb as the 'absolute weapon' that had, in large measure, rendered traditional military establishments redundant and traditional strategic thinking obsolete."[7]

Pipes complained that "a large part of the U.S. scientific community had been convinced as soon as the first atomic bomb was exploded that the nuclear weapon, which that community had conceived and helped to develop, had accomplished a complete revolution in warfare." That conclusion, Pipes wrote, "was reached without much reference to the analysis of the effects of atomic weapons carried out by the military, and indeed without consideration of the traditional principles of warfare." Instead, Pipes argued that this misguided notion was the result of psychological and philosophical distortions of the scientists themselves. "It represented," Pipes wrote, "an act of faith on the part of an intellectual community which held strong pacifist convictions and felt deep guilt at having participated in the creation of a weapon of such destructive power."

Thus Pipes dismissed the anguished concern of many of the scientists who know these weapons best, as if their feelings of guilt and their wishes for peace were absurd or decadent or perhaps even anti-American.

The Soviets, by contrast, according to Pipes, who in a perverse way seems to revel in the heartlessness he assigns to them, were not so sentimental. They believed instead that Clausewitz was right: nukes or no nukes, war was still the pursuit of politics by other means. And because the hard-headed Soviets believe that nuclear weapons can be used successfully in war just as conventional weapons can, the Americans must prepare to emulate the Russians.

The principal Team B analysts, Paul Nitze and William Van Cleave, shared this view. Nitze and Van Cleave had already held discussions for months with Eugene Rostow and others to plan the formation of the Committee on the Present Danger even before these gentlemen, acting as Team B, entered CIA headquarters at Langley, Virginia, to reevaluate the agency's data. Thus their decision to form an activist organization based on the notion that the United States was losing out to the Soviets and pressing for greater arms expenditure predated their look at the CIA's material. So much for pretensions of objectivity.

Team B's conclusions were based on three points: a depiction of Soviet strategic intentions; the claim that the Soviets were engaged in a massive military buildup; and the idea that the Soviets' civil defense program made credible their expectation of surviving a nuclear war with the United States.

Those same three points would later form the core assumptions of the Reagan Administration's strategic policy, including, of course, T. K. Jones's shovel-based plan for protecting the civilian population. Yet while the Team B study is still classified, enough of it has leaked to raise serious questions about the credibility of its analysis.

When George Bush accepted the Team B conclusion that the Soviet buildup was much greater than had previously been assumed by the CIA, he did so, he told the *New York Times*, because of "new evidence and reinterpretation of old information [that] contributed to the reassessment of Soviet intentions."[8] Yet the new evidence to which he referred in fact actually refuted the conclusions of Team B and the subsequent assumptions of the Reagan-Bush Administration.

The "new evidence" available to Team B was the CIA's revised estimate of Soviet defense spending published in October 1976, which held that Soviet military spending as a percentage of GNP had increased from the 6–8 percent range to the 11–13 percent range. This was Team B's proof that the Soviets were building a bigger military force than we had thought.

However, as former CIA analyst Arthur Macy Cox pointed out in an article in the *New York Times*, the revised CIA estimates of 1976 tell us, in fact, nothing of the sort.[9] As Cox observed in another article in the *New York Review of Books*,

> While Team B's report . . . remained classified, the CIA's own official report on Soviet defense spending of October, 1976, had contradicted Team B's conclusions, not supported them. The true meaning of the October [CIA] report has been missed. A gargantuan error has been allowed to stand uncorrected all these years.[10]

Cox then cited the same CIA report on which Team B had relied and to which Bush referred as the "new evidence." "The new estimate of the share of defense in the Soviet GNP is almost twice as high as the six to eight percent previously estimated," the CIA report said, but then added, "This does not mean that the impact of defense programs on the Soviet economy has increased—only that our appreciation of this impact has changed. *It also implies that Soviet defense industries are far less efficient than formerly believed.*"

It was exactly wrong, then, for Bush to have suggested that the CIA had doubled or even measurably increased its estimate of the size of the actual Soviet defense program, for what it revised was only its evaluation of the efficiency of Soviet production, in other words the amount the Russians were paying for what they got. What the CIA showed was that the Soviets were having a harder time punching out the same number of tanks and missiles as the CIA had formerly projected for them; that they were, in other words, paying more for the same level of production. As former CIA analyst Cox noted, "What should have been cause for jubilation became the inspiration for misguided alarm."

As for increases of actual Soviet defense spending during the seventies, the CIA in its official estimate published in January 1980 concluded for the 1970–79 period that "estimated in constant dollars, Soviet defense activities increased at an average annual rate of three percent."[11] This is higher than the U.S. increase during the seventies, and lower than the U.S. rate from 1979 through 1983. For the seventies, NATO expenditures exceeded those of the Warsaw Pact. A 3 percent increase in Soviet military spending is actually no higher than the overall increase of their GNP during the seventies, which is put at between 3 and 5 percent by experts on the subject.

There is much more to be said about the increases that have occurred in the past two decades in the Soviet force posture relative to that of the United States, and of its respective alliances. Later I shall undertake a more detailed comparison of Soviet and U.S. strength. My purpose here is simply to emphasize the serious error that underlay Team B's assertion that U.S. intelligence had underestimated the Soviet buildup and that a new spiral in the arms race was therefore in order.

Team B's somber estimates of Soviet intentions, accepted as the national intelligence estimates under Bush's prodding, were to alter the climate for détente and arms control which the incoming Carter Administration would face from the time of its inauguration. According to the *New York Times* in December 1976: "President-elect Carter will receive an intelligence estimate of long-range Soviet strategic intentions next month that raises the question whether the Russians are shifting their objectives from rough parity with United States military forces to superiority."[12]

The *Times* account added that "previous national estimates of Soviet aims—the supreme products of the intelligence community since 1950—had concluded that the objective was rough parity with United States strategic capabilities." The *Times* then quoted Bush as saying that the shift in estimates was warranted because "there are some worrisome signs," and added that "while Mr. Bush declined to discuss the substance of the estimate, it can be authoritatively reported that the worrisome signs included newly developed guided missiles, a vast program of underground shelters and a continuing buildup of air defenses."

The claims made for Soviet underground shelters and civil defense generally were a critical element in the controversy within the intelligence community even before Team B intervened. The *Times* article stated that the convocation of Team B "came about primarily through continuing dissents by a longterm maverick in the intelligence community," Major General George J. Keegan, who retired as Air Force chief of intelligence soon after the Team B report was completed and who had been a consultant to Team B. The *Times* said, "In 1974 [Keegan's] dissents to the national estimate relating to the significance of the Soviet civil-defense program and new guided missiles provoked such a storm that he was called to the White House to make his case before the [Foreign Intelligence] advisory board."

Keegan convinced Leo Cherne, chairman of the Foreign Intelligence Advisory Board and one of the original architects of the U.S. involvement in Vietnam, to persuade CIA director Bush to convene Team B. Cherne, who heads a private business consulting firm, is also head of the International Rescue Committee, which deals with political refugees. He was one of those Americans who in the early fifties discovered Ngo Dinh Diem living in a Maryknoll seminary in New Jersey and then proposed that he become the George Washington of Vietnam. Back in the 1940s, this same Cherne directed a company that employed William Casey, whom Reagan later appointed CIA Director.

The Foreign Intelligence Advisory Board, of which Cherne has been a member since the Nixon years (he was appointed chairman in 1976), was deactivated during the Carter Administration but resurrected under Reagan, and Cherne is now its vice chairman. This body, which supervises the work of the intelligence agencies, now draws almost half its current roster of nineteen members from the ranks of the Committee on the Present Danger.[13]

The Team B report remains classified, but Lieut. Gen. Daniel O. Graham, retired, who participated in that group's challenge to the previous intelligence estimates of Soviet strength, told the *Washington Post*, when the Team B report was filed at the end of 1976, that Soviet civil defense preparations were crucial to the reappraisal of Soviet strength. This reappraisal also turned on a new evaluation of Soviet intentions, Graham told the *Post*. "I think the largest factor that caused us to err" in the previous intelligence estimates "was putting U.S. concepts into Soviet Russian heads."[14] The most important such concept, he said, was the rejection of nuclear war as an option of policy for the superpowers. Team B had argued that the Soviets rejected the U.S. notion of Mutual Assured Destruction and instead were aiming at nuclear superiority; the Soviets expected not only to survive but to win a nuclear war.

As Graham put it: "The evidence indicates that they [the Soviets] are seeking a war-fighting capability." He added that there were "two catalytic factors" that caused this reevaluation of Soviet intentions. One was the recalculation of the percentage of Soviet GNP going to defense, the meaning of which, as we have seen, was distorted in the Team B report. According to the *Post:* "The other major force in changing the official U.S. perception, Graham said, has been 'the discovery of a very important [Soviet] civil defense effort—very strong and unmistakable evidence that a big effort is on to protect people, industry and to store food.'"

But this "big effort," as much as it may have impressed and alarmed General Graham, is simply the primitive shelter and evacuation scheme that T. K. Jones advocated in his interview with me. When Jones told me that the United States could recover from general nuclear war in an estimated two to four years, he meant that we could do so with a "Soviet-type civil defense." But if digging a hole and covering it with doors is a preposterous defense for Americans, by what logic does the same procedure become "a very important civil defense effort" according to Team B? Why do Soviet manuals telling their people to dig holes in the tundra become a serious problem for American strategic planners? Yet it is these very holes in the ground that are meant to justify the assertion that the Soviets think they can win a nuclear war.

The argument that the Soviets' civil defense proves they are aiming for nuclear superiority and a war-fighting capability was strongly advanced by Team B Chairman Richard Pipes, in his *Commentary* article entitled "Why the Soviet Union Thinks It Could Fight and Win a Nuclear War."[15] Pipes was especially opposed to the notion that Mutual Assured Destruction was an accurate prediction of what would occur should the two superpowers resort to nuclear war.

Pipes claimed that the Soviets thought they could fight and win a nuclear war in part because they could keep their casualties to the level of past conventional wars. Their civil defense program, Pipes said, would permit "acceptable" casualties on the order of twenty million, or about as many Soviet dead as in World War II. The fact, obvious to even the most casual visitor to the Soviet Union, that the Russians still deeply mourn their wartime dead did not trouble Pipes. He simply assumed that the Soviet leadership would see to its own survival and that of its power base in a nuclear conflagration by organizing large-scale civil-defense programs.

The problem with the large-scale civil defense programs envisioned in the Soviet manuals is that to mobilize them takes not the twenty-five minutes required for an ICBM to reach its target, but days, and by some accounts, weeks. The estimate used by civil defense advocates like T. K. Jones and FEMA's William Chipman is three days to a week or more.[16]

But even days of such highly visible preparation would seriously limit the impact of a Soviet first strike on U.S. nuclear-armed submarines and bombers. Clearly, if the Soviets decided to arm their citizens with shovels and evacuate their cities, the United States would put its bombers and submarines on alert, which would make them far more elusive targets, while the American President could simply announce a launch-on-warning policy for the U.S. land-based ICBM force, thus canceling the advantage of a Soviet first strike against our land-based missiles.

For a first strike to make any sense, such a civil defense effort must be on a large scale and therefore highly visible—visible enough, certainly, to alert the other side, which is to say that any attempt to send the people to their shelters could, in itself, provoke an attack. Yet nuclear-war-fighting is inconceivable as a rational policy option without some such highly visible scheme to protect people and machines.

In his *Commentary* article, Pipes turned this argument around and observed that those who believe in the MAD doctrine reject civil defense in order to assure the mutual destruction of both sides.

> The U.S. theory of mutual deterrence postulates that no effective defense can be devised against an all-out nuclear attack: it is this postulate that makes such a war appear totally irrational. In order to make this premise valid, American civilian strategists have argued against a civil-defense program, against the ABM, and against air defenses.

But those who argue against such programs do so not because they want to weaken our defenses and thus create a self-fulfilling prophecy of assured destruction but rather because they feel that ABM and civil defense programs cannot possibly defend a significant portion of the population.[17]

Pipes underscored the importance to his argument of a credible defense against nuclear attack when he wrote: "Nothing illustrates better the fundamental differences between the two strategic doctrines than their attitudes to defense against a nuclear attack."

And he warned that "before dismissing Soviet civil-defense efforts as wishful thinking, as is customary in Western circles," one must recognize that

> its chief function seems to be to protect what in Russia are known as the "cadres," that is, the political and military leaders as well as industrial managers and skilled workers—those who could reestablish the political and economic system once the war was over. Judging by Soviet definitions, civil defense has as much to do with the proper functioning of the country during and immediately after the war as with holding down casualties. Its organization . . . seems to be a kind of shadow government charged with responsibility for administering the country under the extreme stresses of nuclear war and its immediate aftermath.

Thus Pipes apparently believes that despite the extreme stresses of nuclear war, there actually will be an "aftermath" in which enough of the cadre would survive along with sufficient machinery, roads, power facilities, foodstuffs, medical care and all the thousands of other essential items to "reestablish the political and economic system once the war was over."

Unlike T. K. Jones, Pipes was not rash enough to forecast an actual recovery period of two to four years, but his argument clearly assumes that some such recovery is feasible. To help justify this imputed confidence on the part of the Soviet leadership, Pipes added that "the Soviet Union is inherently less vulnerable than the United States to a countervalue attack," meaning an attack on people or industry.

Pipes thinks the Soviets are less vulnerable because, according to the 1970 Soviet census, they had only nine cities with a population of more than one million, which in the aggregate represents 20.5 million, or 8.5 percent of the country's total. By contrast, the 1970 U.S. census showed that 41.5 percent of the United States population lived in thirty-five cities of more than a million people. But what this has to do with anything is not clear from Pipes's argument. As the U.S. Arms Control and Disarmament Agency noted in 1978:

> A comparison was made of the vulnerability of the U.S. and the Soviet Union to nuclear attack. It was found that both countries are roughly equally vulnerable although urban density and population collocation with industry is greater in the Soviet Union.[18]

The two hundred largest cities in either country include most of the population. It would require only the Poseidon missiles on two fleet ballistic submarines to destroy those two hundred Soviet cities. With both superpowers in possession of more than twenty thousand strategic nuclear weapons, what does it matter if the "best" countervalue targets are nine or two hundred? But Pipes believes his comparison of the populations of the two countries' largest cities is crucial to his argument.

> It takes no professional strategist to visualize what these figures mean. In World War II, the Soviet Union lost 20 million inhabitants out of a population of 170 million—i.e. 12 percent; yet the country not only survived but emerged stronger politically and militarily than it had ever been. Allowing for the population growth which has occurred since then, this experience suggests that as of today the USSR could absorb the loss of 30 million of its people and be no worse off, in terms of human casualties, than it had been at the conclusion of World War II.

In case the readers of *Commentary* might miss the point, Pipes added that "in other words, all of the USSR's multimillion [population] cities could be destroyed without trace or survivors, and, provided that its essential cadres had been saved, it would emerge less hurt in terms of casualties than it was in 1945."[19]

Pipes concedes that "such figures are beyond the comprehension of most Americans. But clearly a country that since 1914 has lost, as a result of two world wars, a civil war, famine, and various 'purges,' perhaps up to sixty million citizens, must define 'unacceptable damage' differently from the United States," which has known no such suffering.

But if Pipes is right, then the rest of Europe, including our allies, who also experienced much wartime destruction, should be less squeamish than the United States about the prospect of nuclear war. That this clearly isn't true undercuts Pipes's argument, even if one factors in such theories as the barbaric temper of the East's leadership, or the tendency toward neutralism, which Reagan's first National Security Adviser Richard Allen discerned in the Europeans, or the "Protestant angst" —whatever that might mean—that Richard Perle, Assistant Secretary of Defense for International Security Policy, told me accounts for much of the European peace movement.[20]

Pipes's argument is not much different from T. K. Jones's, except that Jones supplied the details of the Soviet civil defense program while Pipes was careful to omit them. Jones risked ridicule when he talked to me about building primitive shelters with hand shovels, but he was more honest than Pipes, who when he wrote about the Soviet civil defense program disingenuously neglected to say that it was largely a matter of shoveling dirt around factory machinery and over doors atop holes in the ground.

A pamphlet that Pipes and the Committee on the Present Danger drafted says nothing about shoveling three feet of dirt onto some doors, but says instead, "Soviet nuclear offensive and defensive forces are designed to enable the USSR to fight, survive and win an all-out nuclear war should it occur."[21] And how can the Russians be so confident? Because of "the intensive programs," the pamphlet says, "of civil defense and hardening of command and control posts against nuclear attack undertaken in the Soviet Union in recent years . . ." T.K.'s mistake—the one that brought him before a Senate subcommittee— is that he talked about shovels and dirt when he should have talked about "intensive programs."

Perhaps reflecting the more moderate tone adopted by members of the Reagan Administration in response to increasing public objection, Pipes told an interviewer for the *Washington Post* in April 1982 that he doesn't advocate a big increase in civil defense because the American public would not buy it, nor had he ever discussed bomb shelters or evacuation plans with his own family. According to the *Post* story, "Pipes says he is much more worried about his children driving safely, and not getting sick, than nuclear war. He has never thought of building a bomb shelter."[22]

Pipes told the same *Post* reporter that the current probability of nuclear war is 40 percent. How, then, can he simultaneously warn of the Soviets' ability to survive a nuclear war thanks to their civil defense program, believe that nuclear war is highly likely and not advocate a similar program for the United States?

It is possible that Pipes and the others on the Committee on the Present Danger don't really believe their own alarmist rhetoric about the Soviet nuclear threat and the "window of vulnerability."[23]

6

*Window of
Vulnerability*

W HEN you first hear it, the term *window of vulnerability* sounds an elusive but unquestioned alarm.

It was a favorite of Republican candidates during the 1980 election, and while neither my colleagues in the press corps nor I understood exactly what it meant, it sounded provocative enough to keep us listening. What we were told was that this window would open up sometime in the mid-eighties and in would fly thousands of "heavier" and more accurate Soviet ICBMs in a first strike capable of wiping out our own intercontinental missiles. Indeed, as candidate Reagan frequently asserted, the window would be open so wide that "the Russians could just take us with a phone call." He meant that Soviet superiority would be so obvious to our leaders that the Russians could blackmail us into surrendering merely by threatening a first strike.

This claimed vulnerability is the major justification of the massive nuclear arms buildup called for by the Reagan Administration. It was also the basis for Reagan's attacks on the SALT II treaty and for his opposition to a nuclear freeze, both of which, he insists, would lock the United States into a position of strategic inferiority.

According to R. Jeffrey Smith, an editorial staff writer for *Science* magazine:

The scenario [of United States vulnerability to a Soviet first strike] did not achieve wide circulation until it was taken up by the Committee on the Present Danger, a Washington-based lobby that was instrumental in persuading the Senate not to ratify the second Strategic Arms Limitation Agreement. Many of the committee's officials have assumed top positions in the Reagan Administration.[1]

Secretary Weinberger, Smith added, accepted the scenario but he noted that both Harold Brown and the Joint Chiefs of Staff under Carter had pointedly rejected it. Brown had said, "It has never seemed realistic to me," because of the retaliatory power of U.S. submarines and bombers, and then added, "The only thing missing from this scenario is the capability to hit their strategic ICBMs within half an hour instead of ten hours. I submit that is not a central issue in the midst of a thermonuclear war."

But whatever its degree of plausibility, the window of vulnerability was scary stuff in a political campaign, echoing as it did the missile gap of John F. Kennedy's presidential campaign, which, while no more accurately describing an impending real crisis, offered the same kind of simple slogan that voters might buy.

In 1960, Kennedy scored heavily with his accusation that the Republicans had left open a missile gap between us and the Soviets. Once he was elected and read the intelligence data, he discovered that the Soviets had only a few missiles compared to our thousand. But no matter. By the time he discovered the error, he was President.

So, too, the window of vulnerability became a successful election ploy for Reagan and the other Republican candidates who succeeded in scaring voters into believing that our country's strategic posture had been seriously damaged by Carter's policies of "disarmament."

But the analogy with Kennedy ends here, for Reagan became addicted to his campaign rhetoric and as President continued to invoke the window of vulnerability to justify his massive arms buildup. At his October 1981 press conference in which he outlined his strategic program, Reagan once again warned that "a window of vulnerability is opening," and he added that it would "jeopardize not just our hopes for serious productive arms negotiations, but our hopes for peace and freedom." Yet he was not clear about just what this vulnerability entailed. As Christopher Paine, who is on the staff of the Federation of American Scientists, described the press conference in the *Bulletin of the Atomic Scientists:*

"Mr. President," inquired one reporter, "when exactly is the 'window of vulnerability'? We heard yesterday the suggestion that it exists now. Earlier this morning a defense official indicated that it was not until '84 or '87. Are we facing it right now?"

The President appeared confused by the question. He responded, "I think in some areas, we are, yes." As an example he cited the long-standing "imbalance of forces in the Western front—in the NATO line, we are vastly outdistanced there." And then, in an off-the-cuff assessment which must have touched off a few klaxons in the Navy, the President added, "Right now they [the Soviets] have a superiority at sea." What did any of this have to do with silo vulnerability?[2]

Referring to the President's observation about Soviet naval superiority, Roger Molander told me Reagan's comment "demonstrated how poor the President's grasp of this issue was. If there's one area in which the U.S. has acknowledged superiority, it's the Navy—submarines, antisubmarine warfare, aircraft carriers, naval armaments, across the board."[3]

In any case, to link a presumed Soviet naval advantage with the vulnerability of our land-based nuclear weapons to a Soviet first strike was a startling non sequitur. But this sort of exaggeration worked for Reagan as a rhetorical device both during the election and later in the presidency. In a speech to the Veterans of Foreign Wars in August 1980, he said: ". . . we're already in an arms race but only the Soviets are racing." Reagan is convinced that the United States disarmed unilaterally during the seventies while the Soviets barreled ahead in weapons development and deployment; that we accepted parity in nuclear weapons while the Soviet Union pushed forward to attain superiority.[4]

One problem with this argument is that few experts on strategic matters agree that the United States is inferior. While it is possible that the United States may be inferior to the Soviets in specific areas of conventional military power, such as the size of land forces or the number of tanks, it is difficult to understand the charge that the United States is inferior to the Soviets in nuclear weaponry. Perhaps the kindest thing that can be said for such assertions, to quote Gerard Smith, President Nixon's chief negotiator on strategic arms limitations talks, is that they "raise questions about the Administration's common sense and, worse, its credibility."[5]

In an article he wrote for the *New York Times*, Smith called Reagan's claim that the United States is strategically inferior "puzzling, perhaps pernicious," and added,

I believe that almost all American (and, I suspect, Soviet) experts would disagree. Somehow, while being in a position of parity, we have managed to convince many that we are in second place. That specter will be felt at the negotiating table and it is not likely to increase our bargaining power. Until now, negotiations had been based on the assumption that a situation of parity existed between the two parties. It will take some doing to arrive at arrangements that correct a balance now alleged to be out of equilibrium.

Both sides agree that the United States has more nuclear warheads and that the Soviets have a greater amount of megatonnage of explosives packed into their warheads. Those who argue the case for Soviet superiority seized upon this fact. But Herbert York, former director of the Lawrence Livermore Laboratory, points out that

the American strategic megatonnage at the beginning of the 1960s was about three times what it is today. The reason that we came down . . . [is that] we changed over from primarily bombers to primarily missiles. The carrying capacity of the missiles is less and so it's a purely practical result of that changeover that we reduced the megatonnage. But the megatonnage that we had programmed to deliver in the early sixties is the same as the megatonnage that the Russians had programmed to deliver on us today.[6]

York, who currently is a professor of physics and who had helped negotiate the nuclear test ban treaty, added that there is "nothing unprecedented" about the Soviet buildup of the sixties and seventies as the Reagan Administration has charged because "any good Russian intelligence analyst looking at what we had in the early '60s [that is, at the time Brezhnev took over] and adding to that what [former Defense Secretary] McNamara was telling everyone we were going to buy, would have produced a series of numbers identical to what the Soviets have today."

Ironically, it was Carter who first paid official notice to the possibility that our missiles might be vulnerable, an issue that would haunt him during the 1980 presidential campaign. In the aftermath of the events in Iran and Afghanistan, as the public mood grew militant and with an election coming up, Carter adopted a pro-defense line. He advocated the multiple-based MX scheme as a means not only for dealing with American vulnerability but to fend off hawkish critics of SALT

II and as a possible bargaining chip in future arms control negotiations with the Russians.

But the tactic backfired. The Republicans charged that Carter was not serious in his last-minute proposals for beefing up the defense budget and they proceeded to exploit for their own purposes the idea that the country had been exposed to its enemies by years of détente.

The difference between Carter's notion of missile vulnerability and Reagan's window of vulnerability is that while the Democratic President accepted the notion that the Minutemen were vulnerable, he still assumed that there was enough "rough parity" between the strategic forces of both sides so that neither would risk a first strike. Both Carter and his Secretary of Defense, Harold Brown, continued to insist that the Soviets would not risk a first strike against U.S. land-based missiles for fear of retaliation by U.S. nuclear-armed submarines and bombers. Candidate Reagan ignored these two additional legs of the defense triad and expanded the vulnerability argument into a full-blown assertion of U.S. weakness in the face of a threatened Soviet first strike.

Reagan's rhetoric confused a threat to American land-based missiles with a threat to America's overall ability to deter a Soviet first strike. While there is much disagreement among experts as to the percentage of U.S. missiles that would be destroyed by a Soviet attack, no one doubts that the increased accuracy of Soviet missiles has made U.S. land-based missiles more vulnerable to such attack. Meanwhile, Soviet land-based missiles are no less vulnerable to the just as accurate U.S. land-based missiles. Furthermore, we had threatened their land-based missiles before they were able to threaten ours. We improved the accuracy of American missiles—in particular the Mark 12 and 12a warhead for the Minuteman III—before the Soviets could do likewise.

And as the Soviets were improving the accuracy of their land-based missiles, the Pentagon over the past six years spent more than $400 million to enhance the capability of the Minuteman III to destroy hardened Soviet targets. While American observers were surprised by the speed with which the Soviets caught up to the United States in land-based missile accuracy, no one seriously doubted that this would eventually occur.

By 1977, the CIA concluded from satellite sightings of Soviet missile tests that the Russians had attained a suitable level of accuracy and had done so much sooner than had been expected. Because their land-based missiles were more plentiful than ours, they could deploy more of these accurate missiles.

The United States military had anticipated this improvement for some time because the U.S. Minutemen had already achieved the accuracy to threaten Soviet missiles, at least theoretically. (I say theoretically because there are myriad reasons why the Soviet Union or the United States could not hope to succeed with such an attack, ranging from the navigational imperfections of first missile firings over new terrain, to the human error likely as thousands of men handle the weapons, and to the disruption that the first missile fired at a given target might have on the missiles that followed.)

It was precisely because of this expectation that land-based missiles would become more vulnerable that the United States decided to concentrate instead on the other legs of the defense triad—submarine-launched missiles and the bomber fleet. The Soviets have not been able to develop the technology to match this development, and as a result, the survivability of the U.S. nuclear force is unquestionably far greater than that of the presumed enemy.

This last point is important since the literal definition of the window of vulnerability in the Reagan version is the prediction that at some point in the near future, the Soviets will have a strategic advantage of such magnitude that they can launch a first strike sufficient to prevent a devastating U.S. response. This prediction, however, rests on a distortion of elemental facts about the make-up of the U.S. deterrent force and the nature of nuclear war, a distortion so transparent that the prediction of United States vulnerability has the hollow sound of deliberate fabrication.

For the window-of-vulnerability argument to work, its proponents must simply ignore America's submarines and bombers, most of which are on alert at any given time and therefore cannot be taken out in a first strike. Most experts believe that these two legs of the triad of U.S. defense forces would survive a Soviet first strike and, given their fire power, that their use in retaliation following a Soviet first strike would mean the end of Soviet society. As Harold Brown noted in his last Defense Department posture statement, "The retaliatory potential of U.S. forces remaining after a counterforce exchange is substantial even in the worst case and would increase steadily after 1981, with or without SALT, primarily through the ALCM [air-launched cruise missile] and Trident programs. This potential would be much greater in generated alert."[7] A generated alert, which puts U.S. forces in a state of readiness before a Soviet strike, would inevitably occur if we take Soviet civil defense plans seriously, as does the Reagan Administration, for these plans presuppose at minimum three days to a week to evacuate Soviet cities before the Soviets launch their first strike.

Accompanying the American triad are submarine-launched cruise missiles (SLCMs) and ground-launched cruise missiles (GLCMs), as well as the ALCMs launched from B-52s. The cruise missile, which is small and easily avoids satellite detection, has its own built-in guidance system, including a highly accurate terminal terrain-matching capability, and thus is more accurate than the ballistic missile. It also flies beneath the range of conventional radar detection systems, and this, combined with its unerring accuracy, undercuts another mainstay of Reagan's rhetoric—the vulnerability of the U.S. bomber fleet.

During the campaign, Reagan was fond of offering sad-eyed descriptions of "our aging B-52s" punctuated with his inevitable anecdote about encountering a B-52 pilot whose father and grandfather had flown the same plane. The implication was that the plane—part of our deterrent forces against a Soviet first strike—was all but falling apart, hopelessly old-fashioned and in every other way inadequate to the grand defensive task at hand. Carter had disarmed us, or so the Reagan argument went, in part by refusing to fund the B-1 bomber to replace those presumably derelict B-52s.

The fact that the Soviet bomber fleet is a poor shadow of our own, Reagan ignored. Most modern Soviet bombers lack the range to reach the United States, and the airplanes that can reach us are slow and used mostly for reconnaissance. Nor did Reagan mention the air-launched cruise missiles that the Carter Administration had brought into production, at great cost to the taxpayer. One argument against the B-52s is that they are supposed to be increasingly vulnerable to Soviet antiaircraft fire. Yet when cruise missiles are installed on these B-52s, the aging planes become very effective launching platforms far outside Soviet territory, beyond the range of Soviet antiaircraft power. No matter who had won the 1980 election, these air-launched cruise missiles would have been installed beginning in 1982.

This fact prompted the physicist Hans Bethe, who dismissed Reagan's charge that the Carter Administration had somehow "disarmed" America, to note: "On the contrary, the most important progress in weapons in the last decade, I would say, was the cruise missile, which was developed under Carter."

Bethe, a Nobel laureate and a refugee from Nazi Germany, had been head of the Theoretical Physics Division of the Los Alamos Scientific Laboratory, where he worked on the Manhattan Project which de-

signed the first atomic bomb. Now seventy-six, Bethe has continued
working on U.S. strategic weapons systems from the hydrogen bomb
through anti-ballistic missile defenses and helped design the heat shield
for ballistic missiles to protect them as they reenter the atmosphere.
It was therefore from a position of some authority that he challenged
Reagan's vulnerability argument when he told me last winter:

> I don't think that either country is going to make a first strike, because it
> is absolutely crazy to do so. But suppose there were a first strike from the
> Russians, and suppose they could destroy all our Minuteman missiles. It
> wouldn't make the slightest difference. Would we be defenseless? Not at
> all. We have the submarine force with an enormous striking power.[8]

Professor Bethe, as is his custom, referred to careful notes he had
made in preparation for our interview.

> I would like to state that there is no deficiency in armaments in the United
> States, that we don't need to catch up to the Russians, that, if anything,
> the Russians have to catch up to us. The Russians have their forces mostly
> in ICBMs, a type of weapon that is becoming more and more vulnerable.
> I think our military people know this, but they always talk about the
> vulnerability of our nuclear ICBMs, and never talk about those of the
> Soviets. The Russians are much more exposed to a possible first strike from
> us than we are to one from them . . . The submarine-launched missiles, the
> new generation, are going to be extremely accurate. President Reagan
> himself has said the Trident II missile will be accurate enough to hit any
> hard target.

One who agrees with Bethe is former Defense Secretary McNamara.
I asked him how it was possible to argue that the Soviets could now
contemplate a first strike when the United States was not able to pull
that off at a time of massive nuclear superiority, and he replied:

> They no more have a first-strike capability today than we had then. No one
> has demonstrated to me that the Soviets have a capability of destroying our
> Minutemen. But even if they could destroy our Minutemen, that doesn't
> give them a first-strike capability, not when they are facing our Polaris
> submarines and our bombers. The other two legs of the triad are still there.
> . . . The argument is without foundation. It's absurd. To try to destroy the
> 1,054 Minutemen, the Soviets would have to plan to ground-burst two
> nuclear warheads of one megaton each on each site. That is 2,000 megatons,

roughly 160,000 times the megatonnage of the Hiroshima bomb.

What condition do you think our country would be in when 2,000 one-megaton bombs ground-burst? The idea that, in such a situation, we would sit here and say, "Well, we don't want to launch against them because they might come back and hurt us," is inconceivable! And the idea that the Soviets are today sitting in Moscow and thinking, "We've got the U.S. over a barrel because we're capable of putting 2,000 megatons of ground-burst on them and in such a situation we know they will be scared to death and fearful of retaliation; therefore we are free to conduct political blackmail," is too incredible to warrant serious debate.[9]

McNamara believes that nuclear-war-fighting poses risks too considerable for any rational world leader to consider, and that the Soviets are rational. The former Defense Secretary does not believe the Soviets would risk decimating their population by attempting a first strike:

The Russians are people that I would not trust to act in other than their own narrow national interest, so I am not naïve. But they are not mad. They are not mad. They have suffered casualties, and their government feels responsible to their people to avoid those situations in the future. They are more sensitive to the impact of casualties on their people than we appear to be in some of our statements and analyses of fighting and winning nuclear wars which would extend over a period of months.

So they are not mad. They are aggressive; they are ideological; they need to be restrained and contained by the existence of our defensive forces. But they are not mad, and I see no evidence that they would accept the risks associated with a first strike against the United States.

Physicist Kosta Tsipis of MIT goes further than McNamara and argues not only that the United States has a strong deterrent against the Soviets but also that the U.S. strategic arsenal is superior to theirs. Tsipis, in an article in the *Bulletin of the Atomic Scientists*, stated:

The U.S. intercontinental strategic weapons arsenal contains about 9,000 warheads; the Soviet Union will have about 7,000 warheads by 1985. About 3,200 U.S. warheads can be fired from submarines at any one time and they are totally invulnerable; only about 150 Soviet warheads are stationed on submarines at sea and can be considered invulnerable. Therefore, in secure retaliatory capacity the United States is 20 times better off.

On the basis of his accounting, Tsipis concluded, "We have more warheads; we have more survivable warheads; we have new systems, such as cruise missiles and very accurate submarine-launched ballistic missiles. Therefore, we are superior to the Soviet Union in terms of every decisive measure of nuclear capability."[10]

The Reagan Administration makes its case for impending Soviet strategic superiority by downplaying the importance of the submarines and bombers and stressing instead something called hard target kill capability, or counterforce capability, which means the capacity to knock out hardened or protected enemy missiles. This capacity was the substance of an exchange between Reagan and UPI reporter Helen Thomas at Reagan's March 31, 1982, press conference:

THOMAS: Mr. President, the experts say the Russians are far ahead of us in some nuclear weaponry and we are far ahead of them in terms of Polaris missiles and so forth. And we also have the capability of swift massive retaliation against the Soviets. Under these circumstances, why don't we seek negotiations for now and carry on to reduction? That way we can halt the making of doomsday weapons and save billions to help poor people.

REAGAN: Helen, I know that there are people who have tried to figure this out. But the truth of the matter is that on balance the Soviet Union does have a definite margin of superiority—enough so that there is risk and there is what I have called, as you all know, several times, a window of vulnerability. And I think that a freeze would not only be disadvantageous—in fact even dangerous—to us with them in that position, but I believe that it would also militate against any negotiations for reduction . . .

THOMAS: Are you saying that we are vulnerable now, right today, to a nuclear attack that [sic] could not retaliate on?

REAGAN: There [sic] would be possible because of some of triad retaliation, but the Soviets' great edge is one in which they could absorb our retaliatory blow and hit us again.[11]

The heart of Reagan's argument, then, is that the other two legs of the triad are ultimately not effective after a Soviet first strike. But why then have we devoted such vast resources to building and maintaining the subs, B-52s, cruise missiles and the off-again/now on-again B-1 bomber? What we were told when various Administrations including the present one requested funds for these weapons is that they are far better deterrents because they will survive a first strike and yet pack enough power and accuracy to destroy the Soviet Union many times over. Otherwise we should have put our money into more and bigger Minuteman missiles just as the Russians have done. We didn't do it because our experts said it would be wrong, precisely because land-based missiles are ultimately vulnerable while the submarine fleet and the cruise missiles are not.

Former Defense Secretary James Schlesinger made this point in testimony before the Senate Foreign Relations Committee. He told the committee: "The United States has and will continue to have, in my judgment, sufficient surviving and deliverable weapons to destroy the urban-industrial base of the Soviet Union—even after absorbing a Soviet strike . . . Such a capability is frequently considered the ultimate deterrent."[12]

Paul Warnke, too, rejects the notion of U.S. vulnerability. Warnke had been chief counsel in the Johnson Defense Department and was head of the Arms Control and Disarmament Agency during the first two years of the Carter Administration. In an interview for the *Los Angeles Times*, Warnke told me:

I think that it [U.S. vulnerability to a Soviet first strike] quite clearly is not true. We initially started talking about the theoretical vulnerability of [Minuteman missiles]. And now we've gotten to the point where we talk as if it were an accomplished fact and that the Russians could, with a high degree of certainty, launch a counterstrike that would destroy 90 percent of our Minutemen. But really nothing has changed except the rhetoric. The theoretical vulnerability of any fixed target has always existed. That's why we put two thirds of our strategic resources into the non-fixed targets. But having done the sensible things, we now talk as if somehow our security is threatened because this theoretical vulnerability exists.[13]

The Soviets, who lag at least five years behind us in technology, have yet to deploy survivable systems like our cruise and Trident II missiles. If Soviet missiles terrify us, think how the Soviets themselves must have felt all along. As Michael W. Johnson, formerly a senior analyst for the U.S. Army, noted, "Although much is made of the projected Soviet deployment of SS-18s and SS-19s and their capability of destroying all American land-based ICBMs, these Soviet ICBMs will merely be capable of doing in the 1980s what American ICBMs could do in the 1960s."[14]

Thus if we can claim to be threatened by a window of vulnerability to the Soviets' "relentless" buildup of heavier and more accurate missiles, they had even more reason to be threatened by our technological breakthroughs, which for them are still at best five years away. In a superpower nuclear arms race both sides will always be justified in feeling threatened by the weapons breakthroughs of the other side. Each side will then take a step forward in order to enhance its security by augmenting its deterrent. However, the other side will not see this as a deterrent but rather as a new offensive weapon that upsets the balance of power.

When I interviewed Jerome Wiesner, who served as the science adviser to Presidents Kennedy and Johnson and is now president emeritus of the Massachusetts Institute of Technology, he described the dynamic that fuels the arms race:

> The arms race . . . has acquired a psychology—Kennan called it a genetic code—which rides through all kinds of things. The U.S., I eventually became convinced, was fighting a bogeyman. That doesn't mean that [the Soviets] don't have weapons, but that on the whole we were racing with ourselves. We'd invent a weapon, then we'd invent a defense against it, then we'd defend the next weapon because the Russians would have built what we'd invented. We've really been pacing the thing, and we've been doing it for thirty years.
>
> For a long time, we were running against our own intelligence, which wasn't very good. In fact our assessments of the Soviet capabilities tended to be a mirror image of what we were doing. That is really very dangerous. Then in the late 1950s we developed these reconnaissance systems, which gave us the facts, and we saw that we had vastly exaggerated the Soviet forces. At the same time, we upset them because we essentially denuded their protection, which was the secrecy, and they began to build much stronger forces . . . [15]

For example, the United States was not interested in a ban on MIRVing existing missiles during the SALT I talks; "MIRVing" refers to putting more than one independently targeted warhead on each missile to produce a so-called Multiple Independently Targetable Reentry Vehicle. The United States was the first to develop MIRV technology and proceeded to MIRV the Minuteman, which tripled the number of intercontinental warheads on land-based missiles at U.S. command. Inevitably the Soviets mastered the fine art of MIRVing and were able to put even larger numbers of warheads on each of their heavier rockets, giving them the dramatic increase in such warheads which Reagan now claims is a threat to our own Minutemen.

Thus the United States will now build the MX and the Trident D-5, both of which are more accurate than anything the Soviets possess and which carry about ten warheads each. The Soviets have already branded the MX a first-strike weapon, calling it a "fundamentally new-generation weapon designed not for deterrence but for launching the first strike and waging a nuclear war."[16] This was pretty strong language, but no different from Reagan's description of the purpose of the newer Soviet land-based missiles.

Certainly Soviet fears must have been deepened by Reagan's decision to develop the MX missile while rejecting Carter's multiple basing scheme, a shell game in which the MX moves continuously from silo to silo so as to confuse the enemy. Reagan's MX is no longer a clearly survivable weapon, moving at random along its miles of railroad track, but meant to be fixed in its silo or gathered in the so-called "dense pack" pattern, aimed at the U.S.S.R., a weapon ready to play a first-strike role against *their* vulnerable land-based missiles.

While Carter's plan to protect the MX by moving it around on underground tracks was undoubtedly unworkable and too costly, at least it had the merit of presenting itself as a deterrent weapon—as something to use *after* a Soviet first strike. But an MX placed in fixed silos, as Reagan at first proposed, can only be a first-strike, or "launch-on-warning," weapon. By choosing this option over Carter's multiple basing plan, Reagan gave lie to his much proclaimed belief in the existence of a future window of vulnerability, since the fixed-base MX simply becomes another target, no less vulnerable than the Minuteman, unless of course Reagan means to shoot first.

"It's a decision to punt," said James Schlesinger, Secretary of Defense under President Gerald Ford, of Reagan's MX decision. "It does not deal with the vulnerability issue that has been advertised at considerable length . . . it does not close the 'window of vulnerability.' "[17]

Carter's Secretary of Defense, Harold Brown, criticized the decision because "clearly it does nothing to solve the vulnerability problem, which I consider to be real."[18]

As *Washington Post* reporters Lee Lescaze and Martin Schram, who covered Reagan in the 1980 campaign, put it:

The "window of vulnerability" of Reagan's 1980 campaign seems, in a sense, to be going the way of the "missile gap" of John F. Kennedy's 1960 campaign. Last year, Reagan talked at virtually every campaign stop about how increased accuracy of Soviet missiles had made America's missiles vulnerable in their silos. As President, Reagan has now proposed "hardening" these silos to make them less vulnerable to Soviet missiles. But the new MX missiles, when placed in these silos, will be no less vulnerable than any of the Titan or Minuteman missiles would be in them.[19]

Instead of admitting that fears of a window of vulnerability were misplaced, as Kennedy had done with the missile gap, the Reaganites pursued the MX, entangling themselves in severe contradictions, which were summarized in a *Los Angeles Times* editorial urging Reagan to "put the MX on hold," a face-saving way of dropping the whole thing. The *Times* editors wrote:

In his October [1981] announcement, the President said 100 MX missiles would be built while studies continued to determine what would be the most survivable basing system. As an interim measure, the first 36 MXs would be put into fixed, superhardened modifications of the silos now occupied by aging Titan missiles.

Since the extra survivability involved was so expensive and so problematical, however, the scheme had little support in Congress or among Pentagon experts. It was soon dropped, to be replaced by the alternative idea of putting 40 MXs into superhardened Minuteman silos.

But since the missiles would still be in fixed silos, easily targeted by the Russians, it was hard to see how the $3 billion projected cost would buy enough extra survivability to be worth the money. So that approach was ultimately abandoned, too.

Now the Defense Department has recommended that the first 40 missiles be placed in existing unhardened Minuteman silos in Wyoming, Nebraska and Colorado.

Taken alone, this move would not answer the problem of vulnerability. So the idea apparently is to follow up with construction of as many as 14 additional silos around each silo holding an MX missile; the missiles could be moved from silo to silo in a game of hide-and-seek with Soviet spy satellites.

Having gone through all that, the *Times* asked, "why not dig the extra silos in the Minuteman fields but forego the costly production and deployment of the MX?"[20]

The question is intriguing because logically we don't need the MX for defensive purposes. But since the Administration continues illogically to push for $20 billion to $30 billion for MX development, the next question to ask is what Reagan's plan for this weapon actually is.

A possible explanation for Reagan's devotion to the MX is that he needs it to stimulate Cold War fears about U.S. vulnerability to a Soviet buildup, for if all it took to protect America from a first strike were additional Minuteman holes, as the *Times* editorial suggests, how could Reagan continue to argue that a Soviet first strike was a serious threat? To abandon the MX in favor of building a few hundred empty holes is to weaken the hard-line Cold War position that Reagan is so determined to maintain. By abandoning the MX, Reagan would also have to close his window of vulnerability and thus dampen the hysteria, so dear to his politics, that the Russians are coming.

Nor does the Reagan Administration's more recent effort to solve the problem of MX vulnerability—the so-called dense pack solution, which would place the missiles in fixed ground-based silos close to each other —make the weapon any more viable. The dense pack assumption is that an incoming Soviet missile would create sufficient debris to inter- fere with those coming after it aimed at the other U.S. missiles. Ironi- cally, this fratricide effect is often used by critics of the first-strike theory, who argue that because of fratricide, the Minuteman force is not vulnerable.

The Reagan Administration further supports its claim that the densely packed MX missiles could be protected—whereas existing Min- utemen could not—by suggesting that an effective antiballistic system could be created for the more densely grouped MX. Not only would such a defense abrogate the existing restrictions on ABM deployment, there is also serious doubt it would work. As Admiral Stansfield Turner, the director of the CIA under Carter, wrote in the *Los Angeles Times:*

> The illogic of the dense pack concept is reinforced by reports that the Pentagon will also want an anti-ballistic missile defense system to go with it, just in case. If there is one thing that you don't want to do with an anti-ballistic system, it is to bunch your targets close together. That makes it easier for the enemy to saturate the system with attacking missiles.[21]

The problem with efforts to defend against nuclear attack is that any defensive system, no matter how sophisticated and costly, can always be overwhelmed by the production of still more offensive weapons. It was for this reason that the Carter Administration linked the survivabil- ity of its multiple shelter MX system with the passage of SALT II, which established limits on each side's arsenal.

Is it possible ever to establish nuclear security through the develop- ment and deployment of ever more complex and efficient weapons systems? Reagan's alarmist rhetoric ignores the larger truth implied by this question, for without arms control agreements everything, not just land-based ICBMs, sooner or later becomes vulnerable. Even the currently survivable elements of our defense—the submarines and bombers—will eventually become vulnerable to future weapons developments and so, too, will the systems of command and control by which they are directed. But even if a quantity of nuclear weapons should survive, what then? What use will such weapons be if the society that they are meant to defend no longer exists? What purpose will it serve for a few lone submarines, long cut off from any communication with the outside world, to fire their missiles at the enemy's dams, power stations, air fields and cities which, for all their officers know, no longer exist?

Jack Ruina, the MIT engineering professor who served on President Carter's panel to consider the question of Minuteman vulnerability and the need for an MX, told me:

> This business of numbers is just madness, because what is the measure of nuclear capability? If the measure is, can we destroy each other under any possible circumstances, the answer is yes. But you can always make up scenarios where one side or the other will come out ahead. Especially if the scenario starts out that the Soviets attack first. If you want to come out ahead after the Russians attack, you really have to have quite a buildup. But I can think of a lot of scenarios where the U.S. comes out ahead. And you can make up all kinds of games. But given the fundamental truth—and it's a fundamental technological truth at this point in time—neither side could do anything to prevent its destruction if the other side wills it.[22]

Ruina, who served on military panels of the President's Science Advisory Committee from 1963 to 1972 and as an adviser to the National Security Council, and who was the former director of the Defense Department Advanced Research Projects Agency, told me flatly when I asked him about the possibility of defending against nuclear attack:

> There is no technology around, at this point, nor any I can conceive, that suggests that it is possible. The reason for that is very simple, it is no profound technological reason, it's simply that the cost of doing destruction is so cheap for the superpowers. What does it cost to make a bomb, delivered? $10 million? If for $10 million you can do $10 billion worth of damage, if you get a thousand-to-one ratio against you, then the defense has

to be so fantastically good—I'm talking about defense of cities. This was not the case before nuclear weapons.

In Vietnam when we lost 2 percent or 3 percent of the B-52s, per sortie, we thought we were doing very badly. In World War II, when the British shot down 10 percent—that's the highest they ever reached—of German attacking airplanes, the defense was doing very well because those airplanes couldn't be reused. No single attack could do that much damage. But with nuclear weapons that isn't true. The Mount St. Helens eruption was the equivalent of a 10 megaton bomb in its single big explosion. It did $2 billion worth of damage, and it occurred in the middle of nowhere. With nuclear weapons, the superpowers can destroy a thousand times more than it costs to do the destruction. That is the basic truth that makes defense of cities difficult, not all this technological baloney about how we can defend our cities.

But the technological "baloney" persists and along with it the desire for perfecting means of waging nuclear war, a desire which inevitably clashes with the goal of arms control.

7

The Negotiators

The argument, if there is any, will be over which weapons, not whether we should forsake weaponry for treaties and agreements.

—President Reagan, June 1981

WHEN Ronald Reagan, in response to unprecedented public pressure for arms control talks, finally announced his START proposal, he understandably raised hopes that negotiations for arms control might actually get back on track. Were Reagan's START proposal in fact an opening to serious negotiations, his announcement would have been welcome, even though the proposal was on its face unacceptable to the Soviets.

The START proposal was flawed because it called for cuts in what the Soviets valued most, their land-based missiles, while leaving our triad of forces largely intact. START was not an opening toward reciprocal—therefore negotiable—cuts, but a proposal that put the preponderant burden on the Soviets. Nevertheless, defenders of the President's new initiative, including former President Carter, argued that START was a reasonable point with which to begin negotiations with the Soviets, just for this reason. It gave very little away in the first round.[1]

But there was much evidence to support the suspicion expressed by

Carter's Secretary of State Edmund Muskie that the START proposal "may be a secret agenda for sidetracking *disarmament* while the United States gets on with *rearmament.*"[2] The former senator from Maine is not given to wild conspiracy theories or accusations of secret agendas, but there was an unmistakable smell emitted by Reagan's arms control effort and Muskie caught the scent.

To begin with, Reagan had openly subverted the key center of arms control efforts—the Arms Control and Disarmament Agency. The agency, which was set up by Congress in part to lobby for arms control efforts within the government, was now stacked with longtime opponents of such agreements with the Soviets, from the agency's director Eugene Rostow down through the many other Reagan appointees who dealt with arms control.

Whereas the Defense Department continuously urges more weaponry—indeed, it is the Pentagon's responsibility as well as its bureaucratic prerogative to do so—the ACDA was set up to do the opposite. Charles Percy, the Republican chairman of the Senate Foreign Relations Committee, urged Rostow and his counterpart, General Edward L. Rowny, the START negotiator, to be "real advocates for arms control" because

> this is the whole idea behind . . . the legislation establishing the Arms Control Agency. We were there at the creation of it . . . There must be a counterpart to offset the tendency of some in the Administration who never want to see us negotiate with the USSR . . . Instead of having, as you say, SALT turned to START, I am concerned, and others on the committee are concerned, that maybe we would have to rename it STAL, Strategic Talks on Arms Limitations, because that could be the impression gained . . .[3]

But instead of developing a constituency for arms control, as Senator Percy suggested, the Arms Control Agency under Rostow tried to mobilize opposition to the growing peace sentiment. In an unfortunate echo of the antics of Nixon's White House, an echo that revealed a similar paranoia toward citizen critics of government policy, Rostow submitted a secret plan advising the White House how to deflect the impact of Ground Zero Week—the harmless and eminently respectable series of teach-ins and other activities that Roger Molander had organized to increase public understanding of the nuclear war problem. The tactics and players revealed in the memo had been associated with

Rostow's Committee on the Present Danger, which had so effectively opposed SALT II.[4]

According to the *Washington Post:*

A copy of [Rostow's] memorandum was sent anonymously to the Washington Post, and its authenticity was confirmed by the agency.

"The press and electronic media will be full of demagoguery and emotion as journalists hungrily interview tearful mothers and self-righteously indignant clergymen against a mushroom cloud background," the ACDA memo predicted.

. . . The ACDA memo warned that the nuclear war issue was infecting the public. "While this movement includes such perennial elements as the old-line pacifists, the environmentalists, the disaffected left and various communist elements," the memo said, "there is participation, on an increasing scale in the U.S., of three groups whose potential impact should be cause for concern. They are the churches, the 'loyal opposition,' and, perhaps most important, the unpoliticized public."[5]

The memo unintentionally mocked strategic documents of a more serious nature. Saturday, April 17, 1982, it announced, was "Ground Zero Week, minus one," and then for this and each subsequent day it supplied a "scenario" describing Ground Zero's plans and the recommended government response. For example, on "minus one" day, Rostow had anticipated pro-freeze demonstrations at the ruling Social Democratic Party convention in West Germany. The memo did not explain what this meeting had to do with Molander's Ground Zero Week, though Rostow may have felt that the participants in Molander's teach-ins would be heartened by the example of the European rally. Rostow suggested that the government respond with a "Commentary on FRG [Federal Republic of Germany]—demonstrations by Richard Burt and Manfred Von Nordheim: offered to networks and evening news. George Will on Agronsky & Co. (Friday taping). Photo Opportunity—President and Mrs. Reagan at Camp David: spring flowers—atmosphere of calm." And so this foolishness went day by day, including proposed editorial page essays to be placed in the *Washington Post* and the *New York Times*, appearances by Bush on *Meet the Press* and Nitze on *Face the Nation* as well as Colin Gray on ABC's *Nightline*, Richard Perle on *The MacNeil/Lehrer Report* and, to round it all out, a post-mortem editorial page piece by Perle for the *Washington Post* on the Monday following Ground Zero Week.

Perhaps George Will would refuse to perform as Rostow desired, and certainly the *Washington Post* and the *New York Times* could hardly be counted on to print the five editorial page articles that Rostow had assigned to them. The memo in fact tells us nothing at all about the actual ability of the government to manipulate the media, but it does reveal what President Reagan's chief arms control person naïvely thought the possibilities were. Molander, the somewhat bookish former National Security Council staffer during the Nixon, Ford and Carter years, told me he was flattered by the attention. Never before had anyone suspected that he was capable of a radical act, and he couldn't understand what the fuss was about since Ground Zero was interested in nothing more revolutionary than college forums. While the White House displayed good sense by not acting on all the items in Rostow's proposal, the incident revealed the paranoia at the center of the Administration's arms control apparatus.

The memo also revealed much about how Reagan's arms control coordinator understood his responsibilities. Clearly Rostow was more interested in heading off antinuclear sentiment than in heeding its message of concern.

None of this surprised me, for I had interviewed Rostow for several hours in his office a few weeks after his appointment. He had told me then about his concerns as director of the Arms Control Agency and observed, "I do not think the real danger of the situation is nuclear war and mass destruction, I think the danger is political coercion, based on the threat of mass destruction. . . . And that is very real. You can smell it."[6]

I interviewed this sixty-eight-year-old veteran of many causes in his new oak-paneled office in the State Department. This former dean of the Yale Law School can be pleasant and even whimsical when it suits him and is said to have been a very good teacher in his day. One can imagine him even now twitting the liberal prejudices of his students in afternoon seminars. But in the oppressive State Department building, as his conversation meandered, becoming now and then inaudible, and punctuated too often by the demands of brisk and urgent assistants, he seemed out of place. Surely he could hardly have been less suited to the job of supervising the U.S. arms control effort, unless it was Reagan's intention to humble the office and what it once stood for by handing it over to its longtime and implacable enemy.

Though his mind occasionally wanders as he speaks, and he is at times overcome by uncontrollable chuckles, Rostow remains the feisty though worn veteran of forty years of struggle to hold the Soviets at bay. What keeps him ultimately on course, like a blind man with his stick, is his faith in the political line that has sustained him throughout his life.[7]

Rostow told me that he would judge his success or failure in his arms control post not by whether an arms limitation agreement could be signed, but by whether or not there had been a "consolidation of the alliances" against the Soviets. Rostow's view and that of the Reagan Administration is that fears of nuclear war on the part of Americans and other free world citizens simply serve the designs of the Kremlin. As Rostow put it, "The Soviet Union is using, or trying to use, the nuclear question and the threat of nuclear arms, as a device to split our alliances and to threaten them."

The full exchange between Rhode Island's Democratic Senator Claiborne Pell and Rostow at the time of Rostow's confirmation hearing before the Senate Foreign Relations Committee is one of the most telling bits of evidence we have on the state of mind behind the easy slogans of this nuclear hard-liner who, with his like-minded colleagues, has been entrusted with our nuclear future.

The exchange might have revealed more than Rostow intended, for he later attempted, in written correspondence with the Senate Foreign Relations Committee staff, to soften his remarks. Originally I had quoted portions of Rostow's testimony in an article I had written for the *Los Angeles Times* on September 28, 1981, as his statements were read to me over the phone by a Senate committee staffer. Weeks later, I happened to be at the committee's office rechecking the still unpublished Senate committee transcript and learned that Rostow had sent the staff a letter with a different version of his remarks which he wanted to substitute in the published text. Unfortunately, I pointed out to the committee staff, the unexpurgated testimony had already appeared in the *Los Angeles Times,* so that it was a bit late for Rostow to edit his actual remarks. Thus the committee staff did not accede to Rostow's wishes (as too often happens with government spokesmen) and so the following testimony appeared on the record just as it had occurred:

SENATOR PELL: In the event of a full nuclear exchange between the Soviet Union and the United States, do you envision either country surviving to any substantial degree?

MR. ROSTOW: Well, I think that the risks are not so much that of nuclear exchange as of political coercion based on the prospect of a nuclear exchange: the Cuban missile crisis sort of scenario. So far as the risk of survival is concerned, I suppose the answer to your question is, it depends on how extensive the nuclear exchange is. Japan, after all, not only survived but flourished after the nuclear attack, however much we may regret that attack and do regret it. Nevertheless, it happened during the course of the war, and Japan survived. The problem is how extensive.

SENATOR PELL: My question is, in a full nuclear exchange, would a country survive?

MR. ROSTOW: The human race is very resilient, Senator Pell.

SENATOR PELL: Oh, the race is; but I asked if either country would survive.

MR. ROSTOW: Well, there are ghoulish statistical calculations that are made about how many people would die in a nuclear exchange. Depending upon certain assumptions, some estimates predict that there would be ten million casualties on one side and one hundred million on another. But that is not the whole of the population.[8]

Democratic Senator Alan Cranston, a member of the Foreign Relations Committee, voted against Rostow's confirmation. He responded to Rostow's reference to Hiroshima by stating:

That to me is an absolutely incomprehensible, inane comparison of two situations that do not compare in any way. We had only two atomic bombs when we dropped the two on Hiroshima and Nagasaki. Today the U.S. and the Soviet Union could devastate each other with an incredible number of much more powerful nuclear warheads.[9]

Senator Percy, as chairman of the Foreign Relations Committee, lectured Rostow that Reagan had not been granted a mandate to jettison the arms control process. Percy observed that "I was right there in the heart of the campaign at that time, campaigned several days with Governor Reagan . . . It was a war-and-peace campaign issue." Then Percy quoted from Reagan's paid broadcast on CBS two weeks before the election:

As President, I will immediately open negotiations on a SALT III Treaty. My goal is to begin arms reduction. My energies will be directed at reducing destructive nuclear weaponry in the world and doing it in such a way as to protect fully the critical security requirements of our nation.

Percy noted at the confirmation hearings that Rostow would have a key role in determining whether Reagan made good on that pledge and added that the purpose of the arms control agency that Rostow would head "was an offset to those who would just go down the line and say the only way to peace is to arm, arm, and arm; build, build, and build. This was the offset. It says there is an alternate policy that this country can have and that the world can have. Much of the world is devoted to arms control and dedicated to it."

Much of the world may have been devoted to arms control, but Percy must have known that he had no reason to hope that Rostow, who had long been an advocate of the arm, arm, build, build school, would change his mind now. For Rostow's perspective has always been that "appeasement"—not the arms race—is the road to war, a view that, as Senator Cranston observed, would better suit Rostow to an appointment in the Defense Department than as head of the Arms Control and Disarmament Agency. On December 4, 1981, in the *New York Times*, Rostow said, "The greatest risk we face is not nuclear war but political coercion based on the credible threat of nuclear war implicit in overwhelming Soviet nuclear and conventional force superiority."[10] His stance had been the same when I interviewed him some months earlier:

SCHEER: Would it be fair to say that you feel that the dangers inherent in the arms race, the dangers of accidental war, the dangers brought about by more and more weapons piling up, are a less serious threat to peace than the danger of not containing the Soviets and of having the Western alliance break up?

ROSTOW: That is absolutely correct. Wars come about not when power is balanced, but when power is unbalanced. If you look at the wars of this century, or the wars of earlier centuries, they came about when people got panicky that the allies in each case were behind. In a nuclear setting, that becomes twice as dangerous.[11]

Rostow's appointment was a signal that the Reagan Administration was not committed to arms control.

If there were any doubts about this after Rostow's appointment, none could have remained when Reagan appointed Paul Nitze, with whom Rostow founded the Committee on the Present Danger, to be negotiator for the Theater Nuclear Forces talks, which deal with Soviet and U.S. missiles in Europe.

In May 1981, at a conference at the Livermore Laboratory several
months before he was appointed to the Reagan Administration, Nitze
was having lunch with Senator Alan Cranston's foreign policy aide,
Jerry Warburg, several other conference participants and me. We
asked Nitze about the prospects for serious arms control talks and he
said, "There could be serious arms control negotiations, but only after
we have built up our forces." When he was asked how long it would
take to accomplish this, Nitze said, "In ten years."

The seventy-five-year-old Nitze feels there is no sense of urgency
about arms control because, like Rostow, he assumes that the risks lie
not in the arms race itself and the possibility of a misunderstanding or
accident, but in U.S. weakness relative to the Soviets.

Nitze believes that because we have not threatened the security of
the Soviet Union and have been more than generous during the arms
limitation negotiations, there can be no explanation for the Soviets'
continued military buildup other than that they seek strategic superiority. In 1980, Nitze wrote:

A central concern of the Kremlin, however, has been, and must continue
to be in the 1980s . . . the Soviets' ability to deal with the contingency of
a direct confrontation of Soviet military forces with Western military
forces. The Kremlin leaders do not want war; they want the world. They
believe it unlikely, however, that the West will let them have the world
without a fight . . .

The Soviets have for some time had reason to believe that their conventional forces on the Soviet–Warsaw Pact perimeter are superior in capability
to those that might oppose them. They are developing and deploying
non-nuclear forces and theater nuclear forces which can be projected to
considerable distances beyond that perimeter. These will expand the range
of circumstances under which they could expect to achieve local military
superiority. They believe such a capability minimizes the prospect of direct
Western-Soviet military confrontation.

If there nevertheless is such a confrontation, they further believe that,
the stakes being vital, rather than accept their loss the West may escalate
to the use of nuclear weapons. Therefore, the Soviets are driven to put
themselves into the best position they can to achieve military victory in such
a war while assuring the survival, endurance and recovery of the core of
their party and as much as possible of their power base in the Soviet
Union . . .[12]

This is is not a new notion. Nitze has been alarmed by Soviet strategic superiority ever since the Soviets tested their first nuclear device in 1949. It was then that he replaced George Kennan as Director of the State Department's policy planning staff in the Truman Administration. Kennan left the Truman Administration partly because he felt then, as he does now, that the President was overemphasizing military as opposed to political containment of the Soviets in the global struggle.

The thirty-year-old dispute between Nitze and Kennan continues to this day, as Kennan points to the dangers of an uncontrolled arms race while Nitze continues to see danger only in the prospect of our falling behind. As Nitze wrote in that same article:

There are . . . those who, for one motive or another, would seek to depict the United States as starting up a new "arms race." In my judgment, the facts are exactly contrary to any such claim. It is the Soviet Union that failed to respond to the more relaxed policies pursued by the United States in the 1970s, but instead moved relentlessly forward, first to build up its military power and then to extend its whole pattern of expansionist activity culminating in the invasion of Afghanistan. What is needed now is a redressing of the balance, undertaken not for the sake of any expansion of American influence or power, but to prevent further Soviet assaults on the national independence of individual countries and on the security of key regions of the world . . .

Kennan disagrees:

We would have to begin by accepting the validity of two very fundamental appreciations. The first is that there is no issue at stake in our political relations with the Soviet Union—no hope, no fear, nothing to which we aspire, nothing we would like to avoid—which could conceivably be worth a nuclear war. And the second is that there is no way in which nuclear weapons could conceivably be employed in combat that would not involve the possibility—and indeed the prohibitively high probability—of escalation into a general nuclear disaster.[13]

In a report to the Truman government in 1950, the famous NSC-68 document, Nitze advocated "any measures, covert or overt, violent or nonviolent, which serve the purposes of frustrating the Kremlin design . . ." The Kremlin design then under Stalin, later under Khrushchev and now under Brezhnev has always been, in Nitze's view, world domination, and to think otherwise, Nitze feels, is naïve. Although the Soviets possessed only ten to twenty atomic bombs in 1950 and we had many times that number, Nitze was already projecting the first of a series of gaps in which the United States was expected to fall behind the Russians unless we greatly increased defense spending. At that time, he projected that 1954 was the moment of vulnerability in which the Russians would be capable of a first strike against the United States.

In 1950, Nitze was as contemptuous as he is now of the prospects of arms limitation negotiations. According to an article in the *Washington Post,* Nitze's NSC-68 report

> took a cynical view of arms control negotiations. To rally public support for rearmament, it recommended that U.S. leaders constantly put forth reasonable-sounding disarmament proposals which the Soviets were unlikely to accept. Of course, should the Russians show unexpected flexibility, "we would have to consider very seriously whether we could accept such agreements."[14]

As it happened, the year 1954 came and went and the Soviets had not attained a first-strike threat, but that did not keep Nitze from sounding a similar alarm three years later in the Gaither report, which he helped to draft during the Eisenhower Administration.[15] The Gaither report predicted that by 1959 the Soviet Union would achieve "a significant intercontinental missile capability with megaton warheads . . . The United States will probably not have achieved such a capability . . ." Alan Tonelson, who covers arms control issues for the United Nations newspaper, discussed the Gaither report in an article for *Foreign Policy:*

> In the late 1950s, Nitze was in the vanguard of those who detected another Soviet threat to U.S. nuclear superiority that never materialized—the possibility of a so-called missile gap foreseen in the Gaither report of 1957. Formally entitled "Deterrence and Survival in the Nuclear Age," this report became one of the most influential strategic treatises of the postwar period. In particular, its claim that the Soviet Union could win the race to develop ICBMs and achieve a decisive strategic edge before the end of the decade sparked a bitter controversy and provided Kennedy with a major campaign issue in 1960. Nitze was made a special consultant to the project and had a major hand in drafting the study.[16]

The Gaither report, while predicting a Soviet missile capability timetable which again proved incorrect, nevertheless is widely assumed to have stimulated the massive buildup of U.S. offensive power that began with Kennedy. By the time of the 1962 Cuban missile crisis this effort had left the Soviets far behind, and the subsequent Soviet missile buildup proceeded rapidly thereafter. Nitze denies that he and his fellow contributors to the Gaither report helped to create this self-fulfilling prophecy and insists that the Soviet buildup was inevitable even if it didn't follow his predicted timetable. In the *Wall Street Journal* for June 29, 1979, staff writer Kenneth H. Bacon stated:

> In Mr. Nitze's view, one central fact hasn't changed—the Soviet Union seeks to dominate the world, and the U.S. must maintain military superiority to frustrate that goal. What has changed, he says, is that successive American administrations have failed to match the growth of Soviet forces. He concedes that in the past he has predicted faster improvements in Soviet weaponry than actually have occurred, but he thinks the U.S. "edge has slipped away."

When Nitze raised this argument in opposition to SALT II, the Carter Administration attempted to placate him and other critics by endorsing the MX system with its projected $40 to $60 billion price tag. But the obsessed Nitze was in no mood for compromise, and despite the extravagant MX concession, he ended by opposing SALT II. According to the *Wall Street Journal:*

> It is as an outsider—he calls himself "essentially a businessman" managing his extensive investments—that the 72-year-old Mr. Nitze hopes to have his biggest impact on the nation's security policies. He has become a leading critic of the new Strategic Arms Limitation Treaty that President Carter has just signed with the Soviet Union. Over the past two years, the white-haired Mr. Nitze has been crisscrossing the nation to oppose the arms-control treaty as a threat to U.S. security.
>
> "I believe SALT II doesn't reduce the risk of war; it can increase the risk of war," Mr. Nitze argues. He contends that the treaty will lock the U.S. into a position of military inferiority while allowing the Soviets to continue what he sees as a march toward world domination. The treaty, he argues, "could result in a forced accommodation to the Soviet Union," leading to "world retreat" by the U.S.

But in the Reagan Administration, Nitze no longer is an outsider who needs to be pacified. The views he and Rostow have espoused for the past thirty-five years are at long last U.S. policy.[17]

While it can hardly be doubted that Rostow and Nitze are unlikely to approve any serious arms control measures, before his resignation some observers had hoped that then-Secretary of State Haig or Defense Department officials might defend such a treaty over their objections. This possibility was reinforced by repeated leaks to the press of tension between Rostow and Richard Burt, the Assistant Secretary of State who was Haig's key official on arms control efforts. Burt, along with his "good friend," Assistant Secretary of Defense Richard Perle, were the co-chairmen of the interagency working groups dealing with arms control. Burt's influence seriously eroded with Haig's departure and by then his relationship with Perle soured. Whatever their bureaucratic differences, neither Burt nor Perle has ever said a word to encourage arms control advocates. They both opposed SALT II and they take a harsh view of any such dealings with the Soviets.

When I interviewed Burt a month after he was appointed director of the State Department's Bureau of Politico-Military Affairs, he was even tougher than Rostow. Not only did he reveal great hostility to the SALT II treaty, which he had covered as a reporter for the *New York Times* before he joined the Reagan Administration, but he was hostile even to the idea of sitting down with the Soviets in any sort of bilateral arms talks, let alone signing a treaty with them. In his opinion, the mere act of sitting down with the Soviets, no matter what might come out of the talks, legitimized the enemy. In our interview Burt told me that

> to some extent, SALT was a favor to the Russians, because it did demonstrate to the Soviets that they were a co-equal superpower. They were number two through most of the postwar system. The fact that we even sat down with them, and that newspapers around the world saw Nixon and Brezhnev clinking champagne glasses, announced their arrival as a co-equal superpower. They have an interest in sustaining that notion, so that, politically speaking, yes, the whole process of SALT, the bilateral character of SALT, is a favor to the Soviet Union.[18]

Charles Tyroler, director of the Committee on the Present Danger, told me that Burt faithfully attended Paul Nitze's anti-SALT briefings, and that Burt was one of the few sympathetic reporters who attended

Nitze's briefings. Before he joined the *Times*, Burt had learned about strategic studies at the knee of Tufts University Professor Scott Thompson, who is Paul Nitze's son-in-law. In the Rostow memorandum, Thompson was supposed to organize student demonstrations against Ground Zero Week.

In the last months of his job with the *Times*, Burt wrote an article for the quarterly journal *Daedalus* which forcefully denounced the entire arms control process and held out little hope for its future success. "Arms control," Burt wrote, "has developed the same kind of mindless momentum associated with other large scale government pursuits. Conceptual notions of limited durability, such as the doctrine of mutual assured destruction, have gained bureaucratic constituencies and have thus been prolonged beyond their usefulness." And, he added, "There are strong reasons for believing that arms control is unlikely to possess much utility in the coming decade."[19]

How, then, can anyone take Burt seriously as a proponent of the START proposal? For that matter, how can anyone take the START proposal seriously in view of Burt's views on arms control? START is supposed to lead to what President Reagan likes to call deep reductions in the weapons of both sides. Yet in 1981 Burt wrote in *Daedalus* that "regardless of whether the SALT II treaty is ratified, the United States, in any follow-on negotiations, should not seek severe quantitative reductions or tighter qualitative constraints."

Richard Perle, who is Burt's counterpart at the Pentagon, is, if anything, an even stronger advocate of U.S. nuclear superiority. Perle, in his decade of service as the national security adviser to Democratic Senator Henry Jackson of Washington, was a strident critic of Kissinger's détente policies and of the SALT process.[20] In 1980, Perle left Jackson to form a consulting firm with John Lehman, who is currently the Secretary of the Navy. Lehman's brother, Joseph, who wrote Rostow's memo on how to undermine Ground Zero Week, was a third member of the firm. Perle was one of the more active members of the Committee on the Present Danger and has a reputation in Washington as a hawk's hawk.

I interviewed Perle in the autumn of 1981 at his suburban Washington home, at which time he shared with me the intelligence that the massive European movement against the arms race—a movement in which millions of people had demonstrated for peace—was the result of what he called "Protestant angst." The antinuclear movement in Europe was, he told me, a ploy by European church leaders to exploit the fear of nuclear war in order to boost flagging church membership.

"It's a remarkable thing," he told me, "that the churches in countries where organized religion has suffered a decline in recent years should be revitalized over the issues of disarmament and neutralism . . . I had a Dutch friend tell me that the disarmament campaign has been good for the membership drive in the church." He added, "If the way to bring young people into the church is to have seminars on GLCMs [ground-launched cruise missiles] and Pershing IIs, you can hardly blame the clergy for holding seminars on GLCMs and Pershing IIs."

Perle drew a distinction between "Protestant Northern Europe," which had been the scene of massive demonstrations against the new NATO deployment, and the "Catholic South," which he claimed at the time was "solid" for the new weapons. ". . . I refer to it as Protestant angst," he noted, "[because] when you look at Catholic Europe, when you look at Portugal and Spain and Italy, when you look at Greece and Turkey—which are not Catholic, but they're not Protestant either— you find a very different attitude, a much greater awareness of the danger of military imbalance, a greater willingness to make sacrifices for defense."[21]

Perle imparted this theory to me two days before Greek Prime Minister Andreas Papandreou announced his government's intention to ask for withdrawal of U.S. bases and NATO nuclear weapons from Greece, a move that was not unexpected. In our interview, he also told me that there would be no comparable large-scale demonstrations in the United States because "we're in the fortunate position of having been through a similar period during the Vietnam era, and we've pretty much recovered from that." Six months later, the largest demonstration in the nation's history took place in New York City, where an estimated 750,000 people gathered peacefully to protest the nuclear arms buildup.

Perle also told me that the Soviets were involved in the European peace movement. "There is an element of Soviet involvement, of indigenous Communist involvement that is not nearly so well-intentioned, it's not simply a search for a more moral universe . . . There's a united front element in all of this and there is a heavy degree of Soviet involvement . . . Some of these demonstrations have been planned and organized in East Germany." He did not elaborate on this point. But he repeated his Protestant argument, adding that "there's no question" that one of the root causes for the European movement was "angst, it's a sense of fear and anxiety, troubled people, troubled governments, troubled coalitions. And it's happened before and it will happen again, and I think it's a phase that they will have to go through and we will have to go through it holding their hand."

The Europeans, Perle believes, are wrong to be upset by the arms race. "Look, if there were an arms race, the arms race itself should not be a cause of fear," he said, echoing Rostow's similar views. "The arms races that historically led to war were not arms races in which the contending parties maintained a reasonable balance. They were arms races in which one party maintained an advantage sufficient to lead it to believe that it had something to gain by going to war . . ."

Coming from Perle, these statements were not insignificant. Perle's aide, Air Force Major Norman Byers, when I asked him about the power of the interdepartmental groups that Burt and Perle headed, told me, "That's where a lot of the work is done on policy formation. The papers are written and coordinated there." These groups, which include representatives of the CIA, the Defense Intelligence Agency and all the other agencies that deal with arms control policy questions, are at the heart of policy formulation.

The subordinates whom I have mentioned thus far could make life very difficult for a President who sought progress in arms control, but it is also true that the President, were he willing, could sweep aside their opposition. He could, for example, fire them. But there is no reason to believe that these people disagree with Reagan's own views on arms control.

The President's June 17, 1982, speech to the United Nations Disarmament Conference was unprecedented for an American President in the intensity of its Cold War rhetoric. Reagan did not so much as mention Soviet Premier Leonid Brezhnev's call a few days earlier for renouncing first use of nuclear weapons, a proposal which many arms control experts believe would be an important step toward a more stable climate in Europe. Two months earlier, four high-ranking former officials of past Administrations called for a renunciation of the policy of a threatened first use of nuclear weapons.[22] They argued that while the policy might have made some sense in the fifties and early sixties when the United States had a vast edge over a feeble Soviet nuclear force, it no longer did in an age of parity. The four were McGeorge Bundy and Robert McNamara, who were National Security Adviser and Secretary of Defense respectively under Presidents Kennedy and Johnson, along with former Ambassador to the Soviet Union George

Kennan and Gerard Smith, who was chief of the U.S. delegation to the SALT talks from 1969 to 1972.

Anticipating the announcement by the four former officials, the Reagan Administration, in a statement by Haig, reiterated its refusal to renounce first use. And in the President's speech to the United Nations two months later, Reagan did not acknowledge either this or Brezhnev's proposal for renouncing first use of nuclear weapons. But the President did reiterate his START proposal, which would substantially reduce the Soviet arsenals but not our own.[23]

In his speech, Reagan explained that the United States has always taken the lead in disarmament proposals, starting with the Baruch Plan after World War II. But this simply was not true. An exception to Reagan's claim was the American indifference to Soviet interest in a ban on MIRVing missiles—applying multiple warheads to a single missile. Had the United States pursued this, Reagan and his associates might now be unable to claim that the United States is vulnerable to Soviet missiles. For after we rejected the idea of a ban, we MIRVed our Minuteman with three warheads, while the Soviets armed their heavier launchers with ten warheads each. According to Herbert Scoville, Jr., former deputy director of the CIA:

> The United States was about five years ahead of the Soviets in this technology [MIRVing], and rather than attempt to negotiate a halt to MIRV procurement, the United States decided to move ahead without any limitations. Henry Kissinger argued that this program was necessary to get the Soviets to back out of a MIRV race.
>
> As might have been expected, the opposite occurred. The Soviets followed in our MIRV footsteps, first with tests, then with deployment of first generation types and finally with sophisticated guidance systems. Now we see these as a major threat to our ICBMs. President Reagan becomes alarmed over a "window of vulnerability" brought on by the MIRVs, proposes to spend hundreds of billions of dollars as a response to this threat, and now says we can't freeze our nuclear programs until this imagined Soviet superiority is eliminated.[24]

In his United Nations speech, Reagan also announced that any arms control agreement would be worthless unless it could be verified. "Let me stress that for agreements to work, both sides must be able to verify compliance," Reagan said. "The building of mutual confidence in compliance can only be achieved through greater openness."

If by verification Reagan means on-site inspections requiring extensive and unrestricted access to the closed society of the Soviet Union as he has in the past, then there will be no treaty. However, most experts believe that it is possible to negotiate an agreement—like SALT II—which can be verified with satellite detection. In any case, no nation would add weapons without testing them, even if development and production could somehow escape detection. Ironically, Reagan rejects proposals for a nuclear freeze, which would be easier to verify than his own arms control plan. Scoville, who from his CIA experience is familiar with the problems of verification, wrote:

. . . a freeze would mean a stop to *all* activities in any weapons program. The detection of even one missile or bomber would be evidence of a violation. This greatly simplifies verification over that required for monitoring a ceiling such as was agreed to in SALT II. For example, a ceiling on the small, mobile, land- or sea-based cruise missiles would be hard to verify because one could never be sure whether a specific missile was in the allowed quota or not. A total ban on testing, production and deployment could be checked with high confidence since the chances would be high of detecting a single missile out of any significant deployment.

In a freeze, certain elements would have a higher probability of detection than others. Thus, although the production of new missiles is difficult to monitor, particularly small ones that can be confused with other types of hardware, testing and deployment would be much easier by the use of intelligence means . . .

Reagan's United Nations speech was consistent with his previous views. In May 1981 at West Point he had announced that "the era of self-doubt is over" and that the cadets assembled before him were a "chain holding back an evil force."

This speech was President Reagan's first major foreign policy address and provided an important indication of what the President really thinks about arms control treaties:

The argument, if there is any, will be over which weapons, not whether we should forsake weaponry for treaties and agreements. My good friend Laurence Beilenson authored a book a few years ago called *The Treaty Trap*. It was the result of years of research and it makes plain that no nation that placed its faith in parchment or paper, while at the same time it gave up its protective hardware, ever lasted long enough to write many pages in history.

The President then called the cadets' attention to a "thought-provoking" new book by Mr. Beilenson. Its title is *Survival and Peace in the Nuclear Age,* and it affirms that "man has used every weapon he has ever devised . . . it takes no crystal ball to perceive that a nuclear war is likely sooner or later."

Immediately after I read the text of the President's speech, I interviewed Beilenson at his home in Los Angeles. I was curious to meet the man whom the President of the United States regarded so highly for his ideas on arms control. Tucked away in the narrow winding bypasses of the Hollywood Hills lived this feisty but friendly eighty-two-year-old man who, since he retired from the practice of law twenty years ago, has haunted the UCLA library searching for examples of Soviet chicanery, much like countless other old-timers who frequent the public libraries to prove their theories of what ails the world. Many of these prophets merely imagine that they have friends or enemies in high places who support or thwart their home-grown theories, but as Beilenson talked I had to remind myself that this exuberant fellow really did have a line to the President. So I listened respectfully when he told me:

"We ought to try to overthrow any Communist government. I go all the way. I include Yugoslavia. I don't think alliances are worth a whoop in hell to us in a nuclear war." Then he added as an afterthought, "I'd try to overthrow the government of China too . . . so they'd be a non-Communist government so they wouldn't menace us."[25]

When I asked Beilenson whether the President, who calls or writes him every few months, agrees with this extreme position, Beilenson replied: "In my estimate of the Soviet Union and of the Chinese, yes. Philosophically he would agree. Whether he was ready to take the step of announcing that we would help revolution against any Communist country, I don't know."

Reagan's and Beilenson's agreement on the Soviet question goes back to the years just after World War II, years when Reagan was president of the Screen Actors Guild and Beilenson was the guild's general counsel. Beilenson told me that it was Ronald Reagan "who awarded me my gold life membership card. We've been fast friends for years."

Both men fought the "Hollywood Communists" for control of the union. And it is from these struggles that their views of Communist duplicity and subversion hardened into stone. As Beilenson told me:

". . . Reagan, by the time I knew him, he had no doubt about the evils of Communism. He had seen it work pretty well in the Screen Actors Guild. He had seen how they subordinated everything to their Communist principles."

Beilenson recalls that he "saw the meanness of the Communists in the Screen Actors Guild" just as Reagan himself had recalled his own similar experience when I interviewed him during the primary campaign and he explained to me that the Communists were "monsters." But no matter how awful the Hollywood Communists may have been in the forties, these faraway struggles hardly provide an adequate basis for contending with the Soviet Union today.

Yet this is precisely the basis for Beilenson's current rejection of arms control treaties with the Soviets, the same theories that Reagan imparted to the cadets at West Point. Beilenson feels that he, and perhaps he alone, fully grasps the meaning of what he prefers to call "Leninism." It is this Leninist component of Communism that never changes and sustains the current Soviet drive to conquer the world. That is why Beilenson doesn't buy the Sino-Soviet dispute and told me that "in the long run they'll get together. The Chinese will use us as long as they can. But they are still Communists."

Because of his perception of the unchanging imperial ambitions of Communism, Beilenson believes "in what I call 'foreign aid for freedom,' or you can call it subversion, it's the same thing—very simply, offering money openly to anybody who wants to start trouble with a Communist government."

It's not that Beilenson likes war, only that he doesn't believe that diplomacy or other forms of negotiation will contribute much to avoiding it. As he told me,

Where I differ from the [Union of] Concerned Scientists and the Harvard doctors and the preachers about nuclear war—I'm just as scared of it as they are. I just know that it doesn't do any good to say "keep talking." Take diplomacy. There has been diplomacy as long as there has been war . . . diplomacy and treaties have coexisted happily with war all through the ages. If they could prevent war, why haven't they?[26]

Beilenson also differs with T. K. Jones's views on civil defense. Because Beilenson doesn't think there will be time for evacuating American cities, he favors "underground skyscrapers." As he told me, "When the atom bomb was first invented we should have dispersed our population. We should have gone underground. We should be one story above, twelve underground."

I asked Beilenson how much contact he had had with the President on these issues. He said, "Oh, we've been talking for years. He has read all my books." Beilenson added that he had consulted frequently with Reagan when Reagan was active in opposing the Panama Canal Treaty. Beilenson told me: "During the Panama Canal fight for a few days we talked every day, sometimes two or three times a day." The President relied heavily then on Beilenson's book *The Treaty Trap* for evidence that the canal treaty would not hold. Beilenson added that "we talked a lot on the phone," and when I asked when they had last talked he said it had been only a few weeks ago. Reagan had called "from the ranch when he was out here on this last trip. He said, 'Larry, this is Ron.' I said, 'Hello, Ron—excuse me—Mr. President.' And he told me that he had been looking for an opportunity to mention my book, and he was going to do it in his West Point address."

Because I am not privy to their private relationship, I cannot assess the precise impact of Beilenson's work on Reagan's thoughts. But when I asked a top Reaganite about Beilenson's influence, he told me that "the President and Larry are close—they agree on a lot. How many other people get their books plugged in a presidential speech?"

In the case of any of Reagan's strong convictions, one can almost always trace a set of anecdotes and catch phrases that shaped his outlook and to which he more or less compulsively returns in his speeches and other public statements. He will return to these anecdotes for decades whether he's talking about welfare or the federal budget or arms control treaties. In all these cases, there is usually a key individual who first influenced him and to whom he returns for intellectual sustenance. In the case of arms control treaties, we don't have to wonder who that person is, for it was Beilenson's books that Reagan recommended to the cadets and not those of Henry Kissinger or George Kennan.

Beilenson is a foreign policy amateur and his four books have been published only by small right-wing presses. But his views, which just recently would have been dismissed as examples of what the late sociologist C. Wright Mills termed "crackpot realism," have become—odd as it may seem—the conventional wisdom guiding the new Administration.[27]

Although during the first year of the Administration, arms control advocates hoped that more moderate officials would steer the Reagan government onto the arms control track, by the summer of 1982, such hopes had been dashed with the resignation of Haig, following those of Admiral Bobby Ray Inman as deputy director of the CIA and General David C. Jones as chairman of the Joint Chiefs of Staff.

As Leslie H. Gelb, a former top official in the Carter government and currently a Washington correspondent for the *New York Times*, wrote in a *Times* piece on July 24, 1982:

> In recent weeks, the three officials generally regarded as the most moderate voices in the National Security Council have left government, each a man with impressive military credentials.
>
> Their departure is a stark example of just how far the political center of gravity has shifted since the Carter Administration. It is also a reminder of just how steady and deep institutional roots run in Washington, beneath shifting political fashions.
>
> . . . [Haig, Inman and Jones] were classified as conservatives in the Carter Administration. In the Reagan Administration they were classified as moderates . . .
>
> What actually changed was not the three men's views, but the political climate in Washington.
>
> In the inner councils of the Reagan Administration, the three men were the main advocates of arms control talks with the Soviet Union, of a less devilish theory of Soviet behavior, of more tolerance in dealing with the world as it is. As a result, they and the institutions they represented were often out of step with the hard-line approach of the White House.

And it should be remembered that the most hard-line of them all in Reagan's White House, although occasionally masked by an amiable face, is the President himself.

8

Civil Defense

Dᴜʀɪɴɢ the 1980 presidential campaign, on a plane en route from Orlando, Florida, to Columbia, South Carolina, Ronald Reagan paused to stare out the window before telling me of something important he had learned when he visited NORAD, the U.S. attack warning headquarters:

> NORAD is an amazing place—that's out in Colorado, you know, under the mountain there. They actually are tracking several thousand objects in space, meaning satellites of ours and everyone else's, even down to the point that they are tracking a glove lost by an astronaut that is still circling the earth up there. I think the thing that struck me was the irony that here, with this great technology of ours, we can do all of this yet we cannot stop any of the weapons that are coming at us. I don't think there's been a time in history when there wasn't a defense against some kind of thrust, even back in the old-fashioned days when we had coast artillery that would stop invading ships if they came.

These remarks seemed significant to me because usually when people reflect on our advanced technology and the prospect of war, they cite the tragic inability of the otherwise impressive human intellect to have found a way to avoid fighting. "The splitting of the atom," Albert Einstein once observed, "has changed everything save our mode of thinking and thus we drift toward unparalleled catastrophe."

But here was candidate Reagan yearning not for a way to end war but for a means of pursuing it as in the pre-nuclear age. What his statement reflected was a longing for the ultimate antiballistic missile. This wistful desire for the relative simplicity of the past and a belief in the capacity of industrial technology to solve any problem characterizes Reagan's philosophy in general. But in his advocacy of civil defense against nuclear war, these illusions, as I was to discover, reached the point of greatest detachment from reality. Perhaps because he wanted so much to believe that his get-tough stance toward the Soviets really did lessen the risks of global death and destruction, Reagan had come to believe what his advisers had told him: that civil defense can change the deadly implications of the nuclear equation.

This emerged when I asked Reagan, after he complained about our inability to stop incoming Soviet missiles, whether he believed that the Soviets "have a defense against our attacking them." The future President replied: "Yes, they have gone very largely into a great civil defense program, providing shelters, some of their industry is underground, and all of it hardened to the point of being able to withstand a nuclear blast." This last assertion may be only another example of Reagan's well-known habit of extrapolating from the anecdotal briefings on which he thrives. No expert that I can find believes that all of Soviet industry is hardened to the point that it can withstand a nuclear blast. Even such enthusiasts as T. K. Jones, Richard Pipes, Laurence Beilenson and Leon Gouré, author of *War Survival in Soviet Strategy*, [1] go no further than to say that some portion of Soviet industry has been protected, but only against the indirect effects of a bomb. The September 1978 CIA study of the Soviet civil defense program—the only complete CIA study of the subject—could find virtually no evidence that the Russians had hardened their industry. According to this study, "Programs to protect industry by geographic dispersal have not been implemented to a significant extent, however, and there is little evidence of hardening of economic installations . . ."

But such details do not deter the President and should not deter us here, for the point is less whether civil defense works than that Reagan, as he made clear in that interview with me, believes that it works, that a nation sufficiently well prepared can survive and win a nuclear war. He also indicated in our interview that the effective use of civil defense by the Soviets wipes out the deterrent effect of our massive nuclear arsenal—the Mutual Assured Destruction that Robert McNamara pronounced in the 1960s when he was Lyndon Johnson's Secretary of Defense.

Perhaps most serious of all, Reagan believes that we should emulate what he considers the more realistic Soviet view of nuclear war. This becomes clear from the portion of our interview which I offer below in the rambling form in which it occurred. I use this unedited version not to emphasize Reagan's incoherence, for I have learned after listening in interviews with far too many public figures that not all intelligent and well-informed people are verbally articulate. I have used the verbatim transcript as given to me by a professional typist, without additional editing for clarity, because I am not sure exactly what it is that Reagan was saying.

I had asked Reagan if the United States should seek to develop a civil defense program that could protect us from incoming missiles and he replied:

I think we're going to have to start a civil defense program. I think—see, they violated and we kept to the promise that McNamara, in the original getting together and what resulted in our doing away with our antiballistic missile system, at a time when we were ahead of them in technology on that. The idea was the Mutual Assured Destruction plan—MAD, the MAD policy, it was called—and what this policy said was that if neither country defended its citizenry, then neither country could afford to push the button, because they would know that in an exchange of weapons, both countries' populations would be decimated. And they didn't hold to that—and for several years this was a failure of the interpretation of our intelligence, the analysis of the intelligence material we were getting. We paid no attention to the fact that the Soviet Union had put a high-ranking general, who was on the Politburo, in a high command, in charge of civil defense. And they had come to the conclusion that there could be a nuclear war and it could be winnable—by them. And so, in addition to their great military buildup, they have practiced this, they have practiced evacuation, when we finally began to learn the facts, we learned that in one summer alone, they took over 20 million young people out of the cities into the country to give them training in just living off the countryside.

It is unknown where Reagan learned this; the CIA says there is no evidence the Russians have ever practiced evacuating their cities. Reagan's reference to the "failure of the interpretation of our intelligence" is presumably an endorsement of the Team B critique of the CIA's work. However, even after the Team B report, the CIA, as we shall see, continued to deemphasize the importance of Soviet civil defense in the strategic balance. Yet, no matter what the CIA thought, it was safe to assume in view of what Reagan had said in this interview that he would revive the country's dormant civil defense program.

The Reagan Administration eventually presented a program to Congress in the spring of 1982 calling for $4.3 billion for civil defense over a seven-year period. The program's sponsors claimed that it would save 80 percent of the American population in an all-out nuclear war with the Soviet Union. From the outset the program encountered incredulous opposition. For example, California Department of Health Services Director Beverlee A. Myers told a public hearing it would be "unethical" to participate in a plan that "creates the . . . illusion that the public health community can offer any assurance of health protection to the cities of California in the event of a malevolent detonation of nuclear warheads."[2] She added that "to plan for a hoax is a disservice to the people of California." New York City's City Council voted to reject the Reagan Administration's crisis relocation plan and New York Mayor Ed Koch stated that it would be "impossible to evacuate [New York City] in any timely, acceptable way."[3] Hundreds of local governments throughout the nation also refused to cooperate with the new federally sponsored civil defense program even before it was funded.

The New York Times on April 3, 1982, responded with a devastating editorial that went beyond scorn for civil defense to challenge the assumption of nuclear-war-fighting inherent in the Administration's proposal. "The sponsors of this project," the Times said,

contend that the Soviet Union has an elaborate evacuation and shelter program that needs to be matched. In a crisis, they argue, the Kremlin could reinforce a nuclear ultimatum by suddenly evacuating its people and leaving Americans without a credible response.[4]

"Most students of Soviet society," the Times editorial continued,

hold this to be a vast exaggeration. They think the known Soviet instruction manuals, shelter signs and civil defense drills are modest exertions; there is no evidence that the Russians have ever practiced evacuating a city. That would require a miraculous transformation of the Soviet transport and supply networks. And it would be futile. With the twist of a few dials, as former Defense Secretary Brown once observed, America's nuclear weapons could be retargeted to blanket the evacuation sites.

The *Times* concluded that:

The mischief in this kind of planning goes beyond the waste of money. The stability of deterrence that has kept the peace between the Soviet Union and the United States assumes that neither side could ever launch a nuclear strike without suffering an unbearable retaliatory blow. The weapons—and defenses—on each side need to be designed to preserve that condition. Despite serious uncertainties caused by some of the Soviet Union's missiles, the balance of fear persists.

Those who aim to upset it encourage the idea that it is feasible to fight a general nuclear war and to "survive." That idea is not merely irresponsible; it is mad.

The *Times* editorial asked, "Who is the mastermind who thinks this could ever work? And who decided to propose it just as the President was trying finally to calm the public's fear of nuclear weapons? Both should be fired."

But this would be no easy matter, for the mastermind was not, as one might have suspected, T. K. Jones or even Richard Pipes, both of whom by this time were lying low because of the trouble their outrageous remarks had already caused. The mastermind who insisted on the civil defense commitment, the man whom the *Times* called "mad" and said should be fired, was none other than Ronald Reagan himself.

In pushing for the program, according to two top Reagan appointees in the Office of Management and Budget whom I interviewed, President Reagan personally intervened to overrule not only his own Office of Management and Budget but Air Force General David C. Jones, then-chairman of the Joint Chiefs of Staff, as well. Officials from OMB argued that the program had been planned hastily and could end up costing $10 billion over the next five years. General Jones believed the money could be better spent on other defense items.

This new civil defense program, which in its first stage involves planning for the evacuation of the urban population to primitive antiradiation fallout shelters in the countryside, was drawn up by the Federal Emergency Management Agency, which deals with the management of natural and man-made disasters ranging from floods to nuclear war.

The agency's plan was stalled at first by OMB objections and by anticipated congressional opposition. But the agency's director, Louis Giuffrida, contacted presidential counselor Edwin Meese III, who enlisted President Regan's support. Meese and Giuffrida are old friends from the days when Meese was working for Governor Reagan and Giuffrida ran an antiterrorist school in California, teaching business-men how to protect themselves against subversives. I do not know what Giuffrida said to Meese in their conversation, but the two OMB offi-cials to whom I talked both expressed dismay when they told me of Giuffrida's effective pipeline into the White House.

Reagan responded to Meese's entreaties at a December 3, 1981, National Security Council meeting by committing his Administration to the first major increase in funding for the civil defense program in two decades. One of the participants at that meeting provided me with the details of what went on. The President spoke in favor of the Federal Emergency Management Agency's request after Meese called it an essential part of the Administration's strategic policy goals. Later Meese would tell ABC that "we must see that not only our people are protected, but the industrial base of our country could be in a position where it can be rapidly expanded, under the protection which only an adequate civil defense program can give it."

While the President backed the management agency's request "in principle," the specifics were left to subsequent meetings of Adminis-tration budget committees that included Meese and OMB Director David A. Stockman. It was at this stage, in December of 1981 and January of 1982, that the OMB critics effectively attacked the cost figures in the agency's proposals as unrealistic. In particular, the civil defense agency had not accounted for the effects of inflation in the program's future years. Nor had the agency factored in the future costs of such key items as the real estate for blast shelters, or hardened steel and concrete underground structures that could withstand the impact of a bomb.

"They were going to put blast shelters in Manhattan," one OMB critic scoffed, irritated that the FEMA people had not considered the high cost of real estate on that island, "and they just assumed that the cost of the land was insignificant."

One source deeply involved in the budget process predicted that the ultimate cost of the program "could easily go over $10 billion if they end up going for blast shelters."

For fiscal 1983, the commitment was for only part of the agency proposal, a part called Program D^1, which involves an acceleration of planning for the evacuation of American cities and towns prior to a nuclear attack. This program represented an old effort developed during the Carter years which had not been acted upon; now it was taken off the shelf because of Reagan's interest in civil defense. More costly elements, such as the construction of urban blast shelters to protect "key industrial workers" and the hardening of industrial sites to withstand nuclear explosions, were left to the 1984 budget.

According to the agency, its evacuation program, already rejected by local governments across the country, will reduce U.S. fatalities to 20 percent—or almost 42 million people—in the event of an all-out nuclear war. As the proposal said, "Performance in a large-scale, mid-1980s attack would be on the order of 80 percent survival of the U.S. population, if the bulk of the risk-area population had been evacuated to host areas prior to attack and if fallout protection had been developed and other crisis actions taken."[5]

The notion that this goal can be accomplished is at the heart of the difference between those in the Reagan Administration who believe that nuclear war is survivable and their critics, mostly outsiders, who think nuclear war will lead only to mutual suicide on the part of the superpowers.

Civil defense is the talisman of those who believe that nuclear war is survivable and, what's more, that its consequences can be dealt with strategically, morally and politically in the same manner as conventional war. Men like Rostow, Nitze and of course Reagan himself, who obscure the difference between conventional and nuclear war, assert that through some technological means or other, we can defend against its ravages.

These believers often compare the casualties suffered in Hiroshima to those incurred through the non-nuclear bombardments of Dresden or other cities in the world. For example, I asked Charles Kupperman, former defense analyst for the Committee on the Present Danger who was appointed executive director of the Arms Control and Disarmament Agency's General Advisory Committee, about what kind of life we could visualize after a nuclear attack. He responded:

It means that, you know, it would be tough. It would be a struggle to reconstitute the society that we have. It certainly wouldn't be the same society [as] prior to an exchange, there is no question about that. But in terms of having an organized nation, and having enough means left after the war to reconstitute itself, I think that is entirely possible. It may take fifteen years, but geez, look how long it took Europe to recover after the Second World War.[6]

Another comparison was offered by the President's intimate friend and adviser, author Laurence Beilenson, who, while acknowledging the horror of nuclear weapons, noted that "we killed more people when we bombed Tokyo with conventional weapons than we did at Hiroshima and Nagasaki. We also destroyed more houses and made more people homeless than we ever did with nuclear weapons."[7]

The idea is that nuclear weapons may be larger but they are nonetheless like other weapons. In any case we should not flinch in our holy war with the Soviets because of undue concern for the survival of civilization.

"You know, it's an enormous, gigantic explosion," William Chipman, chief of the civil defense division in the Federal Emergency Management Agency, told me as he described the effect that a bomb one hundred times the power of the one dropped on Hiroshima would have on Washington, D.C. He added, "But it's still an explosion, and just as if a shell went off down the road, you'd rather be lying down than standing up, and you'd rather be in a foxhole than lying down. It's the same thing."[8]

One FEMA publication, released in December 1980 and distributed to emergency managers, states, "With reasonable protective measures, the United States could survive nuclear attack and go on to recovery within a relatively few years."[9]

In handouts which resemble newspaper columns that the agency has prepared for publication in local newspapers, FEMA argues that "Americans would not be helpless—and that they could meet and overcome all the challenges of the post attack environment" by taking such protective measures as planning for the evacuation of urban populations, survival training and the construction of simple fallout shelters.

Chipman likened what his agency calls "post-attack recovery" to the problems encountered in other major but survivable historical disasters. He conceded to me in this interview that "there would be a succession of problems, a succession of hurdles to be surmounted." But he then pointed to a fatalities chart indicating distances from a blast and the number of people who would be killed within those distances. The chart showed that most people would pull through. "When they figure fatalities, they figure it on the basis of your Crimean War medical care, which is to say, almost none," he observed as he explained the chart's methodological assumptions. "And yet, if I remember rightly, the people who reached the so-called hospitals of the Crimea—they were more or less like sheds—I think 85 percent eventually survived, essentially unaided, essentially pre-arrival of Ms. Nightingale."[10]

With these remarks Chipman was disputing the goodly number of doctors who had organized in groups, such as Physicians for Social Responsibility, to call attention to the implications of nuclear war. Chipman took particular umbrage at testimony of Dr. Howard Hiatt, dean of the Harvard School of Public Health, who told a Senate committee in June 1980: "Recent talk by public figures about winning or even surviving a nuclear war must reflect a widespread failure to appreciate a medical reality: any nuclear war would inevitably cause death, disease and suffering of epidemic proportions and effective medical interventions on any realistic scale would be impossible."[11]

Hiatt noted in his Senate testimony that after the August 6, 1945, bombing of Hiroshima, most of the doctors in the city were killed or seriously wounded and only six doctors were available to treat the 10,000 wounded who made their way to Hiroshima's 600-bed Red Cross hospital.

There was eventually outside help for Hiroshima's wounded, which Hiatt argued would not be forthcoming in an all-out nuclear attack on the United States. Furthermore, he said, the size of the bombs dropped would be several hundred times larger.

Hiatt cited an Arms Control and Disarmament Agency study which postulated a one-megaton attack on the city of Washington. The result would be that of the area's 2.5 million inhabitants, more than 600,000 would be killed and 800,000 injured. Hiatt said he doubted that there would be one week's notice to evacuate the population, notice on which Chipman and other civil defense officials base their projections. And because medical facilities and supplies are concentrated in the urban area, the surviving population could not be treated.

As Hiatt put it, "Can the seriously injured be treated at George Washington University Hospital? It no longer exists. Georgetown University Hospital? It, too, has been destroyed. In ruins, as well, are Howard University Hospital, D.C. General, Capitol Hospital, and several others . . ."

The Federal Emergency Management Agency concedes in one of its prepared newspaper handouts that

a large-scale nuclear attack on the United States would cause great numbers of casualties, and there would be fewer doctors, nurses and hospitals available to care for them. Even in areas where no nuclear weapons exploded, radioactive fallout could prevent doctors and nurses from reaching injured or sick persons for a considerable period of time.

The answer, according to the agency's handout, is that "people would have to help each other during the emergency" by depending upon their own knowledge of first aid. The agency observes that "both adults and teenagers can acquire these valuable skills by taking free courses that are offered in many communities, such as a Red Cross First Aid course." The agency provides further detail in another publication, which among other things offers a seven-point plan for dealing with burn victims that mostly calls for giving the patient water and covering the burn area with dry gauze. Because burn victims will be numerous and because he did not find the agency's manual adequate, Hiatt went into some detail about the medical procedure he feels will be required. In an editorial in the *Journal of the American Medical Association*, Dr. Hiatt wrote:

A 20-year-old man was recently hospitalized in the burn unit of one of Boston's teaching hospitals after an automobile accident in which the gasoline tank exploded, resulting in extensive third-degree burns. During his hospitalization, he received 281 units of fresh-frozen plasma, 147 units of fresh-frozen RBCs, 37 units of platelets, and 36 units of albumin. He underwent six operative procedures, during which wounds involving 85% of his body surface were closed with homograft, cadaver allograft and artificial skin. Throughout his hospitalization, he required mechanical ventilation and monitoring with central venous lines, arterial lines, and an intermittent pulmonary artery line. Despite these heroic measures, which stretched the resources of one of the country's most comprehensive medical institutions, he died on his 33rd hospital day. His injuries were likened by the person who supervised his care to those described for many of the victims of the atomic bomb that exploded over Hiroshima.[12]

Hiatt quoted the head of the burn unit as saying that "just to keep one such patient alive taxes us." Hiatt added, "No amount of preparation could provide the human and physical resources required for the care of even a few such patients hospitalized simultaneously in any city of the nation. Yet one must assume that at least tens of thousands of such casualties would result in *every* metropolitan center hit by a nuclear weapon."

Mass deaths would also present hazards to the survivors. Physicians argue that pestilence, for example, would be a problem even if tens of millions should manage to survive the effects of the initial blast, fire and radiation. Dr. Herbert L. Abrams of the Harvard Medical School suggested in a report in April 1982 to the American Association for the Advancement of Science that "insects, many of which have an unexplained immunity to radiation, would thrive on the unburied corpses, infest surviving animals and eventually man."[13]

He predicted the resurgence of diseases such as the plague, cholera, smallpox and typhoid, not to mention a huge increase in influenza, pneumonia, meningitis and hepatitis.

The position of the Federal Emergency Management Agency is quite the opposite. A pamphlet dated May 10, 1979, supplied by Chipman, assures readers that "the specter of pestilence and disease stalking the land in the aftermath of nuclear war is probably just that —a specter, not a realistic probability. It need not, and probably would not, occur."[14]

The agency's position is that the major scourge diseases have been eradicated and cannot return. Because knowledge of sanitation and vaccines is widespread, the agency assumes that the survivors would be able to employ such knowledge to good advantage.

"Even under the worst circumstance imaginable," says the pamphlet called "Recovery From Nuclear Attack," "there is no danger of a repetition of the Bubonic Plague that devastated Europe in the mid-14th Century, or other types of potentially catastrophic epidemics."

The bubonic plague is a source of considerable optimism to Chipman, who observed in my interview with him, "It was horrifying at the time, and yet six or eight years later, not only had the English society rebounded . . . but, by God, those people went out on an expeditionary force to France."

Chipman's optimism is typical of the literature that the civil defense agency has produced over the years. "Would Survivors of Nuclear Attack Envy the Dead? . . . Experts Say 'No.'" That question and answer were the headline above one of those fifteen "camera-ready newspaper columns" the agency currently distributes to local "emergency managers" for placement in local newspapers. Most of the columns deal with such details as the construction of a "pre-planned snack bar shelter (Plan D)" in one's basement—which can double as an entertainment center before the attack and, perhaps, after. Some of the columns mean to be useful in everyday emergencies, such as the "special advice on tourniquets," which cautions, "If the situation *forces* use of a tourniquet to keep the patient from bleeding to death (for example, when a hand or foot has been cut off), place the tourniquet *as close to the wound as possible,* between the wound and the patient's heart."[15]

Chipman notes darkly that it was none other than the late Soviet Premier Nikita Khrushchev who first articulated the view that the living will envy the dead. The agency opposes such pessimism. As the agency publication on that topic says:

> In the face of the awesome power of nuclear weapons, the emotional response [to the question of whether the living would envy the dead] often is, "Yes." But data and conclusions drawn from complex and sophisticated studies do not support that view.
>
> . . . A close look at the facts shows with fair certainty that with reasonable protective measures, the United States could survive nuclear attack and go on to recovery within a relatively few years.

To this, civil defense director Chipman adds a personal prediction:

> It's very depressing and horrifying in one sense, but if worse ever came to worst, I really think people would . . . be miserable, but they would in all probability rise to the occasion and . . . restore some kind of a country that would fairly be called the post-attack United States. No one would ever forget what had happened, and I hope to God if it ever happened once, it would never happen again.

I asked him if he thought that democracy and other American institutions would survive. He replied: "I think they would eventually, yeah. As I say, the ants eventually build another anthill."

FEMA and other proponents of a bigger civil defense program cite what they claim is a Soviet annual expenditure of $2 billion in civil defense to support their contention that the current plan of the Reagan Administration to spend only several hundreds of millions each year is not out of line.

But the 1978 CIA report on Soviet civil defense explains this commonly held estimate that the Soviets spend $2 billion a year on civil defense. In fact, the CIA noted, the Soviets do not spend anything near that amount because the figure is a concoction of estimates of what it would cost the United States to duplicate that program; 75 percent of that claimed $2 billion represents manpower costs if they paid their troops the equivalent of United States wages—which, of course, they don't.

Marshall Shulman, the former top Soviet expert in the Carter Administration, told me: "Everything I have seen in the way of studies, both of the initial blast effect and the subsequent radiation effect, indicate that nothing representing our present societies or infrastructure or manner of living would be likely to survive it. Particularly, the long-term effects of radiation would make it difficult to begin the rebuilding process for a long time to come. That is true for the Soviet society, despite the rather limited civil defense program they've had."[16]

Shulman, who currently is the director of the Russian Institute at Columbia University, added: "I see nothing in the Soviet literature that leads me to the conclusion that the Soviet leadership believes that a nuclear exchange would be anything less than total catastrophe. The civil defense program isn't of that substantiality. It is by no means of an order that would give the Soviet leadership confidence that they could substantially reduce their casualties, both their immediate casualties and their long-term casualties. They'd have to be out of their minds to think it would do that."

Walter Slocombe, who was Deputy Under Secretary of Defense for Policy Planning in the Carter Administration and who last year debated Reagan's Deputy Under Secretary of Defense T. K. Jones in four lengthy briefings for congressmen, is also skeptical of the claims made for the Soviets' civil defense program.

He and others told me that it would be a lot easier to evacuate the American population given the much greater number of motor vehicles, vastly superior highway systems and summer homes and motels in the countryside to accommodate the urban refugees, to say nothing of a far greater food supply. It is also true that Soviet industry is more closely aligned with major population centers, and that Soviet cities have a much higher proportion of wooden housing and other structures that are susceptible to nuclear-induced fire storms.

"I don't think the Soviet system works very well," Slocombe told me and added: "The idea that you are going to somehow fundamentally reduce Soviet vulnerability to a nuclear attack . . . directed against cities and industries by evacuating the cities, which is about what the plan is when you strip it of encumbering detail, is just fantastic."[17]

His point was that it would take the Soviets, according to their own estimates as well as those of such U.S. civil defense advocates as T. K. Jones, three days to a week at minimum to evacuate the cities, and that if the United States were interested in maximizing civilian casualties, it could simply retarget to hit the evacuated populations and their water, energy and food supplies. But, in any case, the U.S. targeting plan does not aim at increasing civilian casualties but rather at destroying industrial and military targets.

Jones concedes that the industrial targets are vital to the recovery of any society under thermonuclear attack. But his studies conclude that the Soviets have an effective program for protecting key industrial personnel with shelters and for saving equipment by packing machinery in dirt.[18]

While he was at Boeing, Jones attempted to follow the instructions that he found in Soviet civil defense manuals by covering machinery with soil and exploding TNT in the vicinity. He concluded that Soviet plans for evacuating its urban populations, packing dirt around factory machines, and digging simple shelters covered by doors and dirt were highly effective.

To this, Slocombe responded:

> I find it hard enough to believe evacuation scenarios [but] the burying in dirt and surrounding machine tools with sandbags is even more fantastic. It is one thing to say that if people thought a nuclear war was coming and could somehow be convinced it would help, they would in both countries stream out of the cities, whatever their governments wanted them to do.
>
> And believe me, Americans would stream out of the cities just as well and just as far and to a much more attractive environment than would the Russians. But the idea that people would bury their industry in some useful way before they went—and there is no preparation for this, there is a certain amount of noise but there is not even an allegation that there is any serious preparation for that effort—it's just fantastic. I don't think you could improve on the CIA's conclusions on this subject.

The CIA study to which Slocombe referred was the same interagency report that explained the $2 billion Soviet civil defense investment. This study noted that the actual performance of the Soviet civil defense system was somewhat less effective than a reading of their manuals might indicate:

> Bureaucratic difficulties and apathy on the part of a large segment of the population have retarded implementation in the past, though in wartime such problems would probably diminish. A sustained effort has been made to provide blast shelters for the leadership and essential personnel. Programs to protect industry by geographic dispersal have not been implemented to a significant extent, however, and there is little evidence of hardening of economic installations.

As for the claim by Jones and others that the Soviets have actively been dispersing their industry throughout the country to minimize the effects of bombing, the CIA report concluded: "Soviet measures to protect the economy could not prevent massive industrial damage. The Soviet program for dispersal of industry appears to be offset by a contrary tendency for investments in new facilities to be inside or near previously existing installations . . . ."

The CIA report specifically denied that Soviet civil defense measures would give them the confidence to launch a first-strike attack with the hope of winning a nuclear war, as Reagan, Bush and other Administration members have argued. "They [the Soviets] cannot have confidence, however, in the degree of protection their civil defenses would afford them, given the many uncertainties attendant to a nuclear exchange," the report said. "We do not believe that the Soviets' present civil defenses would embolden them deliberately to expose the USSR to a higher risk of nuclear attack."

Nor did the CIA feel that this uncertainty would lessen in "the foreseeable future."[19]

Just what would be in store for the Soviets, at a minimum, was indicated in a recent report of the International Institute for Strategic Studies in London, which discounted the possibility that nuclear-war-fighting could be limited or controlled. The report's author, Desmond Ball, an authority on targeting plans, wrote that even if the United States followed its current nuclear targeting plan, which aims at military and industrial targets and attempts to spare civilians, the destruction of civilians nonetheless would be unavoidably high.

Simply by virtue of associated industrial and military targets, all of the 200 largest Soviet cities and 80% of the 886 Soviet cities with populations above 25,000 are included in U.S. war plans. Many of these cities would receive more than 10 warheads. Approximately 60 warheads would be detonated within the Moscow city limits; peak overpressures throughout the central Moscow area would be so severe . . . that not a building or tree would remain standing.[20]

Ball added that in addition to upwards of 100 million dead and 30 million injuries, such an attack would destroy 70–90 percent of Soviet manufacturing capacity.

Such estimates of the ravages of nuclear war, Ball warned, "are almost certainly underestimates of the actual casualties" because "esti-

mates of the effects of nuclear war are invariably based on those variables (such as blast and fallout) that are relatively easy to calculate and
generally ignore other effects that would surely take place but whose
magnitude cannot be calculated." Among those effects are the fire
produced by the blast, death due to lack of medical care, long-term
cancer deaths, and death caused by the destruction of crops and live-
stock. Ball estimated that when the above elements are factored in
along with the synergistic effect of all of this mayhem occurring at once
—for example, blood damage due to radiation makes people more
susceptible to blood loss and infection—the fatality figure would be
double the many millions commonly cited.

The assessments of Slocombe and Ball were supported by the former
CIA analyst of Soviet strategic programs—the same one who told me
about the birds caught in a nuclear explosion. He talked about the real
limits of thinking about the unthinkable. Referring to the CIA studies
that he had conducted on civil defense and nuclear war, he said:

We've looked at the blast and primary radiation effects. What we've done
is nothing like what would be required to determine what the total effect
on the population would be. We have not done that study. Because I don't
know how you would do it. We've thought long and hard about how we'd
do it and we don't know. There are too many imponderables. It isn't a
model-able thing.

He then paused and confessed that "I get kind of tired of the issue
after a while" because of the dreary imponderables. Then he said:

What's going to happen? They [burn victims and others] aren't going to
be helped. There are going to be thousands of people that need assistance
immediately, and it's not going to be available. And they're either going to
die or they're going to linger on for a long time. The average level of activity
in the society would be lowered significantly, to mere survival. To helping
your friends and associates do what is necessary to keep on living. No one
is going to be out there running lathes and rebuilding society . . . They're
going to be dying.[21]

9

Postscript

I HAVE referred to some of the men now running our government's foreign policy as neo-hawks because they are more ideological, complex and better informed in their advocacy of a hard military line than the traditional "nuke 'em" crowd. These men came to their militarism not through a love of battle or the gadgetry of war or even a belief in the robust cleansing effect of rough physical contact. They are intellectuals who in their personal demeanor hardly bring to mind Achilles or Hector but instead reveal a fussy, polemical hair-splitting intellectual style that becomes only verbally violent.

Eugene Rostow, Paul Nitze, Richard Perle, Richard Pipes, who initiate policy for the Reagan Administration—who write the position papers and policy options that are then funneled on up the chain of command which sets the parameters for the major decisions—most of these men are academics or at home in academic settings. As I have come to know them I have been struck by this curious gap between the bloodiness of their rhetoric and the apparent absence on their part of any ability to visualize the physical consequences of what they advocate.

My point here is only to suggest that discussions of global violence come to seem absurdly—not to say hideously—abstract when these theorists discuss the prospect of mass destruction as something apart from actual metal tearing human flesh and bodies radiated to oblivion as millions upon millions die either in a blinding flash or unimaginable prolonged agony.

Such thoughts came to mind one evening when Richard Perle, Assistant Defense Secretary for International Security Policy, had invited me home for drinks and an interview on the Administration's nuclear strategy. We sat in his living room with a couple of scotch and sodas chatting about deterrence and such things as whether or not the Soviet buildup had deprived the United States of the option, in Perle's words, of "moving up the escalation ladder," by which he meant our ability to threaten nuclear war if the Soviets threatened us with a conventional defeat in Europe or the Middle East. The specific case he used was Israel, and he argued that the Soviets were able to prevail upon former Secretary of State Henry Kissinger to pressure the Israelis not to destroy the Egyptian army in the Yom Kippur War in 1973 only because we no longer had the nuclear edge.

It was a neat and bloodless discussion that could have been about chess or football—until Perle's two-year-old son climbed up onto his father's lap and, as two-year-olds will do from time to time, smashed him hard in the face. Perle's drink spilled over his lap, he jumped up, the kid fell to the floor, and the father was enraged by this sudden intrusion of actual violence upon the tranquility of his parlor. My own role in this, since I too have a two-year-old child and know what Benjamin Spock meant by the "terrible twos," was to soothe Perle's hurt feelings at being set upon by his little boy.

The point is not that there is anything unusual or unloving about Perle's relationship with his child, for quite the opposite seemed to be true, but that a single episode of tolerable mayhem quite shattered the dispassionate, not to say anemic, civility of our consideration of untold millions who would have to endure far greater suffering than a small fist in the face.

I say this because I do not want to suggest that the neo-hawks are enthusiastic for nuclear war. They are not lunatics who want to destroy the world. They are neither stupid nor insensitive and they know what nuclear war would do to the people they care about. The trouble is that they have become hostages to their own rhetoric, to their compulsive polemical approach to events, and to their obsession with the Soviet threat.

They are not eager for nuclear war any more than I am. But they are as eager for confrontation as they are opposed to accommodation with the Soviet Union. And in that spirit of confrontation—or the full-court press, as Reagan's strategic plan, which these neo-hawks helped to draft, calls it—they want to reestablish the nuclear edge that the United States once had, so that once again, as Perle was explaining to me just before his son interrupted, our side can threaten to move up the escalation ladder.

The ultimate political aim of these nuclear hawks is to intimidate, disrupt and eventually transform the Soviet Union by the threat of nuclear war. What this strategy greatly underestimates is the very real likelihood that it will lead to a very real catastrophe, or as Desmond Ball realistically fears, a confrontation in which our only choices are war or capitulation. As anyone knows who watched the Vietnam War emerge inexorably from an intellectual obsession with the idea of a monolithic and expanding Communist conspiracy to take over the world, intellectual obsessions can lead to vast bloodletting.

Our advantage was real when the Soviets had no nuclear weapons, and then a few, and we had many. The last time we had such an advantage in nuclear as well as conventional weapons was during the Cuban missile crisis, when we made the Soviets blink, to use the language of the Kennedy insiders, and then back down.

The Secretary of Defense at that time, Robert McNamara, helped to codify this response as policy when he referred to the nuclear shield and proposed a flexible response that might include the first use of nuclear weapons. McNamara has since come to oppose that policy as no longer realistic in an age when the Soviets have so many nuclear weapons of their own. It is even doubtful whether the threat of U.S. nuclear superiority was effective during the Cuban missile crisis. As McGeorge Bundy, Carter's National Security Adviser, recalled:

> I myself would argue that what made the Soviets blink was the unfavorable conventional balance in the Cuban missile crisis, not the prospect of a possible U.S. first use of nuclear weapons. The remark about blinking was made by Dean Rusk in response to news that a Soviet ship approaching Cuba had stopped as it reached the blockade line. It was a prudent action in the face of great conventional superiority on the spot.[1]

Whether nuclear superiority was effective in 1962 is debatable. But in the current situation with each side in possession of such massive nuclear arsenals, new weapons systems are simply redundant.

These neo-hawks refuse to acknowledge that reality. They want to threaten the use of nuclear weapons at a time of nuclear parity when such a threat jeopardizes not only the enemy but one's fellow citizens. For the significance of parity is that both sides will now be destroyed if we really do get high enough up the escalation ladder. To climb that ladder, as Perle for example would like to do, requires a fundamental alteration of the most common view of nuclear war—that it is an unspeakable disaster that would reduce both sides to ashes and destroy civilization for longer than anyone cares to contemplate, maybe forever.

These true believers in nuclear-war-fighting, including the President of the United States and most of his key advisers, tell one another what they want to hear: that playing a game of nuclear chicken with the Soviets is not as dangerous as it might seem, for even in the worst case —even if the Soviets don't back off, even if they don't submit to our nuclear pressure—the resulting war will not be so bad; it can be limited and civilization can bounce back sooner or later.[2]

But it is one thing to talk oneself into accepting that the nuclear arms race and the game of threat escalation are not so dangerous and quite another to convince ordinary voters to go along with this madness. This is why in a time of nuclear parity, when both sides are totally at risk, our hawkish leaders invoke the chaste vocabulary of vulnerability and deterrence rather than the blunt language of death and disaster.

Instead of going to the people and saying, "Hey, listen, we want to get back to the good old days of superiority," they pretend that we have actually fallen behind and are simply trying to catch up. Instead of talking openly about nuclear-war-fighting as they did in the first year of their Administration—before their poll-takers advised them to soften their rhetoric—they now stress the need for credible deterrence against the Soviet nuclear-war-fighters. But the neo-hawks have already said too much and written too much to conceal their true intentions.

If this attempt to deceive were simply a matter of special-interest lobbying in some relatively unimportant area of our national life, then one might shrug and say, "So what's new about political chicanery?" But the danger is that these people are dealing with more than commonplace matters, even though most of the violence has so far been verbal. Because of their role in an Administration in which the President sympathizes strongly with their point of view, they have already profoundly affected the commitment to new weapons systems, systems that will make the world far more dangerous, while at the same time they have abandoned the possibility of arms control no matter how many hours we are willing to spend in negotiations with the Soviets.[3]

The danger is that the Soviet Union has no shortage of Perles and Nitzes of its own who are eager to play the same dangerous game, which is, after all, how the nuclear arms race has been sustained for all these decades. This race also now has a technological momentum of its own quite apart from the likely excesses of its human players. Consider a possible scenario: The Soviets deployed the SS-20 in Europe in response to what they claim is their vulnerability. We then deploy the Pershing II missile in Western Europe, which can hit the Soviet Union in six minutes, so the Russians must now go to launch on warning, even if this assumes the risk that the missiles will fly because some birds happen to cross the radar screen, something that actually happened not long ago over Alaska when radar picked up a flight of geese and the computer decided they were missiles. Fortunately on that occasion there was time for the computer to correct the error.

Inevitably in response to our own technological achievements the Soviets will develop more threatening weapons of their own and we will counter, for example with the Navy's D-5, a very powerful and accurate missile, and so on, until the ideological obsessions that have led to this political chaos end where no one—not even Paul Nitze or Richard Pipes—wants them to.[4]

In the first chapter of this book I described a former CIA analyst who who has never forgotten the birds that turned to cinders as he observed them through the pulsing thermal effect of a nuclear explosion many years ago. Like Richard Perle, this man too has a son and this is what he thinks about when he thinks of that young man:

You know, my son just joined the Marine Corps. I don't know why he did it. He went out and joined the Marine Corps. And I think about him. He's a very enthusiastic kid. Goddamn, he's full of life, energy. And he really wants to be a Marine. He wants to be a good Marine. He's seriously involved in that stuff. He's an expert marksman. He does hundreds of push-ups, runs miles in a very few minutes. And I think of him in a nuclear war. I try to personalize what that is like according to the calculations that we do.

I think of my son in a foxhole, and what he's experiencing as this nuclear weapon goes off. And I'm comparing what he's experiencing with what I've seen of a nuclear weapon. Only he's up close—not like me, far away [on a ship], protected with a water wash-down system. He's right there, he's on the front lines. And I'm saying to myself, he's in serious trouble. I can see a variety of things that are going to happen to him, either quickly or afterwards, that are not pleasant. And then I put myself back in this theoretical, strategic stuff, where these guys just calculate megatonnage. But my son is fried.

Notes

1 Nuke War—and Birds

1. Interview with the author, winter, 1981, Washington, D.C.

2. At a press conference in January 1981, in response to the question of whether or not he thought détente with the Soviets was possible, Reagan answered, "Well, so far détente's been a one-way street that the Soviet Union has used to pursue its own aims."

Administration officials do not think that even Reagan's proposed increase in defense spending is sufficient to counter the Soviet threat. *Aviation Week and Space Technology* (March 22, 1982) reported:

> U.S. Defense spending will have to increase throughout this decade to avoid falling farther behind the Soviet Union, a senior Defense official told Congress.
>
> Fred C. Iklé, under secretary of Defense for policy, said, "Even an increase in U.S. military investments as high as 14% per year, continued throughout the decade, would not close the gap in accumulated military assets between the U.S. and the Soviet Union until the early 1990s."
>
> "That is a bleak outlook," Iklé said in recent testimony before a Senate Armed Services subcommittee, "implying either a further deterioration in our security or a need for a Defense increase considerably steeper than what the Administration now proposes." Iklé said that given present trends in Soviet military investments, the accumulation of Soviet armaments and other military assets will continue to exceed the current rearmament program of the West.

The 1980 Republican party platform reflected views similar to those of the Reagan Administration:

> We commend to all Americans the text of House Concurrent Resolution 306, which reads as follows: The foreign policy of the United States should reflect a national strategy of peace through strength. The general principles and goals of this strategy would be:
>   • to inspire, focus, and unite the national will and determination to achieve peace and freedom;
>   • to achieve overall military and technological superiority over the Soviet Union;
>   • to create a strategic and civil defense which would protect the American people against nuclear war at least as well as the Soviet population is protected;
>   • to accept no arms control agreement which in any way jeopardizes the security of the United States or its allies, or which locks the United States into a position of military inferiority;
>   • to reestablish effective security and intelligence capabilities;
>   • to pursue positive nonmilitary means to roll back the growth of communism;
>   • to help our allies and other non-Communist countries defend themselves

against Communist aggression; and

- to maintain a strong economy and protect our overseas sources of energy and other vital raw materials.

Our strategy must encompass the levels of force required to deter each level of foreseeable attack and to prevail in conflict in the event deterrence fails . . .

. . . Nuclear weapons are the ultimate military guarantor of American security and that of our allies. Yet since 1977, the United States has moved from essential equivalence to inferiority in strategic nuclear forces with the Soviet Union . . .

. . . An administration that can defend its interest only by threatening the mass extermination of civilians, as Mr. Carter implied in 1979, dooms itself to strategic, and eventually geo-political, paralysis. Such a strategy is simply not credible and therefore is ineffectual. Yet the declining survivability of the U.S. ICBM force in the early 1980s will make this condition unavoidable unless prompt measures are taken. Our objective must be to assure the survivability of U.S. forces possessing an unquestioned, prompt, hard-target counterforce capability sufficient to disarm Soviet military targets in a second-strike. We reject the mutual-assured-destruction (MAD) strategy of the Carter Administration which limits the President during crises to a Hobson's choice between mass mutual suicide and surrender. We propose, instead, a credible strategy which will deter a Soviet attack by the clear capability of our forces to survive and ultimately to destroy Soviet military targets.

3. "Reagan's World, Republican's Policies Stress Arms Buildup, a Firm Line to Soviet," by Karen Elliott House, the *Wall Street Journal*, June 3, 1980.

Senator Alan Cranston told me in the spring of 1981 that this comment by Reagan was "the greatest oversimplification I've ever encountered regarding the threat by the Soviet Union to the United States." Cranston said, "It overlooks overpopulation, poverty, misery, hunger, nationalistic feuds all over the world, environmental threats, waste disposal—an incredible array of problems that are really as threatening to us and to the world as Soviet behavior. That is the main thrust of our foreign policy at present, that the Soviet Union is the only real problem. It's not a very rounded or sophisticated foreign policy."

4. The origin of Eugene Rostow's remark that we are living in a prewar world was described by Linda Charlton in the *New York Times* ("Groups Favoring Strong Defense Making Gains in Public Acceptance," April 4, 1977):

"You are fully aware, of course," the letter [to Rostow] said, "that in terms of the shifting military balance, the U.S. today is about where Britain was in 1938, with the shadow of Hitler's Germany darkening all of Europe."

These cautionary words, delivered last May in a letter from Frank R. Barnett, a veteran hard-line anti-Communist and strong-defense crusader, to Eugene V. Rostow, the former Under Secretary of State for Political Affairs, may have been straws in the wind, but it is a wind that has been gathering force in the last few years.

Prompted by a general agreement that the Soviet Union's strategic capability has increased greatly over the last decade, established groups that have been preaching the strong-defense gospel for many lean years are coming to the conclusion that America may be ready for their message and others are organizing to join the battle.

The letter from Mr. Barnett to Mr. Rostow was an invitation to join the National Strategy Information Center. The invitation was accepted, as was Mr. Barnett's analogy, which produced the response, "We are living in a prewar and not a postwar world."

Excerpts from Rostow's letter to Frank Barnett are included below:

On the political and political-military side, as you know, our new Committee on the Present Danger, of which you will be an active member, is planning a comparable if more limited operation. It should be no problem to coordinate our activities, and indeed to act jointly on many issues.

I fully agree, as you know, with your estimate that we are living in a pre-war and not a post-war world, and that our posture today is comparable to that of Britain, France, and the United States during the Thirties. Whether we are at the Rhineland or the Munich watershed remains to be seen . . .

(The letter in its entirety was included in an article by Robert Sherrill entitled "Gene Rostow's Propaganda Club" and published in *The Nation*, August 11–18, 1979.)

5. The following exchange took place during Deputy Defense Secretary Frank Carlucci's confirmation hearings (Committee on Armed Services, United States Senate, January 13, 1981):

SENATOR THURMOND: Mr. Carlucci, as you know, the Republican platform called for a degree of military superiority to assure our national security and preserve peace throughout the world. I presume you would support that goal?

AMBASSADOR CARLUCCI: Senator Thurmond, one can get into a lot of debate about the buzzwords that are used in this business.

Secretary-designate Weinberger referred to an imbalance that exists in our strategic forces. I think that is the case. People talk about the window of vulnerability. I think we need to have the strategic capability to survive a Soviet first strike, and retaliate. I think we need to have a counterforce capability. Over and above that, I think we need to have a war-fighting capability.

I think the Soviets are developing a nuclear-war-fighting capability, and we are going to have to do the same. That is a very large order. The indicators are such that whether you call it superiority or essential equivalence, one can never make an absolute judgment. But, as I stated earlier, the prime concern is that the trends are running against us, and the window of vulnerability is going to be upon us very quickly.

6. In a statement presented at Budget Committee hearings (Hearings before the Committee on the Budget, House of Representatives, September 10, 21, 22, 23, 25, and October 1, 1981) Secretary of Defense Caspar Weinberger stated:

turning to specific forces and programs, our top priority is on doing whatever is necessary to ensure nuclear force parity, *across the full range of plausible nuclear war-fighting scenarios*, with the Soviet Union.

. . . concerning the general purpose forces that take the major share of our resources, we will work steadily on expanding our capabilities for deterring or prosecuting a *global* war with the Soviet Union, a war that could be lengthy or be preceded by a prolonged mobilization buildup, rather than confining our planning to address only short wars in selected theaters. This ultimately will lead to larger force requirements . . .

7. On August 14, 1981, Richard Halloran, Leslie H. Gelb and Howell Raines reported in the *New York Times* ("Weinberger Said to Offer Reagan Plan to Regain Atomic Superiority"):

Secretary of Defense Caspar W. Weinberger has prepared for President Reagan a comprehensive proposal to expand the nation's strategic nuclear deterrent forces that goes well beyond previous plans to strengthen those forces, according to senior Administration officials.

The costly plan would encompass intercontinental ballistic missiles, long-range bombers, Trident submarines armed with more accurate missiles and, especially, a vast rebuilding of the extensive communications apparatus through which the strategic forces are controlled.

A key to the proposal, the senior officials said, would be to exploit American technological advantages to offset Soviet strength in numbers of weapons and, more important, to prevent the Soviet Union from concentrating on any single countermeasure.

. . . The proposed plan, the senior officials asserted, was intended to enable the United States to regain nuclear superiority over the Soviet Union within this decade. The Administration intends, the officials said, to build a capacity to fight nuclear wars that range from a limited strike through a protracted conflict to an all-out exchange.

. . . Critical to the success of the concept, the officials said, were weapons and communications that could survive a Soviet attack. They contended that the Soviet Union would be deterred from nuclear or conventional aggression if leaders in Moscow knew that the United States could weather an attack with the President still able to command a missile to be fired directly at the Kremlin and other vital targets . . .

8. Speech printed in *Aviation Week and Space Technology*, November 6, 1978.

9. The following is an exchange from my interview with Charles Kupperman, former defense analyst for the Committee on the Present Danger:

SCHEER: Do you think we are overly influenced by the physicists who emphasize the danger of nuclear war and nuclear escalation?

KUPPERMAN: No, but I think the images Americans have been brought up with on nuclear war are not accurate, and it is certainly a more popular argument to say there's no survivors, no way you can win a nuclear war, that it is too horrible to think about. That appeals to human emotions, and really precludes serious and rational thinking about it.

SCHEER: Do you think it possible for democratic society to survive?

KUPPERMAN: I think it is possible for any society to survive, and I would think that a democratic society would want to survive.

SCHEER: I mean in an all-out nuclear war.

KUPPERMAN: It depends on what one considers all-out. If the objective in a war is to try to destroy as many Soviet civilians and as many American civilians as is feasible, and the casualty levels approached 150 million on each side, then it's going to be tough to say you have a surviving nation after that. But depending on how the nuclear war is fought, it could mean the difference between 150 casualties and 20 million casualties. I think that is a significant difference, and if the country loses 20 million people, you may have a chance of surviving after that.

SCHEER: Would that mean the other nation would survive as well? You're not talking about winning a nuclear war, you're talking about a stalemate of some kind.

KUPPERMAN: It may or may not be a stalemate, depending on who had more surviving national power and military power.

SCHEER: So you think it is possible to win?

KUPPERMAN: I think it is possible to win, in the classical sense.

SCHEER: What does that mean, "in the classical sense"?

KUPPERMAN: It means that it is clear after the war that one side is stronger than the other side, the weaker side is going to accede to the demands of the stronger side.

10. On October 16, 1981, in a meeting with a group of out-of-town newspaper editors, Reagan was questioned about European concerns over U.S.–Soviet relations. Asked if he thought there could be a limited exchange of nuclear weapons in Europe or whether it would inevitably grow into a war directly involving the United States and the Soviet Union, Reagan responded, "I don't honestly know." He added that with each side having equal forces, "I could see where you could have the exchange of tactical weapons against troops in the field without it bringing either one of the major powers to pushing the button."

11. Statement issued by Muskie, May 9, 1982, following Reagan's START proposal announcement.

12. Story by UPI White House correspondent Helen Thomas, May 21, 1982.

13. Quoted in *Washington Post* article by Ronald Steel, March 29, 1981.

In an article entitled "Soviet Global Strategy" published in *Commentary* in April 1980, Richard Pipes articulated his views about reform in the Soviet system:

To frustrate Soviet global strategy, it is necessary, first and foremost, to acknowledge that it exists. We must get rid of the notion, widespread among America's educated and affluent, that the Soviet Union acts out of fear, that its actions are invariably reactions to U.S. initiatives, and that it seizes targets of opportunity like some kind of international pickpocket. We are dealing with an adversary who is driven not by fear but by aggressive impulses, who is generally more innovative in the field of political strategy than we are, and who selects his victim carefully, with long-term objectives in mind.

. . . The ultimate purpose of Western counterstrategy should be to compel the Soviet Union to turn inward—from conquest to reform. Only by blunting its external drive can the Soviet regime be made to confront its citizenry and to give it an account of its policies. It is a well-known fact of modern Russian history that whenever Russian governments suffered serious setbacks abroad—in the Crimean war, in the 1904–05 war with Japan, and in World War I—they were compelled by internal pressure to grant the citizenry political rights. We should help the population of the Soviet Union bring its government under control. A more democratic Russia would be less expansionist and certainly easier to live with.

14. "Pentagon Draws Up First Strategy for Fighting a Long Nuclear War," by Richard Halloran, *New York Times*, May 30, 1982.

15. A White House fact sheet on national space policy which was released by President Reagan at the time of the landing of the space shuttle *Columbia*, July 4, 1982, at Edwards Air Force Base, California, stated that among other principles of the U.S. space program:

—The United States is committed to the exploration and use of space by all nations for peaceful purposes and for the benefit of mankind. "Peaceful purposes" allow activities in pursuit of national security goals . . .
—The United States will pursue activities in space in support of its right of self defense . . .
—The United States will continue to study space arms control options. The United States will consider verifiable and equitable arms control measures that would ban or otherwise limit testing and deployment of specific weapons systems, should those measures be compatible with United States national security.

Under the heading "National Security Space Program," the document states "that the United States will conduct those activities in space that it deems necessary to its national security. National security space programs shall support such functions as command and control, communications, navigation, environmental monitoring, warning, surveillance and space defense."

16. "The Five Year War Plan," *New York Times*, June 10, 1982. Bethe and Gottfried said further:

The Soviet Union has always been blessed with five-year plans. Thanks to the Defense Department, we are to have our own in the "Defense Guidance" that is to form the basis for Pentagon budget requests for the next five fiscal years. This comprehensive plan, which envisions a possibly "protracted" nuclear war, global conventional war and "space-based" fighting with anti-satellite weapons, must be examined with great care. It comes close to a declaration of war on the Soviet Union and contradicts and may destroy President Reagan's initiatives toward nuclear arms control.

The plan reveals a nonchalance toward nuclear war, an inability to distinguish real dangers from farfetched nightmares, an unwillingness to learn that many of our technological breakthroughs have returned to haunt us—that the arms race is an increasingly dangerous treadmill.

. . . The five-year plan displays a profoundly disturbing attitude toward nuclear weapons. In contrast to the statesmanlike posture that President Reagan and Secretary of State Alexander M. Haig Jr. have now adopted, it bristles with nuclear saber-rattling: limited winnable nuclear warfare, nuclear weapons in space, anti-ballistic missile defenses. There are glaring inconsistencies: Our nuclear weapons would "render ineffective the total Soviet . . . power structure," while our "plan" assumes Mr. Reagan and his staff could control a nuclear exchange. That some of these steps could violate treaties (nuclear weapons in space, the A.B.M. pact) appears not to matter to the Pentagon.

. . . If the Pentagon plan becomes Government policy, the arms race will quicken. The plan's notion that we could win such a race reveals an ignorance of post-1945 history.

. . .

In response to the Defense Department's five-year defense plan (as reported by Richard Halloran, *New York Times*, May 30, 1982), Leonard S. Rodberg, former director of policy research of ACDA, wrote in a letter to the *New York Times* (June 10, 1982):

It is disturbing that the Reagan Administration's military planners have prepared a "guidance" document which suggests that they find it realistic to plan for a "protracted" nuclear war.

What is even more appalling, though, is that their nuclear strategy is based on what they call "decapitation," destroying Soviet political and military leadership and communication lines. Apparently they want to leave the Russian military forces leaderless and on their own in deciding what to do with the remaining weapons at their disposal.

Such a notion might have made some sense in an era of conventional warfare, when the individual military unit or soldier could accomplish little. In nuclear war, the individual missile commander, submarine captain, even aircraft pilot has the capacity to destroy, on his own, significant portions of an enemy's society.

That our military planners would want to leave Soviet military forces in a situation where any one of countless individuals could cause millions of American casualties seems irresponsible to the point of being criminal.

It is also inconsistent with the Pentagon's own strategy, which, according to the same document, is intended to "force the Soviet Union to seek earliest termination of hostilities on terms favorable to the United States." If the Soviet leadership is "decapitated," who would be left to seek such an end to hostilities?

This "guidance" document provides renewed evidence (is it still needed at this late date?) that our military planners, and the civilian leaders who direct them and listen to them, are ill-equipped, by training and experience, to address the realities of the nuclear age.

Since the first atom bomb was exploded, farsighted scientists and others have been insisting that nuclear war would have little in common with past wars, and yet our leaders continue to rely on the obsolete ideas of another era.

Perhaps it is time we paid attention to the millions of people now mobilizing in the "nuclear freeze" movement, who recognize that our leaders' current course is a little short of suicidal.

. . .

After the story about the Defense Department's five-year plan appeared in the *New York Times*, Michael Getler reported in the *Washington Post* (June 4, 1982):

Fearing repercussions at home and abroad that could damage President Reagan's new push for arms control, the Pentagon today launched an all-out effort to convince people that the United States did not think a nuclear war was winnable and was not suggesting that such wars, if they occurred, would have to be "protracted."

. . . "No one is suggesting that a protracted war is a good thing, or something that we would want to do or are planning to do," said [a] high official . . . But the ability to deal with a protracted attack is important to deterrence, the official claimed, because Soviet nuclear forces may be large enough to strike several times.

. . . In his speech [at the Army War College in Pennsylvania] [Defense Secretary Caspar] Weinberger urged support for Reagan's new strategic buildup, including the MX missile, B-1 bomber, Trident II submarine missile and new communications systems.

"But nowhere in all of this do we mean to imply that nuclear war is winnable. This notion has no place in our strategy. We see nuclear weapons only as a way of discouraging the Soviets from thinking that they could ever resort to them," Weinberger said.

"That is exactly why we must have a capability for a 'protracted' response—to demonstrate that our strategic forces could survive Soviet strikes over an extended, that is to say, protracted period.

"Our entire strategic program, including the development of a protracted response capability that has been so maligned in the press recently, has been developed with the express intention of assuring that nuclear war will never be fought."

17. "Preparing for Long Nuclear War Is Waste of Funds, General Jones Says," by George C. Wilson, *Washington Post*, June 19, 1982.

On July 22, 1982, in a *New York Times* article entitled "50 in Congress Protest Policy on Protracted A-War," Richard Halloran reported:

Fifty members of Congress, most of them Democrats, have signed a letter to President Reagan protesting the Administration's policy on fighting a protracted nuclear war and urging him to reassess the policy.

. . . The letter said: "We are extremely alarmed with those sections of the guidance calling for planning to wage a protracted nuclear war. In our minds, such a strategy will result in a futile renewal of the nuclear arms race in which neither side will relent."

. . . The letter also objected to plans for space-based weapons, which they said violated international treaties, and to the possibility that the 1972 antiballistic-missile treaty might be abrogated.

It said of the nuclear strategy: "This policy completely contradicts your declared intentions to lessen the risk of nuclear war and undermines the credibility of your offer to negotiate 'meaningful reductions' in nuclear arsenals with the Soviet Union."

. . .

Jack Ruina, who was the director of the Defense Department's Advance Research Project Agency in the Kennedy Administration, and who is now an MIT professor of engineering, said: "We have a peculiar situation in the Pentagon in this Administration, where the civilian leaders are the hardest-liners and the military leaders are the more reasonable. Ironically, in this Administration, we might be better off if we had military control over civilian."

18. Interview with the author, spring, 1982, Washington, D.C.

19. Interview with the author, spring, 1982, New York City, New York.

In an interview in March 1982, former Secretary of State Cyrus Vance discussed the difference between the doctrines of the Carter and Reagan Administrations. He spoke of Presidential Directive 59 and then was asked if it is not the Administration's argument that the Russians think they could fight a sustained nuclear war and that to have a credible deterrence, we must think in similar terms. He responded:

> You can find all kinds of theories on the use of nuclear weapons contained in writings by Russian military authors on the use of nuclear weapons, as you can in the United States. There are articles and papers that have been written about the fighting of a sustained nuclear war in the Soviet bibliographies. But that does not mean that that is the political doctrine of the Soviet Union. The Soviets deny that that is their political doctrine. They draw the distinction between strategy and tactics. So the fact that there are such writings does not mean that that is the policy of the Soviet Union.

. . .

Roger Molander and another top Carter aide who did not want to be identified, both of whom had knowledge of the drafting of PD 59, told me it was done at Brzezinski's insistence. The State Department, by then under Muskie, was not included in the process, and Defense Department officials thought that the attempt to nail down specific targeting language would imply more than was intended. Whatever Brzezinski's purposes, which are still unclear, believers in nuclear-war-fighting were a distinct minority in the Carter Administration. This was confirmed in a telephone interview in the spring of 1982 by Walter Slocombe, Deputy Under Secretary of Defense under Carter, who was co-director of the committee that dealt with the issue of revised military targeting that led eventually to the drafting of PD 59. Slocombe told me:

> One of the problems is, PD 59 was a relatively short document which set forward some basic principles that are reasonably well summarized in Harold's [Brown] posture statements and his speech. I think the place where there is a discontinuity is that if there are people in the present Administration who think that you can fight and win a nuclear war, and that it is reasonable to plan on doing so in the same way the British plan to fight and win the war in the Falklands—if there are people that believe that, then there was nobody at a politically responsible or politically significant level in the Carter Administration who thought that.

20. "The Flexibility of Our Plans," speech delivered at the Naval War College in Newport, Rhode Island, August 20, 1980. Printed in *Vital Speeches of the Day*, 46, number 24, October, 1980.

21. "Victory is Possible," *Foreign Policy*, summer, 1980.

22. Interview with the author, fall, 1981, Washington, D.C.

23. From a letter written to Frank Barnett, printed in an article entitled "Gene Rostow's Propaganda Club," by Robert Sherrill, *The Nation*, August 11–18, 1979.

24. Interview with the author, spring, 1981, Washington, D.C.

25. Interview with the author, spring, 1982, Los Angeles, California. In the interview, Ball stated:

> Since the mid-fifties, there have always been tactical nuclear weapons and conventional forces. What is happening now is that the great weight, the whole reliance, is now on the theater nuclear weapons, the short-range battlefield nuclear weapons, and on the ability to use strategic weapons in limited ways. Reliance on the conventional forces has just decreased.
> The U.S. is going to find itself in a position where all it can do is threaten a limited strategic exchange because that is the only option you've got. They are going to find themselves in a situation where they say, "Oh, no, we can't, we really don't believe we can control a nuclear war." In which case the whole thing doesn't work and the Russians get away with it. Or the characters say, we can do this, and they initiate a limited nuclear exchange. Either way it is dangerous.

26. In his study entitled "Can Nuclear War Be Controlled?" [Adelphi Papers, International Institute for Strategic Studies, Fall 1981], Desmond Ball states:

> A strategic nuclear war between the United States and the Soviet Union would involve so many novel technical and emotional variables that predictions about its course—and especially about whether or not it could be controlled—must remain highly speculative.
> To the extent that there is a typical lay image of a nuclear war, it is that any substantial use of nuclear weapons by either the United States or the Soviet Union against the other's forces or territory would inevitably and rapidly lead to all-out urban-industrial attacks and consequent mutual destruction. As Carl-Friedrich von Weiszacker recently wrote, "as soon as we use nuclear weapons, there are no limits."
> Among strategic analysts on the other hand, the ascendant view is that it is possible to conduct limited and quite protracted nuclear exchanges in such a way that escalation can be controlled and the war terminated at some less than all-out level. Some strategists actually visualize an escalation ladder, with a series of discrete and clearly identifiable steps of increasing levels of intensity of nuclear conflict, which the respective adversaries move up—and down—at will. Current U.S. strategic policy, although extensively and carefully qualified, is closer to this second position: it is hoped that escalation could be controlled and that more survivable command-and-control capabilities should ensure dominance in the escalation process. Indeed, reliance on the ability to control escalation is an essential element of U.S. efforts with respect to extended deterrence.
> Escalation is neither autonomous and inevitable nor subject completely to the decisions of any one national command authority. Whether or not it can be controlled will depend very much on the circumstances at the time. The use of a few

nuclear weapons for some clear demonstrative purposes, for example, could well not lead to further escalation. However, it is most unrealistic to expect that there would be a relatively smooth and controlled progression from limited and selective strikes, through major counterforce exchanges, to termination of the conflict at some level short of urban-industrial attacks. It is likely that beyond some relatively early stage in the conflict the strategic communications systems would suffer interference and disruption, the strikes would become ragged, unco-ordinated, less precise and less discriminating, and the ability to reach an agreed settlement between the adversaries would soon become extremely problematical.

. . . Command and control systems are inherently relatively vulnerable, and concerted attacks on them would very rapidly destroy them, or at least render them inoperable. Despite the increased resources that the US is currently devoting to improving the survivability and endurance of command-and-control systems, the extent of their relative vulnerability remains enormous.

. . . The notion of controlled nuclear war-fighting is essentially astrategic in that it tends to ignore a number of the realities that would necessarily attend any nuclear exchange. The more significant of these include the particular origins of the given conflict and the nature of its progress to the point where the strategic nuclear exchange is initiated; the disparate objectives for which a limited nuclear exchange would be fought; the nature of the decision-making processes within the adversary governments; the political pressures that would be generated by a nuclear exchange; and the problems of terminating the exchange at some less than all-out level. Some of these considerations are so fundamental and so intemperate in their implications as to suggest that there can really be no possibility of controlling a nuclear war.

. . . Furthermore, the technical and strategic uncertainties are such that, regardless of the care and tight control which they attempt to exercise, decision-makers could never be confident that escalation could be controlled. Uncertainties in weapons effects and the accuracy with which weapons can be delivered mean that collateral casualties can never be calculated precisely and that particular strikes could look much less discriminating to the recipient than to the attack planner.

. . . Of course, national security policies and postures are not designed solely for the prosecution of war. In both the United States and the Soviet Union, deterring war remains a primary national objective. It is an axiom in the strategic literature that the criteria for deterrence are different from those of war-fighting, and capabilities which would be deficient for one purpose could well be satisfactory for the other. The large-scale investment of resources in command-and-control capabilities, together with high-level official declarations that the United States would be prepared to conduct limited, selective and tightly controlled strategic strikes (perhaps in support of extended deterrence), could therefore be valuable because they suggest U.S. determination to act in limited ways—the demonstratable problems of control notwithstanding. However, viable deterrent postures require both capabilities and credibility, and it would seem that neither can be assumed to the extent that would be necessary for the concept of controlled nuclear war-fighting to act as a deterrent . . .

27. Interview with the author, spring, 1981, Washington, D.C.

2 "It's the Dirt That Does It"

1. Interviews with the author, fall 1981, in Washington, D.C., and McLean, Virginia.

2. "U.S. Could Survive in Administration's View," *Los Angeles Times*, January 16, 1982.

3. "Defense Aide Spars over Nuclear War," *San Francisco Chronicle*, April 1, 1982.

4. "The Dirt on T. K. Jones," *New York Times*, March 19, 1982:

> Who is the Thomas K. Jones who is saying those funny things about civil defense? Is he only a character in "Doonesbury"? Did he once write lyrics for Tom Lehrer's darker political ballads? Or is T.K., as he is known to friends, the peace movement's mole inside the Reagan Administration?
>
> Senator Larry Pressler, a South Dakota Republican, contends that Mr. Jones is not a made-up figure but is actually serving as Deputy Under Secretary of Defense for Strategic Nuclear Forces. That's how he is listed in the blue book, and Mr. Pressler wants him to appear before an arms control subcommittee.
>
> Three times Mr. Jones—or someone speaking in his name—agreed to testify. Three times he failed to appear. The Pentagon finally sent a pinch-hitter, Assistant Secretary of Defense Richard Perle. But the Senate wants Mr. Jones. It wants an authoritative explanation of his plan to spend $252 million on civil defense. Evidently, most of that money will go for shovels.
>
> For this is how the alleged Mr. Jones describes the alleged civil defense strategy: "Dig a hole, cover it with a couple of doors and then throw three feet of dirt on top. It's the dirt that does it."
>
> Mr. Jones seems to believe that the United States could recover fully, in two to four years, from an all-out nuclear attack. As he was quoted in The Los Angeles Times: "Everybody's going to make it if there are enough shovels to go around."
>
> Dig on, Senator Pressler. We're all curious.

5. Interview with the author, fall, 1981, Los Angeles, California.

6. In the following exchange, which took place during hearings before the Joint Committee on Defense Production, November 17, 1976, T. K. Jones, who at the time was program and product evaluation manager at Boeing, expressed views similar to those expressed during my interviews with him. Senator William Proxmire asked Jones, ". . . if we used every bit of our nuclear potential, are you contending that the Soviet Union can survive, could accept that kind of an unacceptable prospect?"

MR. JONES: Yes, Senator, the assumptions we made in estimating the effectiveness of Soviet protection assumed that they made a fairly light attack on the United States forces and, that our forces were on fully generated alert. Therefore, most of our submarines would be at sea, and we assumed that all of those would survive and be usable, and our bombers would be in a very high state of alert and most of those would survive.

We assumed that the attack on our Minutemen force was quite light, which would allow a very large number of those missiles to survive and be used. Our calculations considered that the United States would in fact dump all of those surviving weapons on the Soviet Union. If the Soviets did not execute their civil defense preparations and evacuate their people, sure enough they would be destroyed, but if they execute their plan, they will survive and recover rather promptly.

The two- to four-year recovery time that we project for their recovery does include recovery from a full-scale total United States response, where we disarmed ourselves in throwing everything we had at the Soviet Union.

SENATOR PROXMIRE: . . . do I misinterpret this as indicating that if they had a full evacuation, that they would be able to save 99 percent, plus, of their people?

MR. JONES: Yes, sir, it is I believe about 98 percent of their people.

SENATOR PROXMIRE: This is an all-out attack by this country with everything we have.

MR. JONES: Yes, sir, and moreover, it was an attack where we actually tried as best we could to destroy their people by targeting the evacuation areas.

Later on in the hearings the following exchange took place:

REPRESENTATIVE MITCHELL: . . . I can understand how your research would reveal or indicate that the Soviets are prepared to effectively protect their industry. It does seem to me to become rather speculative to suggest that their present state of prepared-ness would facilitate a rapid recovery, even after an all-out nuclear war. It is just difficult for me to comprehend—it strains credulity, Mr. Jones, to assume that we throw everything we have, and not only are the people protected, but there is this rapid recovery after a total, all-out nuclear war. Now, this is from a layman's point of view. . . .

MR. JONES: Mr. Mitchell, I must confess that as an expert, my original view, and the view I held during the time I was on the SALT delegation, was that there was no defense against nuclear war and that there was no realistic recovery from it. It was not until we started looking at what the Soviets were doing, and then went back and tried to correlate this with the recovery of Europe in World War II, the recovery of the Japanese cities—Hiroshima and Nagasaki—for example, that we began to realize that recovery is feasible.

REPRESENTATIVE MITCHELL: They are not comparable situations, Mr. Jones. Hiro-shima is not comparable to an all-out, total nuclear offensive on America's part.

MR. JONES: We are aware of that, and as a result—in order to make an adequate assessment, we considered the consequences of a full-scale nuclear war in terms of a large scale model of the total Soviet economy and the total U.S. economy. We used the recovery factors demonstrated in World War II, and some of the wisdom that U.S. economists generated in studies of the European and Japanese recovery.

For example, American impressions, which formerly included my own beliefs, are that Hiroshima was put out of business for a very long time. It turns out, however, that the day after the blast, bridges in downtown Hiroshima were open to traffic. Two days later, the trains started to run again, and three days later, some of the streetcar lines were back in operation.

The U.S. survey team came into the area two months after the bomb, and the surviving residents were back on their original homesites, starting to erect shelter out of whatever materials they could find. It is also very relevant to note, sir, that the U.S. team that surveyed Japanese cities prepared a list of very detailed recommendations as to how you should posture society to survive a nuclear war, and that all of those recommendations are contained in the Soviet civil defense documents, with improvements of their own added.

Most important is the fact that Hiroshima was very concentrated as a city—things were packed in pretty tight. If the Soviet Union had continued to keep all of their industry packed into the central cities, there is no way they could recover rapidly from a nuclear war. But, we have seen in major Soviet cities a pattern of dispersal where the industry is spread out as far as sixty to eighty miles from town. Furthermore, separation distances between factories are about two to five miles. With that kind of dispersal, industry becomes survivable . . .

7. Fortunately I had taped this interview and stored the transcripts and tapes at the *Los Angeles Times*, because later Jones simply denied, when he finally appeared before the subcommittee of the Senate Foreign Relations Committee, that he had said anything about the United States recovering in two to four years. Jones had clearly come under pressure from the Pentagon, as evidenced by the fact that for a long time he was not allowed to appear before the subcommittee.

3 Reagan and Bush

1. Interview with the author, published in the *Los Angeles Times*, January 24, 1980.

2. Interview with the author, published in the *Los Angeles Times*, March 6, 1980. Reagan's statement about the Soviets' regard for human life occurred in the following context:

SCHEER: The last time I talked to you, you said that no President of the United States should rule out the possibility of a preemptive nuclear strike in a potential confrontation [with the Russians] . . . Now . . . would that include the possibility of a preemptive nuclear strike by the United States?

REAGAN: What I'm saying is that the United States should never put itself in a position, as it has many times, of guaranteeing to an enemy or a potential enemy what it won't do . . . For example, when President Johnson, in the Vietnam War, kept over and over again insisting, oh, no, no, no, we'll never use nuclear weapons in Vietnam, I don't think nuclear weapons should have been used in Vietnam, I don't think they were needed; but when somebody's out there killing your young men, you should never free the enemy of the concern he might have for what you might do. So you may feel that way in your heart, but don't say it out loud to him . . .

SCHEER: Do you believe that we could survive a nuclear war?

REAGAN: No, because we have let [the Russians] get so strong and we have let them violate the agreement.

SCHEER: But let's say we get stronger than them again. Do you think we could survive a nuclear war? With the right underground shelter systems, with the right defense systems, could we survive one?

REAGAN: It would be a survival of some of your people and some of your facilities that you could start again. It would not be anything that I think in our society you would consider acceptable but then we have a different regard for human life than those monsters do.

3. Interview with the author, winter, 1980.

4. In an article in the *New York Times* on October 12, 1981 ("Reagan Arms Policy Said to Rely Heavily on Communications"), Richard Halloran described the Reagan Administration's plans for improving the capabilities of U.S. strategic military communications:

> The Reagan Administration's plan to spend $18 billion on strategic military communications over the next five years is intended to provide the United States with a far more effective and flexible capacity to wage nuclear war, according to senior Administration officials.
>
> The communications program is the top priority in President Reagan's recently disclosed $180 billion plan to revitalize the nation's strategic deterrent. Defense Secretary Caspar W. Weinberger has repeatedly complained that the communications project has been overlooked in the controversy surrounding the President's proposal to deploy the MX missile and the B-1 bomber.
>
> The program has been designed, the senior Administration officials said, to make possible at least four courses of action that are not currently within the nation's capabilities. According to the officials, the actions would include these:
>
> The President could order a retaliatory nuclear strike against the Soviet Union, without risking an accidental nuclear war, after ascertaining that Soviet missiles are definitely heading toward the United States. This response, known as "launch under attack," is currently possible but has not been adopted because the strategic warning system's accuracy cannot be trusted. The new plan's goal is to make the system so reliable that evidence of an attack would be unmistakable.
>
> The United States could engage in a protracted nuclear war over days or weeks rather than one spasmodic, all-out retaliatory strike against the Soviet Union. The new communications network would give the President the control to fire only those missiles he thought necessary and to order subsequent strikes. If for instance the Administration later decides to place missiles deep into mountains as a reserve force, in a program named Citadel, the new communications network must be certain of reaching them.
>
> The planned B-1 bombers could be dispersed to increase their chances of survival and their ability to mount more than one strike against the Soviet Union. The bombers, after attacking Soviet targets, would not return to their home bases but would fly on to others, including some outside the United States, to refuel, reload and take off on another mission. Reliable communications would be needed to control such operations.
>
> The United States would have the ability to replace vital parts of the warning and communications network quickly if they are damaged by Soviet weapons. Communications satellites, for instance, would be mounted atop new MX missiles instead of nuclear warheads and lofted immediately into space to replace destroyed satellites. Mobile and backup ground stations would increase the nation's capability to continue military action or to recover after a nuclear battle.
>
> "The thrust of this program is to be sure," said a senior official. "What we're creating is a level of credibility that cannot be ignored." He and others contended that reliable communications between the President and United States forces armed

with nuclear weapons were essential to make the deterrent credible to the Soviet Union.

Other officials said the investment in a communications system that could survive a Soviet attack would cut the cost of the nuclear arsenal since fewer weapons would be necessary. For instance, an ability to launch missiles before they have been destroyed, they said, meant fewer were needed to insure that some survive an attack . . .

5. From statement at a meeting sponsored by the Air Force Electronic Systems Division and the Mitre Corporation, reported by Clarence A. Robinson, Jr., in *Aviation Week and Space Technology*, October 26, 1981.

6. Interview with the author, spring, 1982, New York City, New York.

7. Gray discussed the position of the new Administration concerning survivable communications and protracted nuclear war in an interview in May 1982. I asked Gray if it could be said with confidence that there was a commitment within the defense community to the idea of protracted nuclear war. He responded:

I can speak with confidence about it because I work in the defense community and I know the people involved. Unless everyone is suddenly lying to me, I can say that somewhat undeveloped theory does lie behind the procurements. The C³ modernization story doesn't make any sense if you're not thinking along these lines . . . If you only need your forces to go bang on day one, who cares about survivability of the satellites?

. . .

In an article entitled "MAD Versus NUTS" which appeared in *Foreign Affairs* (Winter, 81/82), Spurgeon M. Keeny, Jr., Scholar-in-Residence at the National Academy of Sciences and former Deputy Director of ACDA, and Wolfgang K. H. Panofsky, director of Stanford's Linear Accelerator Center and former member of the General Advisory Committee on Arms Control and Disarmament, take issue with the warfighting strategies supported by Gray and others:

The theme that nuclear weapons can be successfully employed in war-fighting roles somehow shielded from the MAD world appears to be recurring with increasing frequency and seriousness. Support for Nuclear Utilization Target Selection— NUTS—comes from diverse sources: those who believe that nuclear weapons should be used selectively in anticipated hostilities; those who believe that such capabilities deter a wider range of aggressive Soviet acts; those who assert that we must duplicate an alleged Soviet interest in war-fighting; and those who are simply trying to carry out their military responsibilities in a more "rational" or cost-effective manner. The net effect of this increasing, publicized interest in NUTS is to obscure the almost inevitable link between any use of nuclear weapons and the grim "mutual hostage" realities of the MAD world. The two forces generating this link are the collateral damage associated with the use of nuclear weapons against selected targets and the pressures for escalation of the level of nuclear force once it is used in conflict. Collateral effects and pressures for escalation are themselves closely linked.

. . . The much discussed "window of vulnerability" is based on the fear that the

Soviets might launch a "surgical" attack against vulnerable Minuteman ICBM silos —the land-based component of the U.S. strategic triad—to partially disarm the U.S. retaliatory forces, confident that the United States would not retaliate. The scenario then calls for the United States to capitulate to Soviet dictated peace terms.

Simple arithmetic based on intelligence assessments of the accuracy and yields of the warheads on Soviet missiles and the estimated hardness of Minuteman silos does indeed show that a Soviet attack leaving only a relatively small number of surviving Minuteman ICBMs is mathematically possible in the near future. There is much valid controversy about whether such an attack is in fact operationally feasible with the confidence that a rational decision-maker would require. But what is significant here is the question whether the vulnerability of Minuteman, real or perceptual, could in fact be exploited by the Soviets without risking general nuclear war. Would a U.S. President react any differently in response to an attack against the Minuteman force than to an attack of comparable weight against other targets?

Despite the relatively isolated location of the Minuteman ICBM fields, there would be tremendous collateral damage from such an attack, which under the mathematical scenario would involve at least 2,000 weapons with megaton yields. It has been estimated by the Congressional Office of Technology Assessment that such an attack would result in from two to 20 million American fatalities, primarily from fallout, since at least half the weapons would probably be ground burst to maximize the effect of the attack on the silos. The range of estimated fatalities reflects the inherent uncertainties in fallout calculations due to different assumptions on such factors as meteorological conditions, weapon yield and design, height of burst and amount of protection available and used. Estimates of fatalities below eight to ten million require quite optimistic assumptions.

It seems incredible that any Soviet Leader would count on any President suing for peace in circumstances where some ten million American citizens were doomed to a slow and cruel death but the United States still retained 75 percent of the strategic forces and its entire economic base. Instead, Soviet leadership would perceive a President, confronted with an incoming missile attack of at least 2,000 warheads and possibly many more to follow in minutes, and with the action options of retaliating on warning with his vulnerable land-based forces or riding out the attack and retaliating at a level and manner of his own choosing with substantial surviving air and sea-based strategic forces.

It is hard to imagine that this scenario would give the Soviets much confidence in their ability to control escalation of the conflict. If the Soviets did not choose to attack U.S. command, control, communications and intelligence (C³I) capabilities, the United States would clearly be in a position to retaliate massively or to launch a more selective initial response. If vulnerable control assets were concurrently attacked, selective responses might be jeopardized but the possibility of an automatic massive response would be increased since the nature of the attack would be unclear. But even if these control assets were initially untouched, the Soviets could not be so overly confident of their own control mechanisms or so overly impressed with those of the United States as to imagine that either system could long control such massive levels of violence, with increasing collateral damage, without the situation very rapidly degenerating into general nuclear war.

. . . There is now a great debate, particularly in Europe, about the proposed deployment on European soil of U.S.–controlled long-range Pershing II and ground-based cruise missiles capable of reaching the territory of the Soviet Union, in response to the growing deployment of Soviet SS-20 mobile medium-range ballistic missiles . . . The overriding issue which tends to be submerged in the current debate is the fact that *any* use of nuclear weapons in theater warfare in Europe would almost certainly lead to massive civilian casualties even in the unlikely event the conflict did not escalate to involve the homelands of the two superpowers.

Calculations of collateral casualties accompanying nuclear warfare in Europe tend to be simplistic in the extreme. First, the likely proximity of highly populated areas to the combat zone must be taken into account. One simply cannot assume that invading enemy columns will position themselves so that they offer the most favorable isolated target to nuclear attack. Populated areas could not remain isolated from the battle. Cities would have to be defended or they would become a safe stepping-stone for the enemy's advance. In either case, it is difficult to imagine cities and populated areas remaining sanctuaries in the midst of a tactical nuclear war raging about them. Then one must remember that during past wars in Europe as much as one-half of the population was on the road in the form of masses of refugees. Above all, in the confusion of battle, there is no control system that could assure that weapons would not inadvertently strike populated areas. Beyond immediate effects, nuclear fallout would not recognize restrictions based on population density . . .

The authors discuss the ineffectiveness of missile defense and civil defense in the event of a nuclear war, and conclude:

In sum, we are fated to live in a MAD world. This is inherent in the tremendous power of nuclear weapons, the size of nuclear stockpiles, the collateral damage associated with the use of nuclear weapons against military targets, the technical limitations on strategic area defence, and the uncertainties involved in efforts to control the escalation of nuclear war. There is no reason to believe that this situation will change for the foreseeable future since the problem is far too profound and the pace of technical military development far too slow to overcome the fundamental technical considerations that underlie the mutual hostage relationship of the superpowers . . .

8. "Victory is Possible," *Foreign Policy*, summer, 1980.

9. Telephone interview with the author, spring, 1982.

4 The Committee on the Present Danger

1. The following is a list of members of the Board of Directors of the Committee on the Present Danger who have held positions in the Reagan Administration. Asterisk indicates a member on leave of absence in full-time public service.

*President Ronald Reagan

*Kenneth L. Adelman	U.S. Deputy Representative to the United Nations
Martin Anderson	Member, President's Economic Policy Advisory Board
*James L. Buckley	Under Secretary of State for Security Assistance, Science and Technology
W. Glenn Campbell	Chairman, President's Intelligence Oversight Board, and Member, President's Foreign Intelligence Advisory Board
*William J. Casey	Director, Central Intelligence Agency
John B. Connally	Member, President's Foreign Intelligence Advisory Board
John S. Foster, Jr.	Member, President's Foreign Intelligence Advisory Board
J. Peter Grace	Chairman, President's Private Sector Survey on Cost Control
William R. Graham	Acting Chairman, General Advisory Committee on Arms Control and Disarmament
Colin S. Gray	Member, General Advisory Committee on Arms Control and Disarmament
*Amoretta M. Hoeber	Deputy Assistant Secretary of the Army for Research and Development
Francis P. Hoeber	Member, General Advisory Committee on Arms Control and Disarmament
*Fred Charles Iklé	Under Secretary of Defense for Policy
Max M. Kampelman	Chairman, U.S. Delegation to Conference on Security and Cooperation in Europe
*Geoffrey Kemp	Staff, National Security Council
Lane Kirkland	Commissioner, National Commission on Social Security Reform
*Jeane J. Kirkpatrick	U.S. Representative to the United Nations
*John F. Lehman	Secretary of the Navy
Clare Boothe Luce	Member, President's Foreign Intelligence Advisory Board
Charles Burton Marshall	Member, General Advisory Committee on Arms Control and Disarmament
Edward A. McCabe	Chairman, Board of Directors, Student Loan Marketing Association
Paul W. McCracken	Member, President's Economic Policy Advisory Board
*Paul H. Nitze	Chief Negotiator for Theater Nuclear Forces
*Edward F. Noble	Chairman, U.S. Synthetic Fuels Corporation
Michael Novak	U.S. Representative on the Human Rights Commission of the Economic and Social Council of the United Nations
Peter O'Donnell, Jr.	Member, President's Foreign Intelligence Advisory Board

David Packard	Member, White House Science Council
*Richard N. Perle	Assistant Secretary of Defense for International Security Policy
*Richard Pipes	Staff, National Security Council
John P. Roche	Member, General Advisory Committee on Arms Control and Disarmament
*Eugene V. Rostow	Director, Arms Control and Disarmament Agency
Donald H. Rumsfeld	Member, General Advisory Committee on Arms Control and Disarmament
Richard M. Scaife	Member, President's Commission on Broadcasting to Cuba
Paul Seabury	Member, President's Foreign Intelligence Advisory Board
Frank Shakespeare	Chairman, Board for International Broadcasting
*George P. Shultz	Secretary of State
Laurence H. Silberman	Member, General Advisory Committee on Arms Control and Disarmament
Herbert Stein	Member, President's Economic Policy Advisory Board
*R. G. Stilwell	Deputy Under Secretary of Defense for Policy
Richard B. Stone	Member, President's Economic Policy Advisory Board
*Robert Strausz-Hupé	Ambassador to Turkey
Edward Teller	Member, White House Science Council
*W. Scott Thompson	Acting Associate Director, International Communication Agency
Charles Tyroler II	Member, President's Intelligence Oversight Board
Joe D. Waggonner	Commissioner, National Commission on Social Security Reform
Charls E. Walker	Member, President's Economic Policy Advisory Board
*W. Allen Wallis	Under Secretary of State for Economic Affairs
Seymour Weiss	Member, President's Foreign Intelligence Advisory Board
Edward Bennett Williams	Member, President's Foreign Intelligence Advisory Board
E. R. Zumwalt, Jr.	Member, General Advisory Committee on Arms Control and Disarmament

2. "What is the Soviet Union Up To?" The Committee on the Present Danger, April 4, 1977.

3. Interview with the author, spring, 1981, Washington, D.C.

4. In an interview in April, 1982, Herbert York, director of the program in science,

technology and public affairs at the University of California, former director of Lawrence Livermore Laboratory, and former Ambassador to the Comprehensive Test Ban Negotiations in Geneva, discussed analyses of Soviet defense capabilities:

> . . . Most of the analyses which show how good the Russians are compared to us are very heavily based on the notion that Murphy's law [i.e., that whatever can go wrong will go wrong] does not apply in the Soviet Union, and yet it is fully enforced in the West. The people who make these analyses know every detail about what's wrong with our troops and how badly things go, how when you tell the tanks to do a certain thing in an exercise, they may not do it or they do it at half speed or something like that . . . When they analyze the equivalent Soviet situation, they never take into account the fact that things usually don't work. They utterly ignore Murphy's Law. Every time there's an analysis of what would happen if we sent aircraft East in Europe, all of the Soviet surface-to-air missiles are treated as if every one of them worked according to the engineering manual and as if every soldier who had to push every button always pushed it at exactly the right moment because every radar detects every airplane in just a certain mathematically precise way. So that the whole analytical world is just full of analyses which are mathematically correct but based on nonsense inputs. The notion of garbage in/garbage out is well known in connection with operations analysis . . .

5. In an article entitled "The Case Against SALT II," written for the February 1979 issue of *Commentary*, Eugene Rostow, a founding member of the Committee on the Present Danger, wrote:

> Some experts in the field assume that we must accept SALT II despite its potential for condemning us to strategic inferiority, because the American people are unwilling to take "the giant strides forward" which would be required to assure nuclear parity and to maintain a credible and usable second-strike capacity. This defeatism is altogether unwarranted. The American people will spend and do whatever is required to assure the safety of the nation, if their leaders tell them the truth, as President Truman did, and explain the central importance of nuclear weapons to our security and to the foreign policies we employ to protect it.
>
> Because the debate over SALT II presents a unique opportunity for telling this truth, it may well become a major turning point for the future. If, mesmerized by old illusions about disarmament and new ones about détente, we accept the treaty, we will be taking not a step toward peace but a leap toward the day when a President of the United States will have to choose between the surrender of vital national interests and nuclear holocaust. No President should ever be put into such a corner. But if, overcoming these illusions, we permit ourselves to see the SALT II treaty for what it truly is—an expression of American acquiescence in the Soviet drive for overwhelming military superiority—we will give ourselves a last chance to restore the strategic balance that is the only guarantee of peace in the nuclear age and the only context in which the survival of our civilization and its values can be safely assured.

6. "Détente Yields to Nuclear Superiority," *Los Angeles Times*, September 28, 1981.

7. When I interviewed physicist Hans Bethe in March 1982, he noted, "As one of my friends said, 'The Committee on the Present Danger is the present danger.' These people are now in the saddle . . . They talked in a certain way when they were in the opposition. What I am afraid of is that now they will try to persuade the whole country, and act that way from the government."

SCHEER: What is your assessment of where these people come from?

BETHE: They were always here. They came out of the woodwork . . . Suddenly it has become respectable, that is the only difference.

8. From a letter written November 7, 1980, and reprinted in "The Fifth Year . . . and the New Administration," the Committee on the Present Danger, November 11, 1981.

9. Reagan's comment about the Hollywood Communists ("The Russians sent their first team, their ace string, here to take us over") was quoted in a *Los Angeles Times* article (July 17, 1951) entitled "Russ Imperialism Seen by Veteran." Excerpts from the article are included below:

What is on the ruthless march today is not Communism as much as it is Russian imperialism using the Communist ideology as a camouflage, a former captain of the Army Air Force told some 200 persons at the Town Hall yesterday.

And he made the suggestion that the thing be recognized for what it is and that "pro-Russian" should be used in most of the places where the word Communism is heard.

The ex-captain was Ronald Reagan, president of the AFL Screen Actors Guild, and he was one of a three-man team of top-notchers in the fight against Communism in the Hollywood motion-picture industry who addressed the Biltmore luncheon.

. . . Referring . . . to the Hollywood situation, Reagan warned: "The Communism fight is never won. It always leaves behind a little Trojan Horse."

. . . Reagan portrayed the screen as the great purveyor of information about the American way of life and said it was this that Red Russia cannot match, so it tried to take over. When it failed, he said, it tried various schemes to ruin the industry.

"The Russians sent their first team, their ace string, here to take us over," he said. "We were up against hard-core organizers."

10. Interview with the author, spring, 1980, Washington, D.C.

11. Interview with the author, published in the *Los Angeles Times*, March 6, 1980.

12. The statements Reagan has made concerning the Soviet Union since he has assumed office differ little from those he made during his campaign. The following exchange took place during a press conference on January 29, 1981:

Q: Mr. President, what do you see as the long-range intentions of the Soviet Union? Do you think, for instance, the Kremlin is bent on world domination that might lead to a continuation of the Cold War, or do you think that under the circumstances détente is possible?

THE PRESIDENT: Well, so far détente's been a one-way street that the Soviet Union has used to pursue its own aims. I don't have to think of an answer as to what I think their intentions are; they have repeated it. I know of no leader of the Soviet Union since the revolution, and including the present leadership, that has not more than once repeated in the various Communist congresses they hold their determination that their goal must be the promotion of world revolution and a one-world Socialist or Communist state, whichever word you want to use.

Now, as long as they do that and as long as they, at the same time, have openly and publicly declared that the only morality they recognize is what will further their cause, meaning they reserve unto themselves the right to commit any crime, to lie, to cheat, in order to attain that, and that is moral, not immoral, and we operate on a different set of standards, I think when you do business with them, even at a détente, you keep that in mind.

In January 1982, in a question-and-answer session with *Los Angeles Times* reporters, the following exchange took place:

MR. [RICHARD] COOPER [Deputy Bureau Chief, *Los Angeles Times* Washington Bureau]: . . . What is your personal view of the intentions of the Soviet Union? Do you think, as some people do, that they're primarily a sort of defensive, fearful country, looking in Afghanistan and Poland for buffers, or do you think they still have an appetite for other peoples' territory?

THE PRESIDENT: Well, I think there's a combination of both. At least they talk a great deal about their fear that the world is going to close in on them, but the other, you can't deny that the Marxian theory and Lenin's theory and every Soviet leader since has at some time or other publicly reaffirmed his dedication to this—and that is that Marxism, the theory, can only succeed when the entire world has become Communist.

MR. COOPER: So is it a little naïve, perhaps, to think that if we just reassure them, placate them, that they will moderate their—

THE PRESIDENT: That's it. They've got to, and maybe the failures of their own system, which make them dependent on the rest of us for help—as they are—maybe this will help them see the fallacy of this. But this is why I mean it's a combination not only of fear; it's not just defense. They believe that—that religion of theirs, which is Marxist-Leninism, requires them to support world revolution and bring about the one-world Communist state. And they've never denied that.

13. In Norman Podhoretz's article, "Making the World Safe for Communism," in *Commentary*, April, 1976, he concludes:

If it should turn out that the new isolationism has indeed triumphed among the people as completely as it has among the elites, then the United States will celebrate its two-hundredth birthday by betraying the heritage of liberty which has earned it the wonder and envy of the world from the moment of its founding to this, and by helping to make that world safe for the most determined and ferocious and barbarous enemies of liberty ever to have appeared on the earth.

. . .

When I interviewed Charles Tyroler, director of the Committee on the Present Danger, he told me that both Norman Podhoretz and his wife, Midge Decter, joined the Committee as founding members in 1976. Tyroler continued, "Where do you think he got the title for his book, *The Present Danger*? He named it after us . . . He was down at our meeting in January. A very bright fellow. And *Commentary* has been sort of an adjunct—we've had all our stuff in there . . ."

14. Confirmation Hearings, Committee on Foreign Relations, United States Senate, June 22, 23, 1981.

15. "A Reporter At Large—Some Questions About the War," William Whitworth, *The New Yorker*, July 4, 1970.

16. "Common Sense and the Common Danger," the Committee on the Present Danger, November 11, 1976.

17. Interview with the author, published in the *Los Angeles Times*, April 8, 1982.

In November 1962, then-Secretary of Defense Robert McNamara, in a memorandum for the President concerning strategic retaliatory forces, discussed the Air Force's intention to achieve a first-strike capability:

It has become clear to me that the Air Force proposals, both for the RS-70 and for the rest of their Strategic Retaliatory Forces, are based on the objective of achieving a first-strike capability. In the words of an Air Force report to me: "The Air Force has rather supported the development of forces which provide the United States a first-strike capability credible to the Soviet Union, as well as to our Allies, by virtue of our ability to limit damage to the United States and our Allies to levels acceptable in light of the circumstances and the alternatives available."
Of course, any force designed primarily for a controlled second-strike, and for the limiting of damage to the U.S. and its Allies, will inevitably have in it to an important degree a first-strike capability. What is at issue here is whether our forces should be augmented beyond what I am recommending in an attempt to achieve a capability to start a thermonuclear war in which the resulting damage to ourselves and our Allies could be considered acceptable on some reasonable definition of the term.
In my memorandum to you on this subject last year, I defined a "full first-strike capability" as a capability that "would be achieved if our forces were so large and so effective, in relation to those of the Soviet Union, that we would be able to attack and reduce Soviet retaliatory power to the point at which it could not cause severe damage to U.S. population and industry." I indicated then and I reaffirm now my belief that the "full first-strike capability"—and I now include the Air Force's variant of it—should be rejected as a U.S. policy objective.

McNamara went on to argue in some detail that attainment of first-strike capability is "infeasible," "neither necessary nor particularly useful" and "extremely costly," then concluded, ". . . for these reasons, the following discussion is limited to evaluation of the recommended and alternative forces in second-strike conditions . . ."

18. "The Development of Nuclear Strategy," *International Security*, spring, 1978.

19. Lecture series, University of California, Los Angeles, November 20, 1980.

20. "What is the Soviet Union Up To?" The Committee on the Present Danger,

April 4, 1977.

21. The Committee on the Present Danger has not refrained from criticizing the Reagan Administration. In a pamphlet entitled "Is the Reagan Defense Program Adequate?" (published March 17, 1982), the Committee concludes that it is not:

> The Administration's defense program is a minimal one. It will not halt the unfavorable trends in the U.S.–Soviet military balance, let alone reverse them.
>
> In the nuclear area, timely programs to restore the survivability of U.S. strategic forces are not included in the Administration's program. The program does seek to bolster U.S. strength in conventional forces, but the levels proposed are, in most cases, well below those put forth by the Committee on the Present Danger two years ago.
>
> Consequently, any reduction in the Administration's proposed defense effort would further erode our national security.
>
> The time for the United States to restore its defenses is fleeting. Failure to close the window of vulnerability could tempt the Soviet Union to exploit its vast military power. Regretfully, the conclusions reached by the Committee on the Present Danger in its first Statement on 11 November 1976, remain valid today: Our country is in a period of danger, and the danger is increasing. Unless decisive steps are taken to alert the nation, and to change the course of its policy, our economic and military capacity will become inadequate to assure peace with security.

5 Team B

1. "Handicapping the Arms Race," *New York Times,* January 19, 1977:

> Speaking of the C.I.A. (as we were yesterday in connection with the affair Sorensen) we are still preplexed by the manner in which the once proudly independent agency allowed itself to be drawn into an open debate about the size and shape of the American strategic defense effort.
>
> For reasons that have yet to be explained, the C.I.A.'s leading analysts were persuaded to admit a hand-picked, unofficial panel of hard-line critics of recent arms control policy to sit at their elbows and to influence the estimates of future Soviet military capacities in a "somber" direction. Then, fresh from this inside exercise, the panel—headed by Richard Pipes, a professor of history at Harvard—developed a further report that moved from Soviet "capabilities" to Soviet "intentions." It speculated that Moscow was determined to achieve strategic supremacy and an ability to win a nuclear war by 1985—not necessarily to wage the war but to intimidate the West. The essence of the argument, of course, soon appeared in the press, with vague attributions to the C.I.A.
>
> There are two distinct problems here and we ought to keep them apart, even if the C.I.A. could not during the weeks when no one seems to have been in charge in Washington.
>
> The responsibility for evaluating Soviet military capacities belongs in our Government to the Director of Central Intelligence, who is supported by the information

and analyses of dozens of sources, in and out of Government. Presumably, no available facts or supicions are unavailable to this effort. Demonstrably, no serious dissents from these periodic estimates are denied a hearing in the Government and outside. In particular, there have been ample and sympathetic military channels to the President, the Congress and the public for those who dispute the C.I.A.'s estimate of recent years that neither the United States nor the Soviet Union had much hope of soon attaining nuclear "supremacy" in any meaningful sense, even if they had the desire.

There was no need, therefore, to place a panel of members with predictable views on a privileged inside track in this evaluation process, except to give a propaganda edge to a partisan faction. It seems to us not only a wrongheaded but also short-sighted ploy; policy debates that are won by debasing the intelligence currency in which we all must trade will not long count for much or be worth winning.

Now to the heart of the current dispute. Ever since the humiliation visited upon Nikita Khrushchev in the Cuban missile crisis of 1962, the Soviet Union has been running hard to overtake an American "lead" in strategic nuclear weapons. The Russians are still running, even though we have slowed to a jog. The gap has not been closed, nor will it be in the next year or two. With or without a gap in various technical senses, what already does exist is an "essential equivalence" of armament. The Russians possess more missile throw-weight and the United States possesses more nuclear warheads on its missiles as well as more accurate missiles and more bombers.

By 1985, Russia's big and more accurate multiple warheads and missiles may equal or exceed the destructiveness of the American forces, which rely on bombers to deliver half their payload. They cannot endanger our alert-ready bombers or the missiles aboard submarines, but they may begin to threaten the survival capacity of our fixed Minuteman missiles stored in their underground silos. In other words, they might begin to threaten some of our retaliatory power, assuming a Soviet first strike.

The outgoing Administration, and apparently also the incoming, believe that any current fear of "supremacy" is unfounded. "When casualties will be in the tens of millions," Henry Kissinger has said, it "has practically no operational significance as long as we do what is necessary to maintain a balance."

What is necessary? The Pipes panel, among others, presumably wants a big new effort in strategic weapons to match its "worst case" assumptions about Soviet intentions. It is particularly disturbed by Russian civil defense programs, believing that a capacity to hold down civilian casualties might lead the Soviet leaders, some years hence, to contemplate a first strike against the United States.

Even if these fears are justified, there are ways of adjusting strategy to preserve the threat of comparable casualties. The real problem is the rival build-up of offensive missiles. It is costly and can eventually destabilize the nuclear balance.

That recognition is what led us into the arms limitation talks and agreements of recent years—SALT I and II—which, for all their imperfection, remain the best hope of arrresting and eventually reducing the arms race. We welcome debates that will frame our negotiating positions and assist the public in evaluating the results. We deplore any effort to capture the Government's fact-finding machinery for a fleeting advantage in the discussion.

2. This article by David Binder in the the *New York Times*, entitled "New C.I.A. Estimate Finds Soviet Seeks Superiority in Arms" (December 26, 1976), also describes the discrepancy between the CIA's previous estimates of Soviet strength and those put forth by Team B:

> High-ranking officials of the Central Intelligence Agency said their annual so-called national estimate of Soviet strategic objectives over the next ten years . . . was more somber than any in more than a decade. A top level military intelligence officer who has seen the estimate commented: "It was more than somber—it was very grim. It flatly states the judgment that the Soviet Union is seeking superiority over United States forces. The flat judgment that that is the aim of the Soviet Union is a majority view in the estimate. The questions begin on when they will achieve it."
>
> Previous national estimates of Soviet aims—the supreme products of the intelligence community since 1950—had concluded that the objective was rough parity with United States strategic capabilities . . .

3. "Carter to Inherit Intense Dispute on Soviet Intentions," Murrey Marder, *Washington Post*, January 2, 1977.

4. "New C.I.A. Estimate Finds Soviet Seeks Superiority in Arms," David Binder, *New York Times*, December 26, 1976.

5. Interview with the author, Los Angeles, spring, 1982.

6. "Strategic Superiority," Richard Pipes, *New York Times*, February 6, 1977.

7. "Why the Soviet Union Thinks It Could Fight and Win a Nuclear War," *Commentary*, July 1977.

In a *Washington Post* op-ed piece entitled "A Hawkish Argument with Holes" (July 8, 1977), Stephen S. Rosenfeld wrote:

> For rank hysteria in scholarly garb, it's hard to top Harvard Professor Richard Pipes' *Commentary* article, "Why the Soviet Union Thinks It Could Fight and Win a Nuclear War" . . . It's worth jousting with a bit because it's typical of so much of the worst-case alarmism that the military-intellectual complex passes off as serious argumentation.
>
> Pipes . . . believes that what counts "above all" is Soviet intent, and that such intent can be accurately divined from Soviet military doctrine: Official thoughts on using force abroad. He marshals quote after leaden quote to demonstrate that Moscow feels it could fight and win a nuclear war and has prepared to do so.
>
> . . . It is . . . misleading to ignore the ongoing between-the-lines Soviet debates on nuclear war and to credit only the starkest version argued. It is even more misleading not to ask what relationship military doctrine has to actual Soviet policy . . . In fact, the whole matter of basing policy on a measurement of the other fellow's perceived intent is suspect. That method licenses a reading as narrow, or as extravagant, as the reader's central nervous system. It is too open-ended, too undisciplined, too subjective. Pipes' reading is less analysis than Rorschach test . . .

8. Quoted in "The CIA's Tragic Error," Arthur Macy Cox, *New York Review of Books*, November 6, 1980.

9. "Why the U.S., Since 1977, Has Been Misperceiving Soviet Military Strength," Arthur Macy Cox, *New York Times*, October 20, 1980.

10. "The CIA's Tragic Error," *New York Review of Books*, November 6, 1980.

11. "Soviet and US Defense Activities, 1970–79: A Dollar Cost Comparison," CIA, January 1980.

12. "New C.I.A. Estimate Finds Soviet Seeks Superiority in Arms," David Binder, *New York Times*, December 26, 1976.

13. The following members of the President's Foreign Intelligence Advisory Board are also members of the Committee on the Present Danger: W. Glenn Campbell, John B. Connally, John S. Foster, Jr., Claire Boothe Luce, Peter O'Donnell, Jr., Paul Seabury, Seymour Weiss and Edward Bennett Williams.

14. "Carter to Inherit Intense Dispute on Soviet Intentions," Murrey Marder, *Washington Post*, January 2, 1977.

15. *Commentary*, July 1977.

16. Testimony by Dr. William Chipman, then-director, Population Protection Division, FEMA, before the Subcommittee on Health and Scientific Research, June 19, 1980; and T. K. Jones, interview with the author, fall, 1981.

17. In testimony before the Arms Control Subcommittee of the Senate Foreign Relations Committee (January 20, 1982), Sidney Drell, deputy director of Stanford Linear Accelerator, supported renewal of the 1972 ABM treaty and stated:

> with the technologies in hand and foreseeable for the near future, a nationwide ABM for the defense of cities and industry will be effective *only* against very low levels of attack. Therefore, if nationwide ABM defenses were deployed by the Soviet Union, their greatest potential effect would be to blunt the limited deterrent threats of China, France and Great Britain. Such a development, which is likely to occur if the ABM treaty is terminated, could hardly be viewed as in U.S. interests . . .

> · · ·

In my interview with Hans Bethe (published in the *Los Angeles Times* on April 11, 1982) he expressed a similar view:

> Against missiles there is no defense. This is a subject on which I have worked quite carefully and industriously for many years before '68, looking at many ways how to tell decoys from missiles, and so on. Whatever you did, the offense could always fool the defense and could do it better. So antiballistic missiles for city defense are technically nonsense . . .

> · · ·

Admiral Noel Gaylor, retired, former commander-in-chief of United States forces in the Pacific, and former director of the National Security Agency, described the

futility of civil defense efforts before the Arms Control Subcommittee of the Senate
Foreign Relations Committee on March 16, 1982:

> Civil defense . . . won't work against nuclear attack. There are not only enough
> nuclear warheads for direct hits on every military target, every city or village, but
> also for every relocation area in the US—or the USSR. And if the opponent should
> think there are not enough, he has only to build more.
> Deep shelters would become deep tombs.
> Fallout shelters are impracticable. How long can you and your family live under
> two doors covered with three feet of earth? How do you dig, around New York, or
> Chicago, or Moscow, in the frozen ground of winter?
> Evacuation of major cities in any reasonable length of time is impracticable. It
> would invite attack *during* evacuation—actually increasing casualties. And any evac-
> uation area can itself be targeted if the opponent wishes to do so . . .

18. "An Analysis of Civil Defense in Nuclear War," ACDA, December 1978.

19. In an interview in the fall of 1981 I asked Marshall Shulman, who was Special
Adviser to the Secretary of State for Soviet Affairs in the Carter Administration, if he
agreed with the contention that the Soviet Union is indifferent to the prospect of
millions of civilian casualties:
SCHEER: The way the argument is asserted . . . is that the Soviets are supposed to
be insensitive to the loss of human life because they lost 20 million in the Second
World War.
SHULMAN: I think that is utter nonsense. How can one say that the Soviets are
insensitive to the loss of human life? The fact that they took 20 million casualties in
World War II doesn't mean that they didn't care about it, that they are insensitive
to it, or that they would be willing to accept the risk of nuclear war if they could be
sure it would only result in 20 million casualties. That seems to me a grotesque
statement. I find no evidence that that is true. I think it is a projection, a kind of
Rorschach-type projection of people's own attitudes. In truth, the pattern of Soviet
behavior, even under Stalin, was fairly conservative about the risk of war, about the
involvement of their forces in a way that might lead to a risk of a general war situation,
or even a local war. If anything, my guess is that the Soviet population and the Soviet
leadership, having still the vivid memories of World War II, are extremely cautious
about the dangers of war. I can't see how any American analyst would say that the
Soviet leadership would be willing to run the risk of nuclear war if only they could be
assured that their casualties would be—what? One million, two million, ten million
. . . how can one say that? It seems to me pernicious to assert as a fact that they would
be willing to take 20 million casualties if they could limit it to that.

20. Interview with the author, published in the *Los Angeles Times*, November 26,
1981.

21. "What is the Soviet Union Up To?" The Committee on the Present Danger, April
4, 1977.

22. "The Man Not Worried by the Bomb," Charles Fenyvesi, *Washington Post*, April
11, 1982.

According to the *New York Times* (in an article by Judith Miller, June 10, 1982), members of the Reagan Administration themselves, while advocating an enhanced civil defense program for the the United States, have doubts about the effectiveness of the Soviet program:

Richard N. Perle, Assistant Secretary of Defense for International Security Policy, recently told a Senate subcommittee that he could not make "confident judgments about the efficacy of the Soviet program . . ." But he defended the Administration's program on the ground that it might "help to dispel any possible delusions the Soviet leadership might harbor today or in the future that they can exploit the absence of any civil defense program here to deepen our sense of vulnerability and thereby intimidate the United States."

Privately, Administration officials said they had decided against relying on comparisons to the Soviet program to justify American civil defense planning in part because of persistent skepticism in foreign policy and intelligence circles about the scope and effectiveness of the Soviet effort . . .

23. In his article concerning Team B ("The CIA's Tragic Error," *New York Review of Books,* November 1980), published just before Ronald Reagan was elected President, Arthur Macy Cox describes the long-term effects of the Team B report:

Four years later the views of Team B have become even more influential than they were in 1976 and more in need of scrutiny. For all its conclusions are either wrong, or distorted, or based on misinterpretation of the facts. Many of them have been inadequately challenged by the Carter Administration, or not challenged at all. Along with the Soviet military buildup and the violations of détente . . . the Team B arguments have had enormous consequences for U.S. defense spending. Paul Nitze and several other members of Team B organized the "Committee on the Present Danger" which has become one of the most powerful lobbies for a larger military establishment. Today Richard Pipes and other members of Team B have joined their former sponsor, George Bush, and are serving as senior advisers to Ronald Reagan.

. . . The conclusion of Team B that has perhaps had the most ominous continuing consequences is the finding that Soviet strategic theory has been different from ours —because the Soviets are said to believe that nuclear wars can actually be fought and that limited nuclear wars are a real possibility. Both Carter and Reagan have adopted dangerous doctrines based on this mistaken analysis.

. . . It is true that articles in Soviet military journals have discussed the strategy and tactics of nuclear war. Soviet military leaders say that if they are attacked with nuclear weapons they will fight and win a nuclear war. In this they do not seem different from generals elsewhere. U.S. military planners are constantly engaged in war games in which nuclear wars are fought on paper, and through computers, and in the end are won. When [Secretary of State Harold] Brown said on August 20 [in a speech at the Naval War College] that Soviet leaders take seriously the theoretical possibility of victory, he might also have noted the statement of his own Chairman of the Joint Chiefs of Staff, made as long ago as 1977: "U.S. nuclear strategy maintains military strength sufficient to deter attack, but also in the event deterrence fails, sufficient to provide a warfighting capability to respond to a wide range of conflict in order to control escalation and terminate the war on terms acceptable to the United States."

Neither Soviet nor U.S. leaders, however, have ever talked about launching a first strike to win a nuclear war; nor have the leaders of either country threatened such a strike for coercive political purposes. Brezhnev has explicitly rejected the concept of limited nuclear war: "I am convinced . . . that even one nuclear bomb dropped by one side over the other would result in general nuclear exchange—a nuclear holocaust not only for our two nations, but for the entire world . . . The starting of a nuclear war would spell annihilation for the aggressor himself."

. . .

In an op-ed piece in the *Washington Post* (July 31, 1981), Stephen Rosenfeld traces the continuing influence Team B and its revision of CIA estimates have had on United States intelligence:

Start at Team B, then CIA director George Bush's mid-'70s panel of outside experts set up to critique the CIA-led intelligence community's analysts on the Soviet threat. The argument then was whether Team B was a healthy "competitive review" of a shop that had gone ivory-tower soft, or whether its hard-line membership and assumed political mandate made it a "kangaroo court."

Intellectually, that argument was not resolved. Politically, it was. Team B won. That is, trends in the real world and the emerging political consensus, in some combination, made their inevitable mark on the intelligence bureaucrats, and the darker, more hawkish and more pessimistic estimates prevailed. This happened during the Carter period.

So it was that when [CIA director William] Casey arrived at the CIA and checked out the estimating process, he found it sound, needing attention to performance but not design. You can read this several ways. It could be evidence that the process has indeed achieved the goal, so venerated by analysts, of turning out a politics-proof product. Or it could mean that Casey, inheriting a full set of political biases, didn't think or care to examine them.

. . . I suspect that Casey has reinforced the premises he found when he arrived and that the agency is looking at the world through red-colored glasses. Intelligence cannot be politics-free. It should not be. But is there now the proper tension between politicians with their inevitable demand for crisp answers and (good) analysts with their natural drive for clear questions? I am not suggesting that intelligence is being politically cooked but that it is being politically leaned on. Where is Team B?

6 Window of Vulnerability

1. "An Upheaveal in U.S. Strategic Thought," R. Jeffrey Smith, *Science*, April 2, 1982.

2. "Running in Circles with the MX," *Bulletin of the Atomic Scientists*, December 1981.

3. Telephone interview with the author, July 1982.

4. In a press conference in January 1982, President Reagan stated:

Up until now, in previous negotiations they [the Soviets] haven't had to make any concession, because we were unilaterally disarming. But now I think it's all explained in a cartoon that one of your publications used some time ago, and that was Brezhnev speaking to a general in his own army, and he said, "I liked the arms race better when we were the only ones in it."

5. "Towards Arms Control," *New York Times*, June 29, 1982.

6. Interview with the author, spring, 1982, Los Angeles, California.

7. Report of Secretary of Defense Harold Brown to the Congress on the FY 1982 Budget, FY 1983 Authorization Request and FY 1982–86 Defense Programs, January 19, 1981.

8. Interview with the author, published in the *Los Angeles Times*, April 11, 1982.

9. Interview with the author, published in the *Los Angeles Times*, April 8, 1982.

10. "Extreme Wrong on the Extreme Right," *Bulletin of the Atomic Scientists*, April 1982.

11. Transcript of President's News Conference, *New York Times*, April 1, 1982.
    In response to the President's assertion on March 31, 1982, that the Soviet Union could "absorb our retaliatory blow and hit us again," Adam Clymer reported in the *New York Times* ("Two Senators Deny Soviet Arms Lead," April 5, 1982):

Two Democratic Senators who have often advocated a tough stance toward the Soviet Union said today that President Reagan was wrong when he contended that the Soviet Union possesses superiority in nuclear weapons.
    Senator Henry M. Jackson of Washington said, "In the aggregate, we have the capability now of deterring the Soviets." He cited "the qualitative advantages that we have, both in our bomber force and in our submarine force," as balancing Soviet advantages in heavy missiles.
    . . . Senator Daniel Patrick Moynihan of New York also challenged Mr. Reagan's statement that, "the Soviets' great edge is that they could absorb our retaliatory blow and hit us again." Mr Moynihan said that "either side could destroy the other side in a counter-strike, a second strike," and that all further strikes would do, "to use Churchill's term, is to bounce the rubble."

      ·   ·   ·

Former Secretaries of Defense James Schlesinger and Harold Brown also disagreed with President Reagan's position on Soviet nuclear superiority. According to the *New York Times* (in an article by Charles Mohr, May 1, 1982) in testimony before the Senate Foreign Relations Committee:

Mr. Schlesinger acknowledged that the Soviet Union had "gradually acquired a hard-target kill capability against American forces which now in all probability substantially exceeds" that of the United States. But he added that the United States "should not brood about or overstate" this deficiency and "above all we should not suggest that the deficiency in this single dimension implies inferiority because the word 'inferiority' may suggest to others that our deterrent is, indeed, inadequate.

. . . "The United States has and will continue to have, in my judgment, sufficient surviving and deliverable weapons to destroy the urban-industrial base of the Soviet Union—even after absorbing a Soviet strike . . . such a capability is frequently considered the ultimate deterrent.

"If the present discussions of superiority and inferiority are taken to suggest that the Soviet Union can deny the United States that capability, then the suggestion that the Soviet Union has superiority is invalid," [Schlesinger] said.

. . . [Former Secretary of Defense Harold] Brown expressed similar views . . . Brown said the Russians "do not have anything like strategic superiority in a useable sense."

. . .

During testimony before the Arms Control Subcommittee of the Senate Foreign Relations Committee on January 20, 1982, Stanford physicist Sidney Drell pointed out the connection between the United States refusal to ban MIRVing and the perceived vulnerability of American missiles:

We lost an important opportunity for arms control by the decision to press ahead with the technology of multiple independently targetable warheads, or MIRVs, without first making a serious effort to avoid their extensive deployment. We can now see the dollar and strategic costs of that lost opportunity in the form of the MX program. The MX is designed to be the U.S. response to the growing threat to our land-based Minutemen ICBM force posed by the highly accurate and reliable MIRV'd ICBM's now being deployed by the Soviet Union. The MX is a symbol of the failure of arms control!

. . .

In an op-ed piece published in the *New York Times* on April 11, 1982, Nobel physicist Hans Bethe and Kurt Gottfried of Cornell University discussed President Reagan's contention that the Soviet Union could "absorb our retaliatory blow and hit us again":

Rarely, if ever, has the government of a great power proclaimed its vulnerability to devastating attack by a dangerous adversary. Common sense dictates that a moral weakness should not be advertised. Yet that is what President Reagan and his aides have done: they have stated in the starkest terms that soon we shall have no credible deterrent against a Soviet first strike!

This assertion cannot mean what it says. It is, instead, a reckless move to marshal support for new weapons that are intended to regain the nuclear superiority America once enjoyed.

. . . The Russians have put most of their nuclear "eggs" into one basket— land-based missiles. They were forced to do so because of their technological backwardness and geographical position. Their submarines are inferior to ours; they have no bomber bases close to us, while ours encircle the Soviet Union; and they have not been able to develop cruise missiles, which are now revitalizing our bomber fleet. Their ICBM force is so large because that is all they can do well.

Should present trends continue, the Soviet Union will have more-accurate

ICBM's in a few years. By that time, however, many of our submarines will be able to destroy Soviet missiles in their silos.

It is against this background that one must assess the Reagan doomsday scenario: The new Soviet missiles will be able to eliminate our ICBM's in a bolt from the blue; we would not be able to retaliate because enough Soviet weapons would survive our counterattack to devastate the United States; thus, we would have no choice but to yield to all Soviet demands.

This scenario pretends that United States and Soviet ICBM's face each other in a universe decoupled from the real world. It assumes that these highly complex systems, which have only been tested individually in a quiet environment, would perform their myriad tasks in perfect harmony during the most cataclysmic battle of history; that our weapons will not improve, while the Soviet Union's leap ahead. It assumes that we would be helpless when well over half our nuclear warheads have survived, and that a Soviet attack on our ICBM's, which would kill at least 20 million Americans by radioactive fallout, would not provoke us into pulverizing the Soviet Union with our submarines. Only madmen would contemplate such a gamble. Whatever else they may be, the Soviet leaders are not madmen.

What then is the true rationale for the Administration's stance? Judging from many statements by some of its most prominent figures, the public must conclude that there is a significant faction in the Administration that believes in and aspires to nuclear superiority. This group contends that our technological and economic prowess make this a realistic goal and that its attainment would yield rich political dividends.

Neither of these conclusions is correct, as post-1945 history demonstrates. For two decades, we were immune to Soviet nuclear attack while the Russians lay at our mercy. Did that vulnerability deter them from blockading Berlin, absorbing Czechoslovakia, crushing the revolt in Hungary? On the contrary, it impelled them to a dangerous attempt to place missiles in Cuba in a futile effort to gain some semblance of a deterrent. It imbued them with the determination to build a credible nuclear force, whatever the cost. And only when they reached that goal did they begin to negotiate seriously, as exemplified by SALT I.

The "window of vulnerability" to a Soviet first strike does not exist. In reality, the security of all inhabitants of the Northern Hemisphere is eroding because of the irresponsible policies of both superpowers. While millions of ordinary citizens have come to recognize that security is not measured in megatons, those in positions of power continue to act as if nuclear weapons were spears or shotguns . . .

· · ·

During an interview in April 1982 in Los Angeles I asked Herbert York if he agreed with the assertions of the Reagan Administration that the Soviet Union has pursued an unrelenting and unprecedented arms buildup over the last decade.

YORK: The Soviet buildup, talking now just about the question of strategic nuclear weapons, is not at all unprecedented. The buildup in Soviet weapons over the period from the late sixties to the late seventies essentially parallels the buildup that we went through from the late fifties to the early sixties, in almost every way—the number of systems and, in particular, the megatonnage.

Many people focus on the Soviet megatonnage as being excessive; that's based partly on the ignorance of the people who are talking. The fact of the matter is that the current Soviet strategic megatonnage is several times as big as the current American strategic megatonnage. But even that is not unprecedented. The American strategic megatonnage at the beginning of the 1960s was about three times what it is today. The reason that we came down—this, incidentally, is not a secret, but neither doves nor hawks are aware of it, but we reduced our strategic megatonnage by a factor of around three since the early sixties. That came about because in the early sixties the delivery systems were the large bombers, the B-47s and the B-52s, and we changed over from primarily bombers to primarily missiles. The carrying capacity of the missiles is less and so it's a purely practical result of that changeover that we reduced the megatonnage. But the megatonnage that we had programmed to deliver in the early sixties is the same as the megatonnage the Russians had programmed to deliver on us today. Nothing unprecedented about it. Any good Russian analyst looking at what we had in the early sixties, and adding to that what McNamara was telling everyone we were going to buy, would have produced a series of numbers which is essentially identical to what the Soviets have today. The number of megatons and the number of delivery vehicles the Russians have today is what a Soviet analyst would have predicted in the early sixties . . . and what he would have told Brezhnev that we would have in the early eighties . . .

In an interview in April 1982 in Los Angeles, I asked Desmond Ball, an authority on strategic policy, if he agreed that the Soviet buildup had put the Soviet Union in a position of strategic superiority vis-à-vis the United States. The following is an excerpt from that exchange:

BALL: In 1967 the United States had 1054 ICBMs, all single warhead, 41 Polaris submarines with 16 missiles each, all single warhead, add those two together and you get 1710, plus 450 B-52s, which gives you over 2000. Today there is over 10,000, so there has been a five-fold increase. So the premise that the United States has stood still is nonsense. One also hears it asserted that the Soviets have achieved authority in some critical areas. Well, I don't know what those critical areas are, because there are a number of indices by which you can measure the balance: the number of delivery vehicles, numbers of warheads, accuracy with which those warheads can be delivered, the megatonnage and throw-weight on those delivery vehicles, and other combinations of those indices. Now, on any index that is significant, the U.S. retains superiority.

There are two areas in which the Soviets are ahead. One is delivery vehicles. At the moment they have 2500, whereas the U.S. has only a bit over 2000. So the Soviets are a bit ahead on delivery vehicles. But that's not really the point, it is the number of warheads that count and the U.S. retains a 50 percent lead there. And if you continue to project it out into the 1990s, the U.S. is going to continue to maintain about a 50 percent lead there. The other area in which the Soviets are ahead is megatonnage. But megatonnage is really only good at flattening large areas like cities, and there are only a limited number of cities, so after a certain point megatonnage becomes irrelevant.

There is one sub-index, the one on counter-military potential or counterforce capability, that the U.S. vis-à-vis the Soviets has one disadvantage. The fact is that on counterforce capability overall, the U.S. is quite superior. But in the area of ICBMs versus ICBMs counterforce capability, the Soviets are ahead. This is the so-called window of vulnerability. Ironically, this disparity exists because of the U.S. notion of the triad, and her better balancing of forces. The U.S. has put about a third of its capabilities in terms of warheads and megatonnage in each of the legs of the triad, whereas the Soviets have a very unbalanced force; very few bombers, single-warhead missiles on their subs in general and more than two thirds of their capabilities on their ICBMs. So it would of course follow that they would have the advantage in ICBM to ICBM. But because of the triad, that should not be worrisome because you've got the other two bloody legs.

SCHEER: What about the argument that they hit you with the first strike and the weapons on the submarines and bombers aren't accurate enough to really damage their forces and prevent a second strike?

BALL: If the argument is simply that they are not accurate enough, then that is nonsense. Weapons delivered by bombers are more accurate than weapons delivered by Minutemen—the CEP [circular error probable] of bombs is about 600 feet. So the argument becomes more complicated, but it is certainly not because of accuracy. In any case, on that second strike, after they have knocked out your ICBMs, which is going to use up most of their ICBMs, what are you going to need accuracy for? The targets you are going to go after at that point are other military targets: airfields, army camps, tank concentration, or urban industrial areas. Neither of those require high accuracy. In any case, the accuracy of sub-launched missiles these days is approaching that of the ICBMs. It is certainly good enough to do a lot of hard-target operations that in the past could not have been done by submarines.

SCHEER: What about the contention that the United States has unilaterally disarmed?

BALL: That is nonsense. Not just in strategic nuclear warheads, but in tactical warheads—right across the board. The United States has not disarmed, it still retains not just parity but superiority. What is this disarmament? What is this notion that the U.S. has stood still? They've multiplied five-fold in the last twelve years!

In the spring of 1982, I asked Cyrus Vance if he agreed with the Reagan Administration contention that the United States had disarmed over the last decade.

SCHEER: What about the charge that America was disarmed unilaterally in the seventies?

VANCE: Baloney. That is simply not true . . . There was a period of time when the United States clearly had nuclear superiority. It was inevitable that the Soviet Union would develop a capacity which would be roughly equal to our capacity. This indeed did happen, and the Soviets and the United States reached rough parity. In my judgment that continues to be the situation in the nuclear field. We are ahead in some aspects in the possession of nuclear weapons, they are ahead in others. We have more warheads, they have greater throw-weight. But when you take a look at the equation, you see that there is equivalence, or rough parity between the two countries and neither country is going to let the other get ahead of him. Either is going to insist that this rough parity be maintained. I think anybody is foolish to think anything other than that. Certainly that has been the policy of all the Administrations since the 1960s, and at least up until now remains the policy of the United States.

Secretary of Defense Weinberger stated in a presentation before the House Budget Committee on March 20, 1981:

163 / Notes for Chapter 6

The ultimate back-up for our defense posture resides in our nuclear forces. While modernization of theater nuclear forces will alleviate the nuclear imbalance in Europe, one of the most disturbing developments we confront is the continuing deterioration of the balance in *intercontinental* nuclear arms. We must make large investments in this area to deter the ultimate catastrophe. It is unacceptable to find ourselves today facing the prospect of Soviet strategic superiority and to watch the Soviet Union mass-producing both land-based missiles and a manned bomber fleet, while the United States has an open production line for neither.

Our descent from a position of clear strategic superiority, to the present perilous situation coincided with our strenuous attempt to bring the arms competition under control through negotiated agreements with the Soviet Union. Rarely in history have we or any great nation pursued such noble goals, risked so much, and yet gained so little.

In no area have we ignored reality so long as in our effort to negotiate and enforce arms control. We have pursued the elusive hope that by setting an example by our own actions, we might stabilize and then reduce the level of armaments of others.

But what was the result?

We did succeed in restraining *our* own strategic arms programs, but certainly not those of the Soviet Union. The SALT I accord on offensive arms did not significantly impede the growth of the strategic offensive capacity of the Soviet Union; as for SALT II, had you ratified it in the form proposed, that treaty would have permitted an enormous further increase in Soviet offensive capacity, while presenting the danger of lulling us into a false sense of security.

This Administration remains committed to equitable and verifiable arms control. But, our experience over the last two decades has demonstrated that we are not going to be able to limit the growth in Soviet strategic weapons unless we ourselves are fully prepared to compete.

We are not abandoning hope for arms control, but we are abandoning unwarranted illusions. We must work hard now to design a realistic approach to the limitation of armaments, an approach that will help preserve the peace . . .

. . .

The Stockholm International Peace Research Institute's *World Armaments and Disarmament Yearbook for 1982* discusses the strategic nuclear balance and the nuclear arms race in the following terms:

The balance between the two great powers in intercontinental nuclear weapons is becoming increasingly unstable. The number of warheads has multiplied, they have been made much more accurate, and many of them are targeted on the silos of the other side. Each side is claiming that the other side is trying for some kind of first-strike capability, while denying that its own objective is anything but defensive.

. . . Given that both sides have substantial numbers of submarine-launched ballistic missiles (SLBMs), and given that the threat of a first strike against these is . . . hypothetical, this stress on the present or potential first-strike capability of the other side is at first sight puzzling. The scenario suggested on the United States side goes like this. The Soviet Union launches a strike which eliminates all US land-based missiles. It still has enough strategic nuclear weapons in reserve to inhibit the United States from making any reply—since that reply would then bring total devastation on the United States. So there is no US retaliation, either with sub-marine-launched missiles or with the cruise missiles of the bomber fleet.

There are a number of implausibilities in this scenario . . . Nonetheless it is used, on the United States side, as justification for their new strategic weapons plans—including the development of missiles such as the MX and Trident II, with much greater accuracy than the missiles they replace; the search for a less vulnerable basing system for the MX missile; and the multiplication of cruise missiles. There is also renewed discussion in US strategic journals of the need to establish a "launch-on-warning" system. To prevent US land-based missiles being caught in their silos, these missiles should themselves be fired as soon as there was evidence that Soviet missiles could reach their target. They should be fired on the basis of a computer analysis of the evidence from various detection devices, without reference to the President.

So now, instead of what might once have seemed to be a stable system of deterrence—a balance of mutually assured destruction (MAD)—we have the fear of a first strike being used as the rationale for the very big increases now in prospect in strategic weapon programmes and procurement. Between them, the two great powers, with the nuclear weapons at their command, have a total destructive power which is probably equivalent to about half a million Hiroshima bombs: but that is not enough. There can be no better example of the way in which developments in weapon technology—in this case the increasing accuracy of intercontinental ballistic missiles (ICBMs)—lead to a reduction rather than to an increase in security.

. . . To attempt the launch of a first strike against just one part of another country's strategic weaponry would be an act with a very great risk of total catastrophe to the power which launched it. As a realistic technological and political option it lies in the realm of myth. Yet it is this theme—the fear of first strike—which is presented as the justification for the major new developments in strategic weaponry which seem likely to come about in the next decade. Unfortunately myths are often powerful in political affairs . . .

12. "Soviet Nuclear Superiority Disputed," Charles Mohr, *New York Times*, May 1, 1982.

13. Interview with the author, *Los Angeles Times*, September 29, 1981.

14. "Debunking the 'Window of Vulnerability,' A Comparison of Soviet and American Military Forces," *Technology Review*, January 1982.

15. Interview with the author, spring, 1982, Los Angeles, California.

16. "Soviets Blast Reagan Plan to Build MX," Dusko Doder, *Washington Post*, October 4, 1981.

17. "Reagan's Nuclear Strategy Criticized," Michael Getler, *Washington Post*, October 4, 1981.

18. Ibid.

19. "Making the Decision," Lee Lescaze and Martin Schram, *Washington Post*, October 4, 1981.

20. "MX: Let's Put it on Hold," *Los Angeles Times* editorial, March 3, 1982.

21. " 'Dense Pack': It's the Planning That's Dense," Admiral Stansfield Turner, U.S. Navy, retired, *Los Angeles Times*, May 21, 1982.

22. Interview with the author, spring, 1982, Los Angeles, California.

7 The Negotiators

1. The following detailed summary of President Reagan's START proposal, announced on May 9, 1982, during an address at Eureka College, was published in May 1982 by the Arms Control and Disarmament Agency:

STRATEGIC ARMS REDUCTIONS TALKS (START)— PROPOSED REDUCTIONS

On May 9, the President announced a bold, new proposal to reduce significantly the risks posed by large nuclear arsenals. He has proposed a phased approach to reductions focused on the most destabilizing elements of nuclear forces. The initial phase would reduce the total number of ballistic missile warheads by one-third, to about 5,000, would limit the number of warheads carried on ICBMs to one-half that number, and would cut the total number of ballistic missiles to an equal level about one-half of the current US level. In a second phase, we would seek further reductions in the overall destructive power of each side's arsenal to equal levels, including a mutual ceiling on ballistic missile throw weight below the current US level. We will also treat bombers and other strategic systems in an equitable manner. The proposed reductions, coupled with effective verification, will substantially reduce the nuclear threat and will make a major contribution to the stability of the nuclear balance.

The significant reductions proposed by President Reagan are shown in the following comparison:

	Approximate Current Levels	
FIRST PHASE	US	USSR
Ballistic Missile Warheads (Land-Based and Sea-Based)		
• Proposed ceiling of 5,000	7,200	7,500
Land-Based Ballistic Missile Warheads		
• Proposed ceiling of 2,500	2,150	5,900
Ballistic Missiles (Land-Based and Sea-Based)		
• Proposed ceiling of 850, approximately one-half current U.S. levels	1,600	2,350
SECOND PHASE		
Missile Throw Weight		
• Proposed ceiling below current U.S. levels	2 MKG	5 MKG

STRATEGIC ARMS REDUCTIONS TALKS (START)—
THE US PROPOSAL

The President has opened the door to a more constructive relationship with the Soviet Union based upon the principles of reciprocity and mutual restraint.

Arms control is an important instrument for securing such restraint. Equitable and verifiable agreements, when combined with sound foreign and defense policies, can play a critical role in enhancing deterrence and ensuring a stable military balance.

The President has outlined the objectives of U.S. arms control policy:
—*Significant Reductions:* We seek to reduce the number and destructive potential of nuclear weapons, not just to cap them at high levels as in previous agreements.
—*Equality:* Americans will accept nothing less. We want agreements that will lead to mutual reductions to equal levels in both sides' forces.
—*Verifiability:* We will carefully design the provisions of arms control agreements and insist on measures to ensure that both sides comply. Otherwise, neither side will have the confidence needed to accept the deep reductions that we seek.

On May 9, the President announced a bold and realistic two-phased U.S. approach to the Strategic Arms Reduction Talks (START) aimed at these objectives.
—In the first phase, we will seek to reduce the number of ballistic missile warheads by one-third, to about 5,000. No more than half the remaining ballistic missile warheads will be on land-based missiles. We will also seek to cut the total number of all ballistic missiles to an equal level, about one-half of the current U.S. level.
—In the second phase, we will seek further reductions in overall destructive power of each side's arsenals to equal levels, including a mutual ceiling on ballistic missile throw-weight below the current U.S. level.

The President's proposal attempts to reduce the threat of nuclear war by enhancing deterrence and securing a stable nuclear balance. The main threat to the strategic balance has been the massive Soviet buildup of ballistic missiles forces. Because of their large size, increasing accuracy, and short flight times, these missiles (and particularly land-based ICBMs) pose a significant threat to U.S. deterrent forces.
—To enhance deterrence and ensure a stable nuclear balance, the President's proposal focuses, in the first phase, on significant reductions on ballistic missile warheads and deployed ballistic missiles themselves. This would halt and reverse the destabilizing trend that would have been permitted under the unratified SALT II Treaty.
—In the second phase, we will seek further reductions to equal ceilings on other elements of strategic forces, particularly ballistic missile throw-weight. Throw-weight is an important measure of the size and destructive potential of ballistic missiles. First phase reductions will reduce the current disparity in ballistic missile throw-weight, and lay the groundwork for the second-phase reductions to achieve an equal throw-weight ceiling below current U.S. levels.

The President's approach is reasonable and equitable. It would lead to significant reductions on both sides and a stable nuclear balance, which should be in the interest not only of the U.S. and the U.S.S.R., but of the entire world. The President has emphasized our intention to negotiate in good faith and to consider all serious proposals from the Soviets.

The debate on nuclear weapons issues has focused public attention on a matter of crucial importance. It is now time to demonstrate support for the ambitious, yet realistic, approach to strategic arms control embodied in the U.S. START proposal. The START negotiations will begin on June 29.

In testimony before the Senate Foreign Relations Committee on May 17, 1982, Roger Molander, former member of the National Security Council staff and Executive Director of Ground Zero, provided the following analysis of President Reagan's START proposal:

It is clear that President Reagan's START proposal represents a significant departure from the negotiating approach begun under President Nixon. Rather than emphasizing the control of different avenues of strategic competition, it essentially calls for the Soviets to restructure their strategic missile forces along lines much closer to our own. In that sense, START might be characterized as a call not only for a focus on reductions, but also as "STARTing over."

The focus of the President's proposal is missile warheads and especially ICBM warheads. Today, the Soviet Union has about 8000 missile warheads. The ratio between Soviet ICBM warheads and SLBM warheads is almost four-to-one. President Reagan's proposal calls for a one-to-one ratio. To accomplish this change at the warhead levels called for (a ceiling of 2500 ICBM warheads), the Soviets would have to tear down all 308 of their ten-warhead SS-18 heavy missiles and roughly one hundred of their six-warhead SS-19s or their four-warhead SS-17s. This would leave them with about 400 MIRVed ICBMs, compared to their current level of 818. Obviously, these would be profound changes in the Soviet force structure. However, it should be kept in mind that they would not in any meaningful way decrease the threat which Soviet ICBMs pose to the U.S. silo-based Minuteman ICBM forces.

On the U.S. side, we currently have 2150 ICBM warheads and about 4500 SLBM warheads. We could thus meet the proposed 5000-warhead ceiling by dismantling 500 older single warhead ICBMs and roughly 130 MIRVed Poseidon SLBM launchers.

The deal looks even better when you consider that the proposed agreement does not include strategic bombers, an area where we have a ten-to-one advantage—3000 warheads to less than 300 on the Soviet side.

The proposal also does not deal with cruise missiles, a realm of profound U.S. advantage, although it is clear that certain types of cruise missiles, notably ground-launched cruise missiles, should be included in intermediate range force negotiations.

In sum, the President's proposal would be a very good deal for us, and I think I and every other American would rejoice if the Soviets accepted the proposal.

At the same time, it should be pointed out that historical experience is not encouraging in terms of the likely success of a proposal of this character. First, it should be noted that the President's proposal calls for far and away the most dramatic restructuring of the other side's strategic forces of any proposal ever put forward in the history of the negotiations. Secondly, it is important to know that both bombers and cruise missiles have been included in the negotiations since the Nixon Administration.

I point out these facts because it is important that we all recognize just how far-reaching this proposal is. In the past, the response to such proposals has been either outright rejection or a comparable counter-proposal which leaves the two sides miles apart and struggling to find common ground. The term applied to such proposals is "sweetheart deals," and one of the clear lessons of negotiations to date is that they significantly extend the time required to reach agreement. SALT II started with a pair of much less demanding proposals of this character and it took nearly seven years to complete the negotiations.

Thus, if history is any teacher, an agreement based on the President's new proposal will take, as he and his chief negotiator, Ed Rowny, have both admitted, many years to negotiate . . .

. . .

According to UPI reporter Mathis Chazanov (May 23, 1982), the Soviets had the following reaction to President Reagan's START proposal:

"The renaming of SALT into START," [Soviet strategic planner Lev] Semeiko said, "will change nothing if it is a false start generally."

His comments gave the clearest picture so far of Soviet objections to Reagan's proposals at Eureka College May 9.

Cutting the number of ballistic missile warheads to at least a third below current levels would favor the United States because the U.S. Air Force can carry more warheads in its bombers, he said.

Reagan also said no more than half of these should be land-based, but Semeiko viewed it differently: Since three quarters of the Soviet nuclear weaponry is on the big missiles, they would have to make bigger cuts than the Americans, who carry three quarters of their payloads on other systems such as submarines and bombers.

"Consequently the United States would not change anything in the structure of its might if Reagan's options were accepted," he said, "while the U.S.S.R. would radically refashion it by reducing the number of its intercontinental ballistic missiles.

. . ."One can hardly avoid drawing the conclusion that the position stated by the U.S. president is oriented not to searching for an agreement but to providing conditions for the continuation of Washington's attempts to achieve military superiority over the Soviet Union," Semeiko said.

2. Statement issued by Muskie, May 9, 1982, following Reagan's START proposal announcement.

3. Confirmation hearings, Committee on Foreign Relations, United States Senate, June 22, 23, 1981.

4. The following is the text of the proposed agenda of events to counter Ground Zero Week included in Eugene Rostow's memo to the White House. The memo was published in the *Washington Post* on May 9, 1982. The "scenarios" refer to anticipated Ground Zero activities.

Saturday, April 17--Ground Zero Week, minus one
Scenario--FRG-demonstrations at SPD Congress
If Necessary:

PM   Commentary on FRG-demonstrations by Richard Burt
and Manfred Von Nordheim: offered to networks and
evening news
George Will on Agronsky & Co. (Friday taping)
Photo Opportunity--President and Mrs. Reagan at
Camp David: spring flowers--atmosphere of
calm

Sunday, April 18--Ground Zero Week, day one--
Scenario--Ground Zero Opening Ceremonies in Lafayette Park (White House backdrop) and nationwide

AM   *Meet the Press*--Vice-President Bush
Face the Nation--Ambassador Nitze
Photo Opportunity--President returns to White
House (exits helicopter with briefcase) to confer
with Secretary Haig, etc.
New York Times Op-ed by Rumsfeld (as GAC Chairman) on
the boldness and promise of the Reagan arms control
policy
Washington Post Op-ed by Professor William O'Brien
(Georgetown University) stating moral and religious
justification for prudent self-defense in the
nuclear age

Monday, April 19--Ground Zero Week, day two--
Scenario--Clips of national symposia fed for evening
news

AM   Photo Opportunity--The President meets at the
White House with Archbishop Hickey (pro-freeze) and
Bishop O'Connor (pro-defense)

PM   Eugene Rostow speaks at the National Press Club
(Scheduled)
ABC Nightline--Seymour Weiss and Colin Gray give
critical assessment of Ground Zero Week and
Administration arms control policy

Tuesday, April 20--Ground Zero Week, day three--
Scenario--More cuts of gatherings and demonstrations, interviews with Warnke, LaRocque, Caldicott,
et al.

AM   American Security Council holds press conference
assailing both Kennedy-Hatfield and Jackson-Warner
Today Show--Sen. Warner on Jackson/Warner
Good Morning America--Burt

PM   "Fireside Chat" by the President on peace, the
lessons of World War II, etc. (no hardware or balance
discussions)

Wednesday, April 21--Ground Zero Week, day four--
Scenario--More of the same (religious commentary, etc.)

AM   *CBS Morning News*--Dr. William O'Brien and Bishop
O'Connor discuss the Catholic anti-nuclear movement

(Archbishop Hunthausen, Bishop Matthiesen, etc.)
Photo Opportunity--The President meets with a
moderate women's group in the Oval Office--press
release describes President's concern and attention
to their expressed anxieties about war, etc.
Post Op-ed by respected historian on the lessons of
the 30's

PM   McNeill/Lehrer--Richard Perle--peace/deterrence
(not limited nuclear war)

Thursday, April 22--Ground Zero Week, day five--
Scenario--More of the same (Kennedy demagoguery,
etc.)

AM   *Today Show*--Sen. William Cohen--Congressional
Resolutions
Good Morning America--Rep. G. William Whitehurst--
Congressional Resolutions
Photo Opportunity--Secretary Weinberger tours SAC
Base--informal--conversation with pilots, me-
chanics, etc. (emphasize readiness, patriotism,
etc.)
Demonstration--by Students for Peace and Security
(contact Scott Thompson) against pacifism/
unilateralism (site: White House gates)
Wall Street Journal--editorial about hysteria and
policy development--the need for calm (alterna-
tively interview with Solzhenitsyn on subject of
Ground Zero Week)

PM   Speech by Vice-President Bush to a World Affairs
Council
Photo Opportunity--Rowny meets with Swedish
Ambassador to discuss START/Arms Control
Nightline--Rep. Jack Kemp on arms control and the
Defense budget

Friday, April 23--Ground Zero Week, day six--
Scenario--More of the same (European reaction to
Ground Zero Week, etc.)

AM   *CBS Morning News*--Sen. Tower--criticizes
Administration MX Plan--urges more MX in survivable
mode
Today Show--Anne Armstrong--women in support of a
strong defense
National Public Radio--speech or interview by
Secretary Haig

PM   Discussions with George Will for *Agronsky & Co.*
PM   Photo Opportunity--President or Secretary of State
to visit Arlington National Cemetery (sobering
backdrop of war's consequences)

Saturday, April 24--Ground Zero Week, day seven--
Scenario--Large demonstrations in D.C. and
elsewhere--possible weather factor

AM   Photo Opportunity--President working, meeting
Cabinet members (no President-at-play contrasted
with earnest protestors)
AP/UPI exclusive interviews with Haig on START

Submit Perle Op-ed on Ground Zero Week to *Post* for
Monday printing
PM   George Will on *Agronsky & Co.*

Sunday, April 25--Ground Zero Week, plus one--
Scenario--Ground Zero Week closing remarks in
Lafayette Park--much sound and fury (White House
backdrop)
AM   *David Brinkley*--Eagleburger--on Ground Zero
Week/Europe
Meet the Press--Sen. Baker on Administration
arms control policy/budget
President invites small group (3-5) of Ground Zero
Week leaders (thoroughly screened) to the Oval
Office for discussion (no White House-under-seige a
la Nixon)

Monday, April 26--Ground Zero Week, plus two--
Scenario--Analysis and review of Ground Zero
Week
AM   Perle Op-ed in the *Post*
Good Morning, America--European diplomat or
journalist to comment on similarities and
differences of U.S. and European peace movements
Today Show--Midge Decter of Committee for a Free
World
New York Times Op-ed--Nitze on truth and
diplomacy

According to the article that was printed with the ADCA memo on Ground Zero
in the *Washington Post* (May 9, 1982):

The Arms Control and Disarmament Agency last month proposed to the White
House that the Reagan administration "should begin an immediate media campaign" to deal with "the growing stridency and hysteria" of the antinuclear weapons
movement.

In a memorandum from Eugene V. Rostow, director of ACDA, to William P.
Clark, the national security advisor, the agency said that Ground Zero Week, a
national educational campaign on the dangers of nuclear war, would produce an
"eruption of the issue of nuclear war."

A copy of the memorandum was sent anonymously to the Washington Post, and
its authenticity was confirmed by the agency.

"The press and electronic media will be full of demagoguery and emotion as
journalists hungrily interview tearful mothers and self-righteously indignant clergymen against a mushroom cloud background," the ACDA memo predicted.

. . . The ACDA memo warned that the nuclear war issue was infecting the public.
"While this movement includes such perennial elements as the old-line pacifists, the
environmentalists, the disaffected left and various communist elements," the memo
said, "there is participation, on an increasing scale in the U.S., of three groups whose
potential impact should be cause for concern. They are the churches, the 'loyal
opposition,' and, perhaps most important, the unpoliticized public."

ACDA's public position on Ground Zero was more benign than that reflected in Rostow's memo. According to an article in the *New York Times* on April 18, 1982 ("Drive on Atomic Peril to Open" by Judith Miller):

> Eugene V. Rostow, director of the Administration's Arms Control and Disarmament Agency, also welcomed Ground Zero's campaign. In a statement released Friday, he said that a "bipartisan foreign policy cannot be restored until there has been a thorough, civil and disciplined debate about what our foreign policy is for, what it's supposed to accomplish and by what means . . ."

5. *Washington Post,* May 9, 1982.

6. Interview with the author, spring, 1981, Washington, D.C.

7. A speech delivered for Eugene Rostow by ACDA Deputy Director Robert Gray, at UCLA on March 31, 1982, describes the Soviet Union as follows: "We are not dealing with like-minded people. We are dealing with a corrupt society based upon flawed ideological underpinnings which justify and condone practices which negate honorable behavior and fair dealing . . ."

8. Confirmation Hearings, Committee on Foreign Relations, United States Senate, June 22, 23, 1981.

9. Interview with the author, summer, 1981, Modesto, California.

10. On June 20, 1982, Eugene Rostow appeared on NBC News's *Meet the Press* and, according to the Associated Press (June 21, 1982):

> During the show, host Bill Monroe asked Rostow "whether it's plausible to think that if Soviet troops, artillery, tanks, conventional weapons come into Germany, we will attack the Soviet Union with nuclear weapons."
> Rostow replied, "The question of the uncertainty of that response has been the main element of deterrence now for a generation."
> Monroe then asked, "You're saying yes, that it is plausible that we could counter with nuclear weapons against a conventional attack?"
> Replied Rostow: "It is plausible."
> As for pacifist sentiment in Europe, he said, "I think it's much weaker, and all my European friends tell me it's much weaker today, than it was six or eight months ago," before President Reagan and other U.S. officials began responding to European worries.
> . . . Rostow . . . said that despite pacifist and anti-nuclear weapons movements in Western Europe, the region's political leaders need and support the American "nuclear umbrella."
> "All the NATO allies [are] extremely firm" in their support of attempts to bolster the American nuclear arsenal, he said. "They know that their entire security for the last generation has depended upon our implicit threat, our nuclear guarantee that we would use nuclear weapons if necessary to prevent them from being overrun, even by tanks.
> "The nuclear umbrella on which Europe and Japan and many other countries

have depended . . . is strongly and warmly defended by" American allies . . .

11. Interview with the author, spring, 1981, Washington, D.C.

12. "Strategy in the Decade of the 1980s," *Foreign Affairs*, fall, 1980.

13. "On Nuclear War," *New York Review of Books*, January 21, 1982.

14. The *Washington Post* described Paul Nitze's participation in the preparation of the National Security Council Memorandum (NSC-68) in an article entitled "Paul Nitze: The Nemesis of SALT II" (written by C. Robert Zelnick, June 24, 1979):

> By 1950 the Soviets had learned the secret of nuclear fission and the wartime alliance of the two superpowers had receded into memory. President Truman wanted a strategy which would serve as a blueprint for the transition from accommodation to fierce competition with the Soviet Union and justify the rearmament thought essential.
>
> That task fell largely to Nitze, who had just succeeded George Kennan as director of the State Department's policy planning staff. With colleagues at State, Defense and the National Security Council, Nitze drafted the fabled NSC-68 Memorandum, which set the basic tone for a generation's dealings with the Kremlin.
>
> Critics have found much in the document to deplore. NSC-68 did paint a simplistic picture of U.S.–Soviet competition, matching the forces of "freedom" and "justice" against those of "slavery."
>
> . . . The document also took a cynical view of arms control negotiations. To rally public support for rearmament, it recommended that U.S. leaders constantly put forth reasonable-sounding disarmament proposals which the Soviets were unlikely to accept. Of course, should the Russians show unexpected flexibility, "we would have to consider very seriously whether we could accept such agreements."
>
> In NSC-68 one also sees for the first time what might be called the "clear and future danger" alert. At the time, the United States enjoyed a hefty nuclear advantage over the Soviets' 10 to 20 atomic bombs. But by 1954, it was felt, the Soviets would have 200 such bombs, half of which could be expected to reach U.S. targets. And, given the element of surprise enjoyed by a totalitarian society, 1954 could mark a turning point in our relations, unless the West responded with across-the-board military build-ups . . .

15. The Gaither Commission report that Paul Nitze helped draft during the Eisenhower Administration is described in a UPI article ("1957 Prediction Overrated Soviet Missile Buildup," April 23, 1976) as follows:

> The document was the controversial Gaither Commission report presented to Eisenhower Nov. 7, 1957, which erroneously found the Soviet Union opening up a dangerous "missile gap" between 1959–1960. It recommended vast defense expenditures and an extensive fallout shelter program.
>
> Significantly wrong forecasts in the 45-page document, prepared under the direction of H. Rowan Gaither Jr., of the Ford Foundation, included:
>
> —By 1959, the Soviet Union would achieve "a significant intercontinental missile

capability with megaton warheads . . . The United States will probably not have achieved such a capability." John F. Kennedy campaigned in part on the "missile gap" to win the Presidency in 1960, later acknowledged it to have been false.

—By the 1970s, the United States and Soviet Union would possess defensive systems to shoot down attacking missiles. While both superpowers did develop such weapons, deployment was banned by the SALT I agreements, 1972–1974.

—By the mid-1970s, one superpower might make a "temporary technical advance" in weaponry which could give it life-and-death power over the other. Experts today agree neither the United States nor the Soviet Union has such ability.

—There was little prospect for U.S.–Soviet arms control negotiations, and a perpetual, unstable U.S.–Soviet arms race seemed almost inevitable. One control agreement is in effect, negotiations continue on another.

—There was no mention of such growing threats to world stability as the rich-poor gap, population jump, or scarcity of food, resources and energy . . .

16. "Nitze's World," *Foreign Policy*, summer, 1979.

17. When I interviewed Roger Molander in the fall of 1981 he described Paul Nitze's relationship with T. K. Jones as follows: "What everybody always found astonishing about Paul Nitze is that he bought that junk from T. K. Jones. T. K. Jones became his analyst, his numbers cruncher. When Paul Nitze needed numbers he went to T. K. Jones for his numbers. And you know T. K. Jones."

During my interview with T. K. Jones, he discussed Nitze's role in his research on industrial protection during nuclear attack. Jones told me the studies he conducted while at Boeing concluded that, with adequate protection, industrial machinery would survive nuclear attack, though the buildings housing the machinery would be destroyed:

JONES: A lot of people would think you need the building. The guy who ran the Boeing factory knew that you didn't need the building. As a matter of fact, he'd sent a team of people up to Alaska to rebuild a Japan Airlines 747 out on the end of the runway in some pretty rotten weather . . . So you don't need the building but you do need first, the people, second, the machinery. The Russians know that. In World War II they moved their whole aircraft industry east of the Ural Mountains and, for a while, they had machine tools sitting on pallets out in the middle of fields producing airplane parts. The Germans know it because there are some cases where they deliberately didn't restore bombed-out buildings because they knew if it looked like it was repaired, they'd get bombed again so they left the holes in the roof and the guys were down running the machinery. I remember Paul Nitze telling me that when they surveyed the German production records, they found that in a lot of cases where we'd done heavy damage by bombing, the production rate actually very quickly exceeded what it had been before.

SCHEER: When did you first meet Nitze?

JONES: Well, he was my boss on the SALT delegations.

SCHEER: Did he take an interest in this civil defense stuff?

JONES: He did—we were both outside of the government at that time and I started researching it, and then I went back to draw on his knowledge because he had been vice-chairman of the Strategic Bombing Survey. As a matter of fact he personally had been in Japan surveying the war damage there and was able to get at the shelf of books that had been published as a result of that survey, including the books on Hiroshima and Nagasaki. There was a lot of civil engineering surveys of buildings and some very, very detailed work—and, interestingly enough, a set of recommendations, very explicit recommendations on how to make a society much less susceptible to nuclear weapons. We found every one of those recommendations embodied in the Soviet manuals, plus a bunch of unique Soviet innovations on top of that.

SCHEER: You think they plagiarized Nitze's material?

JONES: Sure. Well, it was all there, it was all published, and we forgot about it and declared it unthinkable and they put it in their manual and proceeded to practice it.

18. Interview with the author, spring, 1981, Washington, D.C.

19. "The Relevance of Arms Control in the 1980s," *Daedalus*, winter, 1981.

20. Richard Perle's role in the SALT debate is discussed in a December 4, 1977, article in the *New York Times* (Richard L. Madden, "Jackson Aide Stirs Criticism In Arms Debate"):

To a Carter Administration official who has dealt with him, Richard Perle is a hardline zealot trying to inject himself and his boss into the negotiations with the Soviet Union on limitation of strategic arms.

To his employer, Senator Henry M. Jackson, Mr. Perle is a close adviser and valued aide who in some respects is almost like a son.

As seen by himself, Mr. Perle is a person who tries to digest a vast array of complicated information on strategic arms and other issues and to prepare detailed analyses on the impact, risk and benefits of any agreement on arms limitation so his Senator and others can make a more informed judgment before they vote.

"I really resent being depicted as some sort of dark mystic, or some demonic power," the 36-year-old Mr. Perle said, adding that he has no troops, no votes, only the power of persuasion. "All I can do is sit down and talk to someone."

While the views may differ, there is widespread agreement that Mr. Perle has become a central figure in the developing debate in the Senate over the terms of a new arms control agreement being put together by Soviet and American negotiators in Geneva.

. . . Mr. Perle has the mundane title of professional staff member of the permanent investigations subcommittee of the Senate Government Affairs Committee. But his influence comes from being Senator Jackson's main adviser on strategic-arms policy. The Washington Democrat, who has an influential voice on arms control in Congress, has been a leading critic of the status of the negotiations with the Russians.

Some Administration officials suspect that Mr. Perle may have been more active in generating criticism than Mr. Jackson. "Richard often has been two or three steps ahead of his boss but has been able to pull his boss along," said an official who asked not to be identified. "This time the risk is that he may have gone four steps ahead."

. . . Other Senate and Administration aides perceive Mr. Perle as playing a very prominent role. The focus of Administration efforts to try to win support for the arms control negotiations has become the Senate Armed Services subcommittee on arms control, which is headed by Mr. Jackson and for which Mr. Perle works on a temporary basis.

. . . Mr. Perle was a key participant in such efforts as Mr. Jackson's "qualification" attached to the Senate's approval of the first strategic-arms accord in 1972 calling for equal force levels on both sides in any future agreement; adoption of the so-called "Jackson amendment" as part of a 1975 trade bill withholding most-favored-nation status from countries that restrict emigration, and Mr. Jackson's fight earlier this year that produced a surprisingly large vote—40—against President Carter's nomination of Paul C. Warnke as director of the Arms Control and Disarmament Agency.

. . ."I don't think I'm intellectually rigid," [Perle] said. "I think I try very hard to see all sides of an issue." Any Administration, he went on, presents its view in a "very tendentious manner" and no one questions the right of Congress to raise questions about unpopular things.

But a strategic-arms agreement, he said, "is regarded as good. So there is a certain amount of resentment when you ask questions," he said.

21. Published in the *Los Angeles Times*, November 26, 1981.

22. In an article entitled "Nuclear Weapons and the Atlantic Alliance" (*Foreign Affairs*, spring, 1982) Robert McNamara, McGeorge Bundy, Gerard Smith and George Kennan advocated the adoption of a policy of no first use of nuclear weapons and stated:

It is time to recognize that no one has ever succeeded in advancing any persuasive reason to believe that any use of nuclear weapons, even on the smallest scale, could reliably be expected to remain limited. Every serious analysis and every military exercise, for over 25 years, has demonstrated that even the most restrained battlefield use would be enormously destructive to civilian life and property. There is no way for anyone to have any confidence that such a nuclear action will not lead to further and more devastating exchanges. Any use of nuclear weapons in Europe, by the Alliance or against it, carries with it a high and inescapable risk of escalation into the general nuclear war which would bring ruin to all and victory to none.

The one clearly definable firebreak against the worldwide disaster of general nuclear war is the one that stands between all other kinds of conflict and any use whatsoever of nuclear weapons. To keep that firebreak wide and strong is in the deepest interest of all mankind. In retrospect, indeed, it is remarkable that this country has not responded to this reality more quickly. Given the appalling consequences of even the most limited use of nuclear weapons and the total impossibility for both sides of any guarantee against unlimited escalation, there must be the gravest doubt about the wisdom of a policy which asserts the effectiveness of any first use of nuclear weapons by either side . . .

23. Excerpts from Brezhnev's statement, delivered before the U.N. Special Session on Disarmament, are included below (*New York Times*, June 16, 1982):

This session is faced with great and responsible tasks. Its agenda includes a number of items of paramount importance.

But if we are to single out what is the most important, the most urgent, what now animates people in all corners of the globe, what preoccupies the minds of statesmen and public figures in many countries of the world, this is concern for halting the endless buildup of ever more destructive types of weapons; insuring a breakthrough in improving international relations, and preventing a nuclear disaster.

Concern for peace is the dominant feature of the Soviet Union's policy. We are convinced that no contradictions between states or groups of states, no differences in social systems, ways of life or ideologies, and no transient interests can eclipse the fundamental need common to all peoples, the need to safeguard peace and avert a nuclear war.

Today, as never before, purposeful considered action is required of all states in order to achieve this lofty goal. Guided by the desire to do all in its power to deliver the peoples from the threat of nuclear devastation and ultimately to exclude its very possibility from the life of mankind, the Soviet state solemnly declares the Union of Soviet Socialist Republics assumes an obligation not to be the first to use nuclear weapons.

This obligation shall become effective immediately at the moment it is made public from the rostrum of the United Nations General Assembly.

Why is it that the Soviet Union is taking this step in conditions where the nuclear powers participating in the NATO grouping, including the United States, make no secret of the fact that not only does their military doctrine not rule out the possibility of the first use of nuclear weapons, it is actually based on this dangerous premise?

In taking this decision, the Soviet Union proceeds from the indisputable fact which plays a determining role in the present-day international situation that, should a nuclear war start, it could mean the destruction of human civilization and perhaps the end of life itself on earth.

Consequently, the supreme duty of leaders of states, conscious of their responsibility for the destinies of the world, is to exert every effort to insure that nuclear weapons never be used. The peoples of the world have the right to expect that the decision of the Soviet Union will be followed by reciprocal steps on the part of the other nuclear states.

If the other nuclear powers assume an equally precise and clear obligation not to be the first to use nuclear weapons, that would be tantamount in practice to a ban on the use of nuclear weapons altogether, which is espoused by the overwhelming majority of the countries of the world.

. . . I would like further to invite the attention of the representatives of states attending the special session of the U.N. General Assembly to the following question: In the search for measures which would actually halt the arms race, many political and public figures of various countries have recently turned to the idea of a freeze; in other words, stopping a further buildup of nuclear potentials.

The considerations advanced in this connection are not all in the same vein; still, on the whole, we believe they go in the right direction. We see in them the reflection of peoples' profound concern for their destinies. To use a figure of speech, people are voting for preserving the supreme value in the world, which is human life . . .

. . . .

Excerpts from President Reagan's U.N. speech on the nuclear arms race are included below (as published in the *New York Times*, June 18, 1982):

. . . We look around the world and see rampant conflict and aggression. There are many sources of this conflict—expansionist ambitions, local rivalries, the striving to obtain justice and security. We must all work to resolve such discords by peaceful means and to prevent them from escalation.

In the nuclear era, the major powers bear a special responsibility to ease these sources of conflict and to refrain from aggression.

And that's why we're so deeply concerned by Soviet conduct. Since World War II, the record of tyranny has included Soviet violation of the Yalta Agreements, leading to domination of Eastern Europe, symbolized by the Berlin wall, a grim, gray monument to repression that I visited just a week ago. It includes the takeovers of Czechoslovakia, Hungary, and Afghanistan and the ruthless repression of the proud people of Poland.

Soviet sponsored guerrillas and terrorists are at work in Central and South America, in Africa, the Middle East, in the Carribbean and in Europe, violating human rights and unnerving the world with violence. Communist atrocities in Southeast Asia, Afghanistan and elsewhere continue to shock the free world as refugees escape to tell of their horror.

The decade of so-called détente witnessed the most massive Soviet buildup of military power in history.

They increased their defense spending by 40 percent while American defense actually declined in the same real terms.

Soviet aggression and support for violence around the world have eroded the confidence needed for arms negotiations.

While we exercised unilateral restraint, they forged ahead and today possess nuclear and conventional forces far in excess of an adequate deterrent capability. Soviet oppression is not limited to the countries they invade. At the very time the Soviet Union is trying to manipulate the peace movement in the West, it is stifling a budding peace movement at home. In Moscow, banners are scuttled, buttons are snatched and demonstrators are arrested when even a few people dare to speak about their fears.

. . . My country learned a bitter lesson in this century. The scourge of tyranny cannot be stopped with words alone. So we have embarked on an effort to renew our strength that had fallen dangerously low. We refuse to become weaker while potential adversaries remain committed to their imperialist adventures.

. . . Agreements on arms control and disarmament can be useful in reinforcing peace, but they're not magic. We should not confuse the signing of agreements with the solving of problems. Simply collecting agreements will not bring peace. Agreements genuinely reinforce peace only when they are kept. Otherwise we are building a paper castle that will be blown away by the winds of war.

. . . Since the end of World War II, the United States has been the leader in serious disarmament and arms control proposals. In 1946, in what became known as the Baruch Plan, the United States submitted a proposal for control of nuclear weapons and nuclear energy by an international authority. The Soviets rejected this plan.

In 1955, President Eisenhower made his open skies proposal, under which the United States and the Soviet Union would have exchanged blue prints of military establishments and provided for aerial reconnaissance. The Soviets rejected this plan.

In 1963, the limited test ban treaty came into force. This treaty ended nuclear weapons testing in the atmosphere, outer space or under water by participating nations.

In 1970 the treaty on the nonproliferation of nuclear weapons took effect. The United States played a major role in this key effort to prevent the spread of nuclear explosives and to provide for international safeguards on civil nuclear activities.

. . . In the early 1970's, again at United States urging, agreements were reached between the United States and the U.S.S.R. providing for ceilings on some categories of weapons. They could have been more meaningful if Soviet actions had shown restraint and commitment to stability at lower levels of force.

The United Nations designated the 1970's as the first disarmament decade. But good intentions were not enough. In reality that 10-year period included an unprecedented buildup in military weapons and the flaring of aggression and use of force in almost every region of the world.

We are now in the second disarmament decade. The task at hand is to assure civilized behavior among nations, to unite behind an agenda of peace.

. . . Let me stress that for agreements to work, both sides must be able to verify compliance. The building of mutual confidence in compliance can only be achieved through greater openness . . .

. . . Isn't it time for us to really represent the deepest, most heartfelt yearnings of all of our people? Let no nation abuse this common longing to be free of fear. We must not manipulate our people by playing upon their nightmares. We must serve mankind through genuine disarmament . . .

24. "Ex-CIA Official Says Nuclear Weapons Freeze Could Be Verified," *Los Angeles Times*, April 11, 1982.

25. Interview with the author, summer, 1981, by telephone and in Los Angeles, California.

26. In an article entitled "A New Nuclear Strategy," written for the *New York Times Magazine* (January 24, 1982), Laurence W. Beilenson and nuclear scientist Samuel T. Cohen wrote:

. . . We must accept the virtual certainty that any war between the United States and the Soviet Union involving the defense of our major allies will start as—or will rapidly become—a nuclear war, in which the Russians will deliver a massive nuclear strike against the United States. In our present defenseless condition, such a strike against our military installations might kill tens of millions of Americans, an enormous calamity. If our counterstrike were against Soviet cities and the Russians responded in kind, our toll could well exceed 100 million, an unspeakable horror.

Rightly appalled by this dismal prospect, peace groups urge us to do something to preclude the catastrophe. They argue that diplomacy can save us from nuclear disaster, that reasonable men will find solutions to overcome man's unreasonable nature. A popular European movement, which appears to be spreading across the Atlantic, demands that governments renounce nuclear weapons altogether as instruments of national policy.

Diplomacy has sometimes averted war, and is not to be dismissed. At best, however, it is a patching device. The fruit of diplomacy is a treaty, and all nations, including our own, have habitually broken treaties. The champion treaty breaker, the Soviet Union, believes that violating compacts for the sake of advantage is a virtue.

But why not, as many Americans urge, take a chance on the treaty process, accepting the risks involved for the sake of peace? Because reliance on that approach increases the chance of war by lowering our guard. Our arms-control agreements with Moscow have not restrained the growth of nuclear stockpiles on both sides. Yet, lulled into a false security by the treaty procedure, we have sunk from superiority to inferiority in strategic nuclear capabilities . . .

The "new nuclear strategy" advocated by Beilenson and Cohen includes

devising new nuclear weapons that can best protect the United States against nuclear attack. This will call for developing offensive weapons in great quantities, and exploiting mobility, concealment and dispersion to make them invulnerable to any conceivable nuclear strike. It will call for removing the shackles placed by the strategic arms treaty of 1972 on the development of antimissile weapons capable of protecting our population and economy. It will call for restoring our emaciated air defense against bombers, so as to meet an impending Soviet threat in that category of weapons. And it will require a program, following the Swiss example, for providing our cities with civil defense shelters, which can save enormous numbers of American lives . . .

27. In an article entitled "U.S. Puts Defense Over Arms Control" published in *Aviation Week and Space Technology*, August 3, 1981, Clarence A. Robinson, Jr., reported:

Reagan Administration U.S. military strategy for the period through the 1980s mandates that arms control policy with the Soviet Union will frame any agreements so that they support U.S. defense needs instead of allowing arms control considerations to affect defense programs.

In the strategy recently provided to the Pentagon and the armed forces, the White House made clear that in formulating military programs, decisions will be independent of arms control.

"Our first priority must be to formulate and implement our defense program so as to redress the current imbalance," the Reagan strategy said.

The strategy pinpoints ways to correct the imbalance, which favors the Soviet Union, through modernization.

The guidance to the military also recognizes that successful arms control agreements can make a significant contribution to the defense effort, but enjoins the Pentagon from relying on such agreements for "any essential security needs . . ."

John Newhouse, in an article entitled "Arms and Orthodoxy" (*The New Yorker,* June 7, 1982), discussed the Reagan Administration's attitude toward arms control:

Each of the four previous Administrations had internal divisions of opinion on SALT issues but not on the desirability of the process. When I asked a military officer with long experience in these matters why the present Administration was having so much trouble, he said, "This crowd is different from every other. There is no one among them who has any sympathy for the SALT process. Haig and a few others in the State Department are for it, partly because it's their turf, and Haig is very turf-conscious. Rostow is no help at all, and everyone in the Defense Department is very anti-SALT. The Joint Chiefs of Staff are the only unambiguously sympathetic agency in town, but they can't do much about it. They can't let themselves get too far afield from Weinberger and the Defense Department. In every other Administration, there was intense activity right from the beginning. Options and positions, accompanied by highly analytical backup papers, were ground out. This time, we've done nothing until very recently that has any practical value or relevance to the process."

A number of people working on arms-control and security matters in other parts of the government told me much the same thing. Each of them compared the Administration's negative attitude with the more orthodox position of the Joint Chiefs of Staff; they all stressed the continuing support of the Chiefs for the SALT II treaty. (In the present climate, it doesn't even strike people as ironic that the Joint Chiefs of Staff, who were never among the keenest advocates of SALT, are now its strongest official supporters. The Chiefs want the bird in hand, the SALT-imposed restrictions on Soviet forces, whereas their civilian colleagues in the Defense Department want the birds in the bush, new strategic systems awaiting development and deployment.) Each deplored the amount of time that had been lost. A State Department official said, "Nothing was done on SALT for nine months other than ponderous papers discussing why it would have to be done differently from before. Neither Haig nor Weinberger has focussed on it. The Defense Department is wholly preoccupied with nuclear-war-fighting scenarios."

8 Civil Defense

1. *War Survival in Soviet Strategy,* Advanced International Studies Institute, 1976.

2. "State Official Labels Nuclear Evacuation Plan Hoax on Public," Carl Ingram, *Los Angeles Times,* March 18, 1982.

3. "New York Rejects Disaster Plan," Leslie Bennetts, *New York Times,* June 10, 1982.

4. The complete text of the *New York Times* editorial entitled "The Shelter Fraud," published on April 3, 1982, follows:

The Pentagon has already begun to play down its formal claim this week that a multibillion-dollar civil defense program could "provide for survival" of 80 percent of the population in a general nuclear war. Still, we have two questions:

Who is the mastermind who thinks this could ever work? And who decided to propose it just as the President was trying finally to calm the public's fear of nuclear weapons? Both should be fired.

There may be a need to prepare for the manageable damage of natural disasters, nuclear power plant failures or even an accidental or small-scale nuclear attack. But any promise of recovery from Armageddon is a fraud. Based on hallucinations about Soviet civil defense, it damages public morale and undermines the balance of nuclear terror.

People who think that even with a week's warning they could evacuate two-thirds of the American people, feed them for a month in remote fallout shelters and then resume life in 300 or more devastated cities ought themselves to be evacuated from Government forthwith. That they think all this "crisis relocation" could be prepared in seven years on a Federal budget of $4 billion, plus perhaps $2 billion from the states, further evidences their incapacity.

The sponsors of this project contend that the Soviet Union has an elaborate evacuation and shelter program that needs to be matched. In a crisis, they argue, the Kremlin could reinforce a nuclear ultimatum by suddenly evacuating its people and leaving Americans without a credible response.

Most students of Soviet society hold this to be a vast exaggeration. They think the known Soviet instruction manuals, shelter signs and civil defense drills are modest exertions; there is no evidence that the Russians have ever practiced evacuating a city. That would require a miraculous transformation of the Soviet transport and supply networks. And it would be futile. With the twist of a few dials, as former Defense Secretary Brown once observed, America's nuclear weapons could be retargeted to blanket the evacuation sites.

The mischief in this kind of planning goes beyond the waste of money. The stability of deterrence that has kept the peace between the Soviet Union and the United States assumes that neither side could ever launch a nuclear strike without suffering an unbearable retaliatory blow. The weapons—and defenses—on each side need to be designed to preserve that condition. Despite serious uncertainties caused by some of the Soviet Union's missiles, the balance of fear persists.

Those who aim to upset it encourage the idea that it is feasible to fight a general nuclear war and to "survive." That idea is not merely irresponsible; it is mad.

· · ·

In an article published in the *New York Times* ("Russians, Too, Joke Sadly on Atom-War Survival," June 11, 1982), reporter John Burns described the attitude of Soviet citizens to the Soviet Union's civil defense program:

Much of the [Soviet civil defense] effort seems to have gone into lectures and demonstrations. It is these that have given rise to much of the cynicism among ordinary people since the precautions advocated are widely regarded as inadequate to the threat.

Public apathy is suggested by the nickname given to the program—"grob," an acronym drawn from the program's full title, Grazhdanskaya Oborona, meaning civil defense. Grob is also the Russian word for coffin . . .

According to a *New York Times* article (Judith Miller, June 10, 1982), many American experts have doubts about the efficacy of Soviet civil defense programs:

Malcolm Toon and Thomas J. Watson, former American ambassadors to Moscow, repeatedly tried to evaluate the Russian program while serving there. They concluded that the country did not appear to have a program that could effectively shelter a large part of the population.

"The Soviets are very good at establishing lots of bureaus to work on projects that never fly," said Mr. Watson, the former chairman of the International Business Machines Corporation, who left Moscow in 1981.

"Their civil defense program is a turkey, as they are beginning to realize," said Adm. Noel Gayler, retired, former director of the National Security Agency and former Commander-in-Chief of United States forces in the Pacific.

According to intelligence sources, however, Russia spends considerable sums to insure that key personnel would survive a nuclear exchange.

"But it's a mistake," said William Hyland, a top official in the Nixon and Ford Administrations, "to confuse a program to protect leaders and key industrial personnel with effective civil defense for the population."

5. "Enhanced Civil Defense Program to Implement PD 41 Policies," FEMA, March 30, 1981.

6. Telephone interview with the author, spring, 1981.

When I interviewed Charles Kupperman, executive director for ACDA's General Advisory Board and former defense analyst for the Committee on the Present Danger, in the fall of 1981, he discussed his image of nuclear war, and how it differed from that of the Physicians for Social Responsibility:

KUPPERMAN: What they [the Physicians] are talking about is a very individual thing, but I'm concerned about the survival of this nation, and the preservation of our freedom and independance. At some point, as it has been the point in the past, people have had to fight and die to preserve our freedom and independence. Of course it bothers me that any American has to give his life.

SCHEER: What do you mean that they are looking at it from an individual point of view?

KUPPERMAN: They are doctors, they are not politicians, they are not a national security analyst, they are not a leader of this country that has to take the responsibility for keeping our nation free and secure. Their concerns are different, as well they should be.

SCHEER: The question is, what is the reality of—

KUPPERMAN: Okay, how about the reality of the Second World War, when the British knew that the Germans were going to bomb Coventry, but they couldn't alert the citizens because that would tip the Germans off that they had cracked their code? Certainly the British must have been upset about the victims of Coventry, but they had a higher objective and that was to defeat the German war machine. Therefore they had to accept those kind of casualties until they were in a position to win the war. That isn't a pleasant choice.

SCHEER: What I am trying to get at here is the image of the kind of casualties, an image of what happens. Those doctors obviously were presenting a view of what happens. What I'm interested in is contrasting that . . . with your view of what happens.

KUPPERMAN: I don't know how to contrast it, really. I don't look at it that way . . . I'm not a doctor. Their concern about a burn victim is from their own perspective as a medical person. My concern is that of a strategist, a member of an Administration that is charged with keeping the United States free and secure and independent, and carrying out our foreign policy objectives. That is my focal point. Of course it bothers me, but it also bothers me that people die from cancer. It bothers me that they haven't solved heart disease either . . . All those things bother me. But there are so few areas that I'm competent to do anything about, I've got to be pretty selective in where I put my emphasis.

SCHEER: But in terms of your image of nuclear war, do you factor in what those doctors were saying?

KUPPERMAN: Yes, that is why I want to have a civil defense system, because it can be very effective in reducing casualties. That is my point. If doctors are so concerned about it, the answer isn't necessarily disarming the United States or cutting our weapons programs . . . it might be having a civil defense program. You can make a very good case that that is exactly what those doctors ought to be shouting for.

SCHEER: But they say that it is impossible to protect the population from nuclear attack.

KUPPERMAN: Yes, but the thing is, nuclear weapons have certain effects and if you take steps to deny those effects, you save a lot of people. And unless you are right in the middle of ground zero, you are not going to have a lot of burn victims if you take those steps. And if you evacuate these people out of the targeted areas, or what you think are targeted areas, they are not going to get burned or destroyed . . .

At another point in the interview I asked Kupperman if he believed it possible to survive a nuclear war.

KUPPERMAN: . . . Well, again, it is relative. If you are trying to assure the survivability of 100 million of your people or 20 million of them—the demands are different. . . . I think there are certain things that can be done that can reduce casualties, and as far as those things go, they lead to a better chance of recovery.

SCHEER: So you think it is possible to survive and recover?

KUPPERMAN: I think it is possible to survive a nuclear war. But again, it depends on a variety of assumption and variables. It also depends on the relative position of the United States and the Soviet Union after a nuclear exchange.

SCHEER: Is it possible to survive it with your civilization intact?

KUPPERMAN: Well, it is possible to survive it with a certain amount of society intact, it depends on what steps we take to ensure that survivability. It certainly won't be the same as before the war. But generally societies have been intact—like Germany and Japan and Western Europe in the Second World War weren't the same after the war as they were before. But generally societies have been intact. The question really gets down to political credibility in the conduct of your foreign policy. If you look like you are serious about defending yourself and your allies with real civil defense programs and other measures, I think that has political credibility with the adversary. An adversary isn't going to take somebody seriously if they don't take steps to protect themselves.

Nuclear war is a destructive thing, but it is still in large part a physics problem.

SCHEER: What do you mean?

KUPPERMAN: Well, sheltering yourself against nuclear effects can be done, it just depends on how much effort and money one wants to spend on it, but a certain layer of dirt and some reinforced construction materials can assure the survivability of somebody, assuming they aren't at ground zero of a detonation.

Hiroshima, after it was bombed, was back and operating three days later. So it is certainly a destructive weapon, and nobody wants a nuclear war, but I don't think the United States in the past has been serious enough about planning for its survival in the event of a nuclear war . . .

·   ·   ·

I asked Nobel physicist Hans Bethe whether he thought the destructive power of nuclear weapons and conventional weapons was in any way comparable.

BETHE: The difference in quantity means a difference in kind. There were fire raids in the Second World War. There was destruction of buildings in the Second World War. If you have atomic weapons, a single plane will destroy a city. A single missile will destroy a city without having any soldier putting his life on the line. We have some 9,000 strategic weapons. Every one of them is bigger than the Hiroshima bomb. The Russians have a similar force . . . If you direct [them] against cities, you can destroy at least five thousand cities of over a hundred thousand—there are maybe two hundred of those in each country. Why would you need more than two hundred weapons?

Warfare has become totally different because the destructive power is greater than the totality of the things you can destroy. That has never happened before. That is the difference. The destruction can happen in an hour or two, instead of in five years. If it happens over five years, you can recover in part, again and again, you can adjust to it, you can bring help to the city which has been hit. If in two hours all our cities are destroyed, no help can be brought. That is not a difference in size but a difference in kind.

7. Interview with the author, summer, 1981.

8. Interview with the author, winter, 1981, Washington, D.C.

9. Handout to Emergency Managers, FEMA, December 1980.

10. During hearings before the Subcommittee on Health and Human Research on June 19, 1980, Senator Edward Kennedy asked William Chipman, then-director of FEMA's Population Protection Division, about conditions in the post–nuclear attack environment. Chipman responded:

Senator, we have done, through the last decade or so, a great deal of post-attack research. People have looked at radiological problems, economic problems, psychological problems, problems of disease control and public health in the year or so following an attack. And in all these years of research, no factor has been found which would preclude recovery. In other words, it is not a question of black and white—of perfect survival, however that may be defined, versus national extinction. It is a question of degree. And what you have done has an impact, of course, on whether there is more misery and suffering or less, and whether you are going to hope for recovery in a somewhat lesser period of years or longer. There are no certainties in this area.

Someone mentioned the Black Death, and I was impressed a few weeks ago in reading about that during the period of the Hundred Years' War. Here was a catastrophe that killed a third of the population of England. And yet these people were able to mount an expeditionary force to France and fight the Battle of Poitiers six or eight years after the epidemic. I do not know what this says about the ethics of the human race, but it shows there is a certain resilience and toughness to society.

We hope that we will never see anything like this. But if such a catastrophe should ever occur—a failure of deterrence—it is almost sure that the survivors would put back together some kind of society, some kind of economy. It would not be a question of back to the trees. Grimness, privation, suffering, yes; but not total extinction or going back to barbarism.

The important thing, it seems to me, is that what we have done by way of preparedness affects the outcome. There are many things that need more research, but there are many things that can be done.

11. Hearings before the Subcommittee on Health and Scientific Research of the Committee on Labor and Human Resources, United States Senate, June 19, 1980.

12. "Preventing the Last Epidemic," *Journal of the American Medical Association*, November 21, 1980.

13. "Nuclear War Would Leave U.S. Devastated by Disease," Daniel Gilmore, UPI, April 19, 1982.

Dr. Abrams, in a report entitled "Medical Problems of Survivors of Nuclear War" (published in the *New England Journal of Medicine,* November 12, 1981), concludes:

Several factors point to an increased risk of serious infection and communicable disease in the post-attack environment. These include the effects on susceptibility of irradiation, malnutrition, and exposure; the effects on disease transmittal of unsanitary conditions, lengthy stays in shelters, and the growth of insect populations; and the effects on attempted countermeasures of depleted antibiotic stocks, shortages of physicians, the destruction of laboratories, and the general disorganization sure to follow an attack.

Although this threat has been considered small in comparison to the direct effects of nuclear weapons, its potential impact both on survivors and on the recovery process itself requires careful consideration. Previous studies may have been overly optimistic in their assumptions and analyses. First of all, the synergistic effects of increased susceptibility, easier disease transmittal, and less effective countermeasures are uncertain. Secondly, some studies have assumed the post-attack survival situation to be favorable, with plentiful food, and functioning governmental and health organizations. Thirdly, the profound effects of epidemics on post-attack recovery— leading to further famine and disease—have not been adequately calculated. Fourthly, lethal, highly infectious, and largely uncontrollable diseases of low incidence in the United States have been assumed to stay at low incidence in the post-attack period. A breakout of one or more could greatly increase the number of deaths.

Although no existing data prove that catastrophic epidemics will occur in the post-attack period, the matter is one of overwhelming importance and uncertainty.

What is certain is that infection will pose a substantial threat to health and recovery for all those injured by blast, heat, and radiation, and that the resources to grapple with this threat will be inadequate.

14. "Recovery From Nuclear Attack," published by DCPA (now FEMA), May 10, 1979.

15. Handout to Emergency Managers, FEMA, December 1980.

16. Interview with the author, fall, 1981, New York City, New York.
That the Soviets clearly recognize the devastating effects of nuclear war is illustrated in an article by John Burns that was published in the *New York Times* on June 11, 1982:

A recent edition of the Communist Party daily Pravda carried a stark forecast of the impact of a new war on the Soviet homeland. The article was attributed to Nikolai N. Blokhin, one of the country's leading cancer specialists. He is also a leader of a Soviet doctors' group formed as a counterpart to similar groups in the United States and other Western countries that have been urging a reduction in nuclear weapon stockpiles.
"If during the Second World war our country sacrificed 20 million lives to the god of war, now in a few hours the number of victims on the territories of the combatants would exceed that many times over," Dr. Blokhin wrote.
"In a city with one million people, according to experts, hundreds of thousands would die in the first moments after an explosion and one can hardly call lucky those who would avoid death or direct injury, but get irradiated instead. They would be threatened with leukemia and other cancer forms, and their genetic make-up would be disrupted, raising the risk of having deformed children.
"Would life on earth still be viable?" he asked.

17. Interview with the author, fall, 1981, Washington, D.C.

18. See "Central War and Civil Defense," T. K. Jones and W. Scott Thompson, *ORBIS*, fall, 1978.

19. "Soviet Civil Defense," CIA, July 1978.

20. "Can Nuclear War Be Controlled?" Adelphi Papers, International Institute for Strategic Studies, fall, 1981.

21. Interview with the author, spring, 1981, Washington, D.C.

The Royal Swedish Academy of Sciences devoted an entire issue of their publication, *Ambio*, to different aspects of the environmental effects of nuclear war (Volume XI, Number 2–3, 1982). The nuclear war scenario considered likely by the authors would have the following consequences:

The number of immediate or early deaths resulting from the effects of blast, fire, and heat in the nuclear exchange described here will approach 750 million (slightly more than half of the population of the cities bombed) and about 340 million will be seriously injured. To these casualties must be added those who will succumb to or be incapacitated by fire and heat. A considerable proportion of those who survive the blast, fire and heat will suffer from acute radiation sickness as a result of exposure to fallout. In addition, sublethal levels of ionizing radiation will lower resistance to infection, and diseases such as cholera and dysentery will spread rapidly in the absence of proper water and sanitation facilities.

About one-third of the urban survivors will be in a state of acute anxiety, and about 20 percent of the other survivors will be so incapacitated by psychological and pathopsychological conditions that they will be unable to care for themselves or others. Those who have witnessed the annihilation of their societies may suffer from profound apathy and disorientation. The staggering numbers of corpses to be cleared away and the pressing need to care for the wounded and ill will absorb much of the time and energy of those who are still capable of purposeful action.

. . . Rainwater, and surface water . . . will be contaminated, and many of the water supply systems destroyed . . . Rainwater in early fallout areas will contain such a high concentration of toxic material that it will be a lethal poison. Those caught in such areas will experience burns through the full thickness of the exposed skin.

Faced with food shortages, people will almost certainly be unable to avoid eating food contaminated with radioactivity.

. . . Enormous amounts of light-absorbing and light-reflecting particulate debris will cloak the atmosphere in a dark veil which will hinder sunlight for weeks and perhaps months. In the Northern Hemisphere vast fires will almost certainly sweep over expanses of forest land and agricultural fields, and these fires along with those in oil and gas fields ignited by the thousands of nuclear explosions will load the lower atmosphere with tiny particles of tar, soot and ash. When the fires burn out and the particles eventually fall to the ground, the changed chemistry of the atmosphere would be such that a severe photochemical smog could form over much of the Northern Hemisphere. This smog, together with a shortage of all types of supplies and a state of chaos, will tend to make agriculture extremely difficult. A large reduction of the stratospheric ozone layer is also possible. It would last for several years and lead to an increased intensity of solar UV-radiation received at the earth's surface, with serious consequences for humans, plants and animals.

Agricultural and natural ecosystems weakened by radiation and other environmental stress will be vulnerable to attack by pests that thrive on ailing plants. Cockroaches and rats, carrion birds and organisms of decay will increase in frequency. Pests, those small-bodied, fast-multiplying organisms that are often in competition with human beings, are relatively resistant to radiation, and will thrive in the conditions of the aftermath.

All these factors will cause enormous problems for the survivors in the Northern Hemisphere and severe food shortages will persist in large areas for months or years following the war. Widespread famines will return to areas where they have long been absent.

. . . Societies will be drastically changed. The economies of the Northern Hemisphere will collapse and there will be a return to the barter system. Commodities and services now taken for granted will no longer exist. No modern economic system based on economies of scale, specialization and international exchange would be likely to survive the war. Decades, or even centuries might pass before any social and economic recovery could be possible.

Industrially less developed countries with large populations and inadequate food production—even if not directly involved—will be swept by waves of famine, disease and social unrest. The complete breakdown of the system of international trade in fertilizers, fuel, farm machinery and technology and funds, would also deprive many Third World countries of resources that are currently needed to sustain them, thus creating a lethal gap between the number of people and the resources available to support them.

In the face of such anarchy, post-nuclear "governments" would most likely be highly authoritarian, and of necessity dependent on Draconian laws. Surviving "societies" would have to be highly restricted, dedicated to the virtually impossible task of managing scarce resources, and closely governed by the exigencies of survival.

. . . Although the impact of nuclear war described in this issue would be widespread and terrible, there would probably be survivors. Their fate, however, is extremely uncertain. The human and social environment in which they will have to live will be changed far beyond our comprehension. In addition to wartime destruction and poisoning, the natural environment might suffer such grave long-term changes as to severely threaten the survivors' fight for recovery. In any case societies as we know them today will most certainly cease to exist.

9 Postscript

1. Memorandum to Jason Epstein, Vice President and Editorial Director, Random House, July 7, 1982.

2. In an article entitled "Two Views of the Soviet Problem" (*The New Yorker*, November 2, 1981), former Soviet Ambassador George Kennan contrasts his view of the Soviet Union with that of those he describes as his "critics and opponents in recent years":

My opponents seem to see the nuclear explosive as just a weapon like any other weapon, only more destructive; and they think that because it is more destructive it is a better and more powerful weapon. I deny that the nuclear explosive is a proper weapon. It conforms, in my view, to none of the criteria traditionally applied to conventional weapons. It can serve no useful purpose. It cannot be used without bringing disaster upon everyone concerned. I regard it as the reflection of a vast misunderstanding of the true purposes of warfare and the true usefulness of weaponry.

My opponents see the Soviet Union as having sought and achieved some sort of statistical superiority over the NATO powers in this kind of weaponry. I myself have not seen the evidence that it has achieved that sort of superiority; nor do I see any reason to assume that that is what it would like to do. The evidence seems to me to suggest that it is striving for what it would view as equivalence, in the statistical sense—not for superiority. My opponents believe that differences of superiority or inferiority, in the statistical sense, have meaning: that if you have more of these weapons than your adversary has, you are in a stronger position to stand up against intimidation or against an actual attack. I challenge that view. I submit that if you are talking, as all of us are talking today, about what are in reality grotesque quantities of overkill—arsenals so excessive that they would suffice to destroy the adversary's homeland many times over—statistical disparities between the arsenals on the two sides are quite meaningless. But precisely that—the absurd excessiveness of the existing arsenals—is the situation we have before us.

. . . My opponents say: We must have these weapons for purposes of deterrence. The use of this term carries two implications: first, that it is the Russians who have taken the lead in the development of these weapons, and that we are only reacting to what they have done; and, secondly, that the Russians are such monsters that unless they are deterred they would assuredly launch upon us a nuclear attack, with all the horrors and suffering that would bring. I question both these implications; and I question in particular the wisdom of suggesting the latter implication thousands of times a year to the general public, thus schooling the public mind to believe that Soviet adversary has lost every semblance of humanity and is concerned only with wreaking unlimited destruction for destruction's sake. I am not sure, furthermore, that the stationing of these weapons on one's territory is not more of a provocation of their use by others than a means of dissuading others from using them. I have never been an advocate of unilateral disarmament, and I see no necessity for anything of that sort today. But I must say that if we Americans had no nuclear weapons whatsoever on our soil instead of the tens of thousands of nuclear warheads we are now said to have deployed, I would feel the future of my children and grandchildren to be far safer than I do at this moment; for if there is any incentive for the Russians to use such weapons against us, it surely comes in overwhelming degree—probably, in fact, entirely—from our own enormous deployment of them.

. . . I see the danger not in the number or quality of the weapons or in the intentions of those who hold them but in the very existence of weapons of this nature, regardless of whose hands they are in. I believe that until we consent to recognize that the nuclear weapons we hold in our own hands are as much a danger to us as those that respose in the hands of our supposed adversaries there will be no escape from the confusions and dilemmas to which such weapons have now brought us, and must bring us increasingly as time goes on. For this reason, I see no solution to the problem other than the complete elimination of these and all other weapons of mass destruction from national arsenals; and the sooner we move toward that solution, and the greater courage we show in doing so, the safer we will be.

3. According to the *Washington Post* in an article by reporter Dusko Doder (April 11, 1982), Reagan's arms buildup has caused significant concern in the Soviet Union:

A senior Soviet arms control specialist was quoted today as saying that the Soviet Union may adopt a "launch-on-warning" defense posture—which provides for quick firing of nuclear missiles—as a relatively cheap way of responding to President Reagan's planned buildup of U.S. strategic might.

Under "launch on warning," Soviet nuclear missiles capable of reaching the United States would be programmed for almost instant action if computerized Soviet intelligence monitoring facilities reported an imminent American threat to the Soviet Union.

A group of American academic specialists and antinuclear activists, who asked that the Soviet official not be identified, quoted him as saying that "launch on warning" would almost "eliminate the human element" from calculations in emergencies.

From the Soviets' point of view, the new posture would better protect their missiles from a surprise U.S. strike. But it would also increase the possibility that the Soviets would launch an attack by mistake because of computer error.

"We cannot afford to match you ruble for dollar," the official was quoted as saying by the Americans, "but you'd be making a great mistake to think that you could gain strategic superiority" over the Soviet Union.

. . . The Americans met a number of top officials in Moscow and said the Soviets think that the United States is "pulling ahead in the arms race." As a result, the suggestion that Moscow may adopt "launch on warning" may have been calculated either to convey the gravity of Soviet concerns or perhaps to increase psychological pressure on Washington by signaling that automatic massive retaliation is being seriously considered.

. . . The Soviets believe that Reagan is trying to build up the U.S. ability to knock out their land-based missiles—which account for 70 percent of the Soviet strategic force—by developing the MX missile and the D5 warhead for the submarine-launched Trident missile and by planning to deploy Pershing II and cruise missiles in Western Europe, the Americans said . . .

• • •

In a speech at UCLA in April 1982, Jerry Hough, a Russian specialist who is a professor at Duke University and a staff member of the Brookings Institution, described the current debates in the Soviet Union regarding Soviet defense policies vis-à-vis the United States:

The most alarmist participants in the debates have been the military. The most sophisticated of the Soviet generals, Nikolai Ogarkov, the leading Soviet military representative on the SALT-1 delegation, has argued in print that the situation in the world today has many similarities to those in the 1930s—that is, on the eve of World War II. In a remarkable article in the theoretical journal, *Kommunist,* he argued . . . that "sometimes questions of the struggle for peace is understood not from class positions, but somewhat more simply: any peace is good, any war is bad. This can lead to lack of concern, indifference, and self-satisfaction, to the underestimation of the threat of war." Ogarkov emphasized that war is very different from what it was in the past, that surprise and mobility are far more important, and that old military doctrines need to be discarded. He strongly emphasized the need for quick mobilization and called for defense committees such as existed during World War II . . . The exact meaning of Ogarkov's article is the subject of intense debate in Washington . . . At a minimum, however, Ogarkov certainly was saying that the Soviet Union must increase its military budget in response to the American buildup. His talk about mobilization was absolutely chilling to a Russian audience that remembers that mobilization on the eve of World War I had a momentum that led to war, and his remarks [about] the similarities to the 1930s had a similar impact.

. . . None of the major civilian participants in the debate have been as alarmist about the danger of war as Ogarkov and the military press, but some are very hard-line. For example, Korionov, the longtime columnist of *Pravda*, is probably the closest Soviet equivalent to the American Richard Pipes or Norman Podhoretz— that is, a person with an unrelievedly black picture of the adversary who sees the struggle as relentless and unmitigating. Korionov has been writing for *Pravda* for years, and he generally is put on the shelf by the editors when relations with the West are going well. In 1981, as can be imagined, he appeared very frequently . . . Korionov claims that American policy has been unchanging over the decades and remains completely hostile on ideological or class grounds. Last summer he quoted a U.S. Chief of Staff document from right after World War II that asserted —or at least allegedly asserted—that American policy "should be based on the following supposition: we shouldn't permit a political system alien to our own to survive." He asserted that "this strategy was incorporated into real military prepara- tions," and indicated that it still lay at the basis of American policy. As for NATO countries, Korionov treats them as quite united and threatening.

. . . A series of hard-liners do not go as far as Korionov . . . nevertheless this group . . . agree that the Carter and Reagan Administrations have been extremely aggres- sive and threatening. Unlike Korionov, they do not emphasize the imperialistic nature of capitalism, but instead what they see as the basically aggressive tradition of American foreign policy—the chauvinism, the messianism, the assumptions of superiority . . . Thus in July Bogdanov argued in *Kommunist* that a strong hegemo- nistic tendency has been inherent in the American tradition. "Regular failures [of American policy] now and then . . . has forced [the American] strategists . . . to make a more somber assessment of their own possibilities and of international reality, but the tendency to world domination has remained and has broken through . . . to each generation of American politicians." These scholars assert—and reportedly sincerely believe—that the United States has a real desire to achieve military superiority, and they interpret the American MX and the Pershing rockets in Europe as part of a real American war-winning strategy, one based on a first strike doctrine.

. . . General Milshtein of the University of the USA seems more concerned about the possibility of an American technological breakthrough in weaponry and seems to be advocating more money for research and development . . . Trofimenko explic- itly has warned against the Soviet Union spending money to answer the American first-strike force (that is, against building a Soviet MX) and he seems more worried about American military action in the Third World. A third seems to think that American economic difficulties and Allied pressure may moderate American hegemonism somewhat . . . Nevertheless, this type of hard-liner give the readers little reason to believe that meaningful détente with the United States is possible.

At the other end of the political spectrum, the most consistent and outspoken proponent of détente has been Fedor Burlatsky, the head of the philosophy depart- ment of the Institute of Social Sciences of the Central Committee . . . Burlatsky has emphasized three major themes. The first is the great catastrophe that nuclear war would be, and the overwhelming priority of preventing it. If Marshal Ogarkov harks back to the 1930s to evoke the memory of military threat, Burlasky goes back to the wartime period to emphasize the cooperation of the Soviet Union and the United States against a common threat, Hitler. Now, however, he argues that the common enemy is greater than Hitler: it is nuclear war itself. Burlatsky's second theme . . . is the outmoded nature of dogmatic ideology . . . The Chinese alliance with the United States, he has said, shows that "dogmatism and abstract schematizing . . . does not stand up to reality."

. . . Burlatsky's third theme is that the American threat should not be exaggerated. The really impossible statement to make in the Soviet press is that the United States is rearming because of the threat of Soviet armaments. However, in 1980 Burlatsky went as far as he could go in this direction by suggesting that maybe the West had a mistaken idea that they were being defensive.

. . . Other proponents of détente have been emphasizing other arguments . . . The first deputy director of the Institute of the World Economy and International Relations stresses the importance of measures that build trust . . . the son of the USA institute director, Georgii Arbatov, repeatedly asserts . . . that "military superiority in its traditional sense—the ability to win in military actions—loses its meaning in a nuclear age . . ." Georgii Arbatov, the Director of the Institute of the USA, and Aleksander Bovin, a columnist in *Izvestia* and probably Brezhnev's leading speechwriter, have been warning against hysteria and overreacting, and Arbatov . . . has warned that creating an emotional situation by painting a picture of a foreign threat already takes a country a long way on the path to war . . .

. . .

The unpublished working papers prepared in November 1981 by John Steinbruner, Director of Foreign Policy Studies at the Brookings Institution, and Edward A. Hewett, Senior Fellow in Foreign Policy Studies at the Brookings Institution, are included below:

Current United States defense policies assume that Soviet military capabilities are constantly and indefinitely increasing, that the dominant thrust of Soviet policy is to use those capabilities to expand their political control throughout the world, and that the appropriate United States response is an expansion of our own military forces financed at the cost of social expenditures. Though these assumptions enjoy strong political support within the United States, they are increasingly doubted in Western Europe and elsewhere, most significantly by people who share our security objectives but reject these premises of our policy.

Ultimately this dissent will have to be reflected in the United States as well, for there is supporting evidence too important to be indefinitely ignored. Though not yet reflected in American public discussion, there are in fact strong reasons to believe that the assumptions of current U.S. defense policy represent a fundamental miscalculation of the trend in Soviet military development, a misinterpretation of the defense policies underlying the Soviet force structure; and a distortion of economic considerations in Soviet policy.

. . . The prevailing sense of alarm at Soviet military development derives largely from the sharp increase in major weapons deployments that has occurred in the past decade. Soviet forces have been supplied with technically improved missiles, tanks, submarines, medium bombers and tactical aircraft. As a result, the balance of weapons inventories has become more favorable to the Soviet Union than it was a decade ago. In the merciful absence of actual fighting, impressions of the overall balance of military power are largely dominated by these comparisons between weapons inventories. Thus the appearance of superior strategic power which the

United States enjoyed in the 1960s has disappeared and those who fear the emergence of global Soviet superiority are not easily reassured.

In recording the relative changes in weapons inventories United States defense officials have usually characterized the increase in Soviet weapons as a sustained military buildup with constant or even increasing momentum. Though detailed force projections have been somewhat more cautious, the general impression has been conveyed that the Soviets can be expected to improve their weapons inventories in the 1980s at about the same rate they did in the 1970s. That expectation constitutes a principal justification for major increases in the U.S. defense effort.

There are concrete reasons for doubting the validity of this simple extrapolation in analyzing Soviet military programs. Soviet weapons emerge from a centralized planning process in which military requirements are established and political authorization is provided long before weapons deployments are actually undertaken. For major weapons programs the final stages of deployment—the supply of weapons to active Soviet military units—are completed ten to fifteen years after the basic political decisions have been made. To a first approximation therefore the increase in Soviet weapons inventories in the 1970s was the result of planning targets set in the 1960s—a period of strong political tension when the Soviet Union experienced significant disadvantages in the balance of weapons. Since these planning targets have largely been met, those historical decisions will not produce major increases in Soviet forces in the 1980s . . . For major Soviet strategic programs, the rate of activity in the pipeline—the production and construction that intervenes between authoritative planning decisions and the final deployment—appears to have slowed during the 1970s as compared with early periods.

Surface warship construction is an exception to this pattern in that significant increases did occur during the 1970s. For that reason this is an area that merits special attention. For the moment, however, these increases seem to reflect the downstream implications of a 1960s commitment; namely, the necessity of protecting Soviet ballistic missile submarines deployed in sea areas adjacent to the Soviet Union.

. . . These observations do not yield a firm, certain projection of Soviet forces but they do identify a serious possibility that must be considered in the design of U.S. security policy. The much discussed Soviet military buildup may have reached its peak in the 1970s and we may be in the early stages of a natural stabilization of Soviet deployments resulting from the absence of major initiatives from the planning system during the 1970s. If that is the basic trend, then the main issue is whether Soviet planners will continue or can be induced to continue a pattern of relatively stable military commitments or whether in the context of current events they will react against planning targets of the past decade and set major new initiatives in motion. If the latter occurs now, the consequences would not be experienced by the United States until the 1990s. By then they would be irrevocable.

. . . In the current setting Soviet planners have strong incentive to reduce considerably the growth rate of military expenditures in order to free resources for use in consumption and investment. That probably is their basic inclination. Nonetheless there is considerable danger that first the rhetoric, and then the reality of a military buildup in the United States will force Soviet leaders, however reluctant they might be, to engage in a new phase of arms competition. It would be foolish to suppose that the Soviet Union is unable to compete after thirty years of doing so; it would be unwise not to encourage the contrary incentive.

It is not in the United States' interest to promote exaggerated fears of the Soviet Union or to indulge in emotional reactions to aggressive Soviet actions as a substitute for effective prevention or resistance. Belligerence is no more appropriate a base for United States policy than complacence. United States military development will have to continue at a judicious pace, particularly in the conventional forces. There will continue to be instances, as in Afghanistan and in Poland, where the United States must pursue effective means to oppose Soviet policy. In designing countervailing military power and in resisting objectional actions, however, we must preserve reasonable balance in the overall U.S.–Soviet relationship lest we create the monster we profess to fear . . .

4. In my interview with former Secretary of State Cyrus R. Vance in March 1982, he discussed the world view of the Reagan Administration:

I honestly don't know what the position of the new Administration is, as I've said on a number of occasions. I know what their rhetoric is. Their rhetoric is very strongly anti-Soviet. It implies that the source of most problems that arise around the world is Moscow, and that therefore that problem presents a basic confrontation between East and West. I think that's a vast oversimplification and is incorrect and will lead us into making erroneous decisions. The world is much more complex than that. It is a world of great change. It is a world where problems which have local roots—economic, political and social—have produced local conflicts which can only be resolved by dealing with the grassroots causes, and not by trying to make it into an East-West confrontation. And if we don't realize that and we don't attack those problems in a way that gets at the root causes, we are going to get ourselves into situations where we will make great mistakes and perhaps get hurt.

. . .

When I interviewed Marshall Shulman, director of the Russian Institute at Columbia and former Special Adviser to the Secretary of State in the Carter Administration, in the fall of 1981, he discussed the issue of Soviet-American relations and mutual perceptions:

It does seem to me that at least the articulated voices we have had in this country the last few years reflect an essentially nationalist point of view. This point of view may reflect itself at times in a kind of hair-chested militancy about the Soviets, in charges that previously people were too soft, and that they should be harder, in opposition to arms control, opposition to a moderating level of tension in the Soviet competition and so on. But I think that phenomenon has to be interpreted in terms of the shifts in the tides in our political and psychological life, more than changes in the objective situation. I don't see shifts in Soviet behavior sufficient to account for these tides of feeling. That is not to say—I want to make this emphatically clear —that I don't see the Soviets as a problem, or a challenge, or as a competitive problem for us. But the issue of how to manage it is still there, and it produced a situation in which some people favor a high confrontation relationship in the belief that we can spend the Soviets into the ground, into capitulation or collapse. This

196 / Notes for Chapter 9

view would have us raise the degree of confrontation at every level: political, propagandistic, economic, and so on. Others, including myself, have no illusions, I hope, about the Soviet Union and the seriousness of the challenge, but nevertheless feel that our own interests suggest a managed competition. And particularly an effort to stabilize the strategic military competition on the grounds that not to do so is contrary to our own interests, that it would make every problem in the world more difficult, more complicated and more dangerous. Whether this is Central America, Latin America, relations with Europeans, the Middle East, the Persian Gulf—every one of those problems becomes more explosive when we and the Soviets are locked into a high tension relationship. Moreover, the effect of a high confrontation policy tends to encourage those forces within the Soviet situation that we would least like to see ascendant in the Soviet Union. It encourages a mobilization in the Soviet Union, it encourages tighter political and police control of the society, it diminishes any prospect of easement of the repugnant aspects of the regime. It tends to encourage the military and makes them stronger as a result. This is not in our interest. So it isn't really a case of soft versus hard, the question is: What are our own interests in the management of this competitive relationship?

Appendices

Warnke Interview

The following interview, which ran in the *Los Angeles Times* on September 29, 1981, is excerpted from an interview I conducted with Paul Warnke, head of the Arms Control and Disarmament Agency under President Carter, in the spring and summer of 1981.

SCHEER: The Reagan Administration has launched a massive military buildup, partially on the assumption that the United States is vulnerable to a Soviet first strike due to increased Soviet missile accuracy. Is this danger a hoax or is it true?

WARNKE: I think that it quite clearly is not true. We initially started talking about the theoretical vulnerability of [Minuteman missiles]. And now we've gotten to the point where we talk as if it were an accomplished fact and that the Russians could, with a high degree of certainty, launch a counterstrike that would destroy 90 percent of our Minutemen. But really nothing has changed except the rhetoric. The theoretical vulnerability of any fixed target has always existed. That's why we put two thirds of our strategic resources into the non-fixed targets. But having done the sensible things, we now talk as if somehow our security is threatened because this theoretical vulnerability exists.

SCHEER: But didn't the Soviets vastly increase their nuclear arsenal during the years of SALT negotiations?

WARNKE: Well, yes, but what that assumes is that there is no momentum for the American nuclear arms buildup, and there is just the Soviets' [buildup]. I forgot what the exact figures are, but we've been adding something like three warheads a day to our strategic arsenal ever since SALT I. During that period of time, we've developed the cruise missile, we've developed the Trident missile, we're developing the Trident II missile, and we're going ahead with the MX. That covers your entire triad. We're modernizing the ICBMs, the SLBMs and the strategic bomber force. It seems to me that is indication of sufficient ability to keep up the pace.

SCHEER: But the Soviets have been spending more than the United States over the last ten years.

WARNKE: Well, one of the reasons is the fact that at that earlier point we had numerical superiority over the Soviets in just about every conceivable respect. The other factor which is often left out of this is you have to look at it from the standpoint of the threat which is made up of the United States, plus the NATO allies, plus China, plus their problems on their western border with Eastern Europe. NATO up until quite recently has been outspending the Warsaw Pact—including the Soviet Union—by something like 25 percent.

SCHEER: But what about the charts and figures that show them pulling ahead of us? Where do these figures come from?

WARNKE: Nobody's phonying them up, but any time you've got asymmetrical forces, you can put together comparisons that make you look to be at a disadvantage. The ICBMs represent something like 30 percent of our strategic nuclear resources and something like 75 percent of the Soviets'. Well, if you compare 75 percent of their force with 30 percent of our force, we're going to be at a tremendous disadvantage. It's sort of like comparing tanks in Europe, where they have something like a five-to-one edge. Well, why is that? It's because we have chosen not to put that much money into tanks. Instead of that, we put it into tactical aircraft and antitank weapons. Why? Because we have no intention whatsoever of storming over the border to try and invade the Soviet Union and we don't need that number of tanks.

SCHEER: What about the nuclear blackmail thesis, that the Soviets are preparing for a massive first strike and that a U.S. President would surrender rather than retaliate for fear of the Soviet's response?

WARNKE: I don't accept the thesis at all. First of all, who's going to be there to surrender? Do you figure that Washington is going to go unscathed? Do you figure that everyone's going to be in Storm Mountain, or wherever it is that I used to have a helicopter pass to? I'd say if there are just a couple of nuclear submarine captains out there, they'll see to it that the Soviet Union suffers. I know if I were one of them, I'd see to it that there was no Moscow. And it doesn't take that much to destroy the Soviet empire. Once Soviet headquarters is gone, how many wet eyes are there going to be in Armenia or Latvia? I'd like to think there might be a few people in California who might mourn if Washington disappears, but if you get outside greater Russia, how many people are going to be sad that there isn't any Kremlin? They're more vulnerable than we are. They know that.

SCHEER: It has been said by spokesmen for the Reagan Administration that the United States must attain a nuclear-war-fighting capability.

WARNKE: What that assumes is that there will be some real gradations in a nuclear war, and that makes no sense. Under what circumstances would you have this sort of protracted, controlled nuclear war? Do you just sort of test the other side and say, "I'm going to take Minsk," and see what his reaction is? Then he blows up Dubuque, so you say, "I see your Dubuque and raise you Vladivostok." What kind of crazy poker game is that? It's war-gaming, not war-fighting.

SCHEER: But your successor, Eugene Rostow, argues that the Russians think they can win a nuclear war and we have to respond.

WARNKE: No matter how ideological they are, they are not crazy. Now, if you want to hypothesize insanity on the part of your adversary, then I submit that deterrence loses any meaning. I've dealt with the Russians, probably to a greater extent than Gene Rostow, and although you might say a lot of other things about them, they are not crazy. And they have a very healthy respect for nuclear weapons, and they have a far greater appreciation than any American of the ravages that even conventional war can inflict upon a country. You know, since the last Civil War musket hit a tree in Pennsylvania, we haven't had war in this country. You can find crazy statements on both sides of the Atlantic. Read the confirmation hearings of Alexander Haig and Caspar Weinberger. Certainly some of their statements are consistent with the idea that we might fight a nuclear war.

SCHEER: What about the counterarguments about the Soviets' fallout shelters and other preparations to survive a nuclear war?

WARNKE: What kind of civil defense program is going to defend you against 6,000 nuclear warheads? It depends upon whether you want to die in the field or die in a hole. Would you rather be roasted or boiled? It doesn't make any real difference. There *is* no civil defense against the number of warheads that we and the Soviet Union have deployed against one another. And you're just kidding yourself if you think there is. If you take a look at any of the intelligence analysis, it will demonstrate that a civil defense program would *not* protect the Soviet Union from unacceptable damage.

Just take the question of evacuation. Remember the time of the Three Mile Island crisis, and one of the real problems was that if something went wrong, how would you get everybody out of that area —a fairly limited area? How would you evacuate New York? Or Moscow? And in the case of the Soviet Union, where would they go? How far out of Moscow do you have to get before you're at a two-track road, and sometimes there's not even enough room to pass.

So what is the civil defense program? Now, if they put them in shelters in the urban areas themselves, those shelters are going to become ovens. Then what happens when the people come out of the holes, those that have survived? Where do they go? What do they do? Where do they work? Where do they find food? We lack imagination when we talk about a limited nuclear war in which the Soviet Union or we would emerge as the winners.

SCHEER: Eugene Rostow and others argue that increased Soviet military strength over the past ten years has given them political victories. Do you agree?

WARNKE: Oh, hell, if you compare this situation with 1972, we've won the big ones ever since. Back in 1972, they had a major position in the Middle East. There isn't a country in the Middle East, with the exception of South Yemen, that they can point to as being a client state. At that point, they were very big in Egypt. They certainly had better relations with Syria and Iraq than they have today, so that certainly can't be viewed as anything but a Soviet setback in a very key area. And look at the situation with regard to the U.S.-Soviet-Chinese triangle relationship. In 1972, we were in the middle of a divisive war in which American troops were being killed by weapons that were being supplied by the Soviet Union and the People's Republic of China. Now we have a situation in which we are actually talking about arming the Red Chinese, those billion Chinese armed with nuclear weapons that we used to talk about back during the Vietnam War.

SCHEER: Doesn't Soviet penetration of various countries alter the balance of power?

WARNKE: Certainly, if you had an Ethiopian-style government in Saudi Arabia, in Kuwait, and in the rest of the oil-producing areas, it would be distinctly disadvantageous to us. But Angola does not show itself as being subservient to the Soviet Union. Even though we've got the massive example of China, we still tend to assume that if a country is Marxist, it's going to be pro–Soviet Union and anti–United States, and that's demonstrably not the case.

SCHEER: What about the argument that the Soviets betrayed the SALT process with their foreign adventures and aggressions?

WARNKE: What has that got to do with strategic arms control? If you figure you can't have arms control unless the Russians are nice guys, then it seems to me that you're being totally illogical. If the Russians could be trusted to be nice guys, you wouldn't need strategic arms control. And you wouldn't need strategic arms. Happy days would be here again. I think you have to start off with the premise that they are going to do a lot of things that are quite objectionable to us, and the question is, can you channel the competition in a fashion that doesn't result in you both being destroyed? And that to me is a sufficient goal in itself. I don't have to like them to want to save my country.

SCHEER: So when you read these counterarguments to SALT II?

WARNKE: I'm singularly unimpressed. In a lot of instances what they do is to rely on the fact that there are asymmetries in the force structures. And they point to the respects that the Soviets are ahead of us and say SALT is no good because we don't eliminate those respects in which the Soviets are ahead of us. But, at the same time, they wouldn't conceive of eliminating the asymmetries that make us ahead of them. Take, for example, the fact that we have about 70 percent of our strategic resources in the non-fixed systems—the ballistic submarines and the strategic armaments—and 30 percent in the fixed ICBMs. They have almost the reverse figures. They have something like 75 percent of their resources in the fixed ICBMs, so you can find a lot of critics of SALT pointing to the fact that 75 percent of their force is bigger than 30 percent of ours. But if we compare 100 percent against 100 percent, we have the better forces and we have the more survivable forces. And SALT preserves that. They talk about the fact that the Soviets were allowed to keep their 308 heavy missiles. We don't have heavy missiles because we don't want them. We could have made the MX as big as the SS-18 [a Soviet missile].

SCHEER: Is it conceivable to you that some progress toward arms control could be made under Rostow?

WARNKE: Not on arms control, no. I have considerable respect for Mr. Rostow. I worked with him in the Johnson Administration. He is an intelligent man; he's a man of good will. I think he is a genuine skeptic about merits of arms control. I think he thinks it will never work.

SCHEER: So what do we lose?

WARNKE: We lose the ability to restrict the development of nuclear arms that could lead to a very substantial increase in the likelihood of nuclear war.

SCHEER: You live in a world which most of us avoid thinking about. What have you learned about the people involved in this debate—the Rostows, the Warnkes? How do they live with this information? Are they different than the rest of us?

WARNKE: I think that the average American doesn't think much about nuclear war. He doesn't think much about it because, in the first place, it's almost unthinkable and, secondly, because he assumes there's nothing he can do about it anyway. So he puts it out of his mind, but there are some people that are forced to think about it because of the nature of the activities that they've undertaken, because they become experts in strategic nuclear weapons, and I think that a lot of us tend to get to a point of abstraction in which you lose sight of reality.

I remember back when I was doing my best to get Ed Muskie nominated and elected. It must have been about 1970. At one point, he asked me to talk to him about strategic arms and strategic nuclear doctrine. I did for about forty minutes, and I thought I was being extraordinarily eloquent. And at the end of it, he looked at me and said, "You've got to be nuts." I think that's the general reaction people have.

SCHEER: But how should one think about these weapons?

WARNKE: You can't conceive of nuclear weapons in terms that are traditional. It's not like a time when you were trying to limit battleships. Now it made a real difference in terms of military capability whether you had ten battleships and the other guy had two or whether he had ten and you had two. For one thing, you could afford to expend three to kill his two and then you'd be the battleship monopolist. You'd have seven left. It's very different with strategic nuclear weapons.

SCHEER: But isn't there a risk in forgetting it's different?

WARNKE: Yes, it's a real risk. It's a real risk that at this point there are a lot of people that talk as though nuclear war is not only conceivable but it's winnable. Then you have Carter's Presidential Directive 59 that talks about—apparently, because I haven't seen the text, but from the descriptions—it talks about the fact that we ought to have the ability to fight a protracted and limited nuclear war. There is an increasing tendency to suggest that it would be just another war in which there would be a winner and a loser. And I think this is very dangerous.

SCHEER: How dangerous is the current moment? Should people be scared?

WARNKE: They ought to be increasingly scared, yes, because of the fact that we are getting to this point at which both sides are developing this counterforce capability. And if we begin to talk about fighting and winning a nuclear war, so will the Soviets. I mean, we'll match one another in that respect and there is this obvious competition that exists, bitter competition. The Soviets are not good world citizens. They are not going to behave well. There are going to be crises. There are going to be confrontations and if we end up with a situation in which each side operates on the doctrine of "launch on warning," then a nuclear war could start because of panic, not because of any kind of rational calculation of advantage, but just the idea that at least I'm going to diminish this other guy's ability to destroy me. I think that's the risk.

And there's only one way out of it and that's getting SALT back on track. We're still talking as though the use of military force against the Soviet Union, or Soviet use of military force against us, is a conceivable way of implementing national objectives. And the nuclear age has changed that. Remember the Einstein quotation where he said the unleashing of the power of the atom has changed everything except our way of thinking? That's the problem. It's changed everything but our way of thinking. We still talk in Clausewitzian terms as though war is the continuation of diplomacy by other means. That's no longer the case, and it never will be again, unless you're talking about low-level conflicts between superpowers and the Third World. But if you talk about a war between the United States and the Soviet Union, it's going to mean that neither one of us will be a superpower anymore.

Rostow Interview

The following excerpt, which ran in the *Los Angeles Times* on September 29, 1981, is from interviews that I conducted with Eugene Victor Rostow in the spring and summer of 1981.

SCHEER: Does the Reagan Administration base its defense policy on the assumption that there is a very real prospect of a Soviet nuclear first strike?

ROSTOW: "Prospect" is the only word I question there. There is a very real potentiality for a first strike. The calculation now is that with the heavy Soviet ICBMs alone, they can knock out all our ICBMs, a considerable part of our bomber fleet and any submarines we had in port . . .

SCHEER: There are a number of scientific studies that say because of the missile bias problem—the gravitational pull, weather conditions, accuracy and so forth—no one would dare a first strike because you would have to hit more than 90 percent of your targets within 600 feet, and that the technology doesn't exist to do that. The argument is that people like yourself have exaggerated the possibility of a first strike.

ROSTOW: I'm not trying to exaggerate it . . . All I'm saying is that somewhere in this period there is vulnerability of our ICBMs and of a good deal else, and a terrific asymmetry in the arsenal, and that has to be remedied.

SCHEER: When you say "asymmetry in the arsenal," you don't mean that they have more nuclear bombs?

ROSTOW: They have more accurate ones. You get into a position where, if you have a conceivable first strike against our ICBMs, then what do we do? We have a lot of missiles on submarines, but they are not so accurate . . .

SCHEER: When you say their missiles are more accurate, you mean that's because more of theirs are land-based. They are not more accurate than our land-based missiles?

ROSTOW: I don't suppose so. They are much more accurate than they used to be.

SCHEER: And they are much more accurate than missiles on the submarines or the B-52s, by the nature of the beast. Were you opposed to the decision to station portions of our nuclear forces on submarines and in airplanes—to have a triad of defense?

ROSTOW: No, I think the triad is a very good idea, because you are dealing with the uncertainties of technology . . .

SCHEER: So the way you purchase a greater measure of security is by developing things like the MX, which allow you a second strike to do what? Take out their missiles after a first strike?

ROSTOW: That's right, so you have deterrence that becomes even moderately credible . . .

SCHEER: Don't you instead get a never-ending arms race? They will counter our MX with something bigger and more varied, and then we have to counter with something bigger and more varied on our part.

ROSTOW: Well, we've now gone through ten years in which we didn't race, and things have just gotten worse, and our political situation, the Cold War, has gotten very much worse . . .

SCHEER: Yet one can look at important areas of the world, for instance China, which the Soviets lost and where there are a billion people we are now talking about arming. Egypt, the most powerful Arab country in the Middle East, with which we now have joint maneuvers. Isn't it possible from the Soviet side to think that whether their goal is expansion or not, they're not doing very well at it?

ROSTOW: Well, you can't win them all . . . But they stick with their program and they are moving ahead now into very sensitive areas which could affect the balance of power itself. Vietnam and Cambodia may be peripheral or secondary targets, but Iran is not. Neither is the Persian Gulf area.

SCHEER: What would we have done differently in Iran if the Soviets had been weaker in nuclear power? How does the nuclear equation affect what we did or did not do in relation to Iran?

ROSTOW: . . . The state of nuclear balance vitally affects your capacity to use conventional force.

SCHEER: What conventional force would we have used in Iran which we were not able to use?

ROSTOW: I don't know. There are lots of things about the Iranian affair that we don't know. . . . I'm saying that the state of the nuclear equation there made it very problematical about the use of conventional forces, which we used perfectly comfortably in Korea.

SCHEER: But we did send troops to Iran. We sent the helicopters and they failed, at least on one level, not because we don't have nuclear weapons but because we don't have helicopters that work. Aren't we really looking for scapegoats? Instead of asking, why didn't the helicopters work, or why did the Shah tumble, or why did the Ayatollah get in power . . .

ROSTOW: There are a lot of factors there, but the fundamental factor was that we didn't dream of handling that situation as we handled the situation in Korea. I didn't advocate the sending of troops in to rescue the hostages, and I'm here as the arms control fellow, and not as a free citizen just discussing things at large. The state of the nuclear equation does, however, affect your capacity to use or consider using conventional forces in many possible situations.

SCHEER: Is it true, as your predecessor Paul Warnke claims, that NATO's defense expenditures exceed those of the Warsaw Pact nations?

ROSTOW: I don't believe that's right.

SCHEER: Figures which come from the Arms Control and Disarmament Agency and the Central Intelligence Agency show that over the last ten years, NATO has spent $200 billion more than the Warsaw Pact.

ROSTOW: We may have been outspending them, I don't know. But no one doubts that they have been making more tanks and have more troops and more kinds of military hardware, including many that we do not make.

SCHEER: Do you believe that the Soviet Union has any legitimate grievances against us?

ROSTOW: None whatever.

SCHEER: You don't think that they can correctly feel that, for instance, our policy toward China or the Vietnam War or the Korean

War or towards Cuba violated the United Nations Charter?

ROSTOW: No. Impossible. It's impossible to take that position. Cuba is the closest case, but I would strongly defend what Kennedy did with Cuba, yes.

SCHEER: For instance, supporting efforts to assassinate Castro, which we have admitted to—is that not a violation of the U.N. Charter?

ROSTOW: There has been testimony to that effect. The government hasn't admitted it. No, I don't mean to say that if we ever undertook to assassinate another person, that wouldn't violate the U.N. Charter, and other things besides, the laws of the United States, for example. Those charges were made, but they were also denied . . .

SCHEER: When you look at the world, there is no sense that we could possibly have done anything similar in any of these areas? The Soviets claim they were invited into Afghanistan; we claim we were invited into Vietnam to save the legitimate government. You don't feel that there is any serious duplicity on the part of both major powers in some of these cases?

ROSTOW: No, I don't. And I think it is a great mistake to try to evade responsibility by taking that easy option.

SCHEER: But when we characterize the motives of other countries, what seems aggressive to one side can seem defensive to the other side.

ROSTOW: Not really. Not really.

SCHEER: You think the Soviets can see anything offensive about our developing military alliance with China, right on their border? And the threat of giving major weapons systems to a government that has said it believes war is inevitable with the Soviet Union?

ROSTOW: I talked this point over when I was in China in 1978, about the inevitability of war. Mr. Deng Xiaoping [Vice Chairman of the Chinese Communist party] said that no, he agreed that war could be postponed for a very long time. Of course, the doctrine of the inevitability of war was there, but still it could be postponed.

SCHEER: When you appeared before the Senate Foreign Relations Committee, Senator Alan Cranston [D–Calif.] was troubled that you compared a nuclear war that would occur at this time with the two nuclear bombs that dropped on Japan, when those were the only two such bombs in existence. His feeling was that you were being naïve to think that war could be limited to the level of what were primitive bombs, when the world nuclear arsenal is so colossal.

ROSTOW: But I think it is equally naïve to suppose that one use of a nuclear weapon would immediately detonate the whole arsenal. I think there is a tremendous risk of escalation in the nuclear field, and I will use every influence I have in the government to try to keep the tracks separate. But they are closely linked in their nature, and they cannot be kept separate forever. That's why I think deterrence is so important, and why I think the problems before us are important. That's why I think it is so important to try to prevent war.

SCHEER: What are your main objectives in running the Arms Control and Disarmament Agency? What if you are here four years, eight years, and you have not concluded any major arms reduction agreement? Will that disappoint you?

ROSTOW: . . . Surely I'd be disappointed not to have reached an agreement, but I think that chances for reaching an agreement are good but they're not very good. They depend on a lot of extrinsic factors about the political conditions in the Soviet Union. I think that my second objective is to make sure that the arms control issue becomes a factor in increasing the solidarity of our alliances, rather than dividing them. The Soviet Union is using this as one of the main themes of its propaganda, to arrest rearmament and to split us from our allies. I'm going to try, through consultations, through understandings, through explanations . . . to see to it that people understand this issue, what it means and doesn't mean, and the role it plays, and thus to consolidate these alliances and bring them closer together, rather than allow them to be split.

SCHEER: Would it be fair to say that you feel that the dangers inherent in the arms race, the dangers of accidental war, the dangers brought about by more and more weapons piling up, are a less serious threat to peace than the danger of not containing the Soviets and of having the Western alliance break up?

ROSTOW: That is absolutely correct. Wars come about not when power is balanced, but when power is unbalanced. If you look at the wars of this century, or the wars of earlier centuries, they came about when people got panicky that the allies in each case were behind. In a nuclear setting, that becomes twice as dangerous. People always ask, will nuclear war mean the end of civilization? The damage to the quality of civilization brought about by the First and Second World Wars was very great. The damage that could be imposed on civilization by a nuclear war is even worse.

SCHEER: Paul Warnke states that the Soviets have observed the conditions of SALT, that they need arms control for their economy, that they are not preparing to engage in a first strike. He says that only a madman would prepare for a first strike, and the Soviets are not mad, whatever else they may be.

ROSTOW: . . . I do not think that nuclear war is the main threat. It is a possibility. But I don't think it is the main threat to the future. I think the main threat to the future is political coercion based on nuclear blackmail.

SCHEER: You told the Foreign Relations Committee, "What we need now is an agreement on how to go forward. We certainly aren't going to abandon all that's been done." I took that to mean that you will adhere to SALT.

ROSTOW: We'll do nothing inconsistent with those treaties so long as the Soviets behave in a similar way.

SCHEER: Why adhere to SALT II if it was, as you have said, a bad treaty and it put us at a disadvantage?

ROSTOW: Because, at the moment, to behave in a way inconsistent with it is incompatible with our interest. And there is nothing that we want to do or have decided to do that is incompatible with the treaty, at the moment. We're struggling to make the MX decision and the bomber decision—all that is years away, so there is no reason for us to do it. It is a perfectly normal thing to do in the conduct of international relations, not to rock the boat when you have a treaty relation that is pending. You might want to modify it, renegotiate it and so on, but it is prudent and normal international behavior . . .

SCHEER: But you had argued that SALT is incompatible with our interest.

ROSTOW: Of course, but that was to ratify it as a treaty because it would bind us. At the present time, there is nothing we can do within the SALT period that would violate its terms . . .

SCHEER: The protocol on SALT which bans the deployment of cruise missiles runs out in December. Are you in favor of extending the protocol?

ROSTOW: No.

SCHEER: Why not?

ROSTOW: Because it is part of a treaty that hasn't been ratified, and its whole meaning was in terms of the structure of that treaty.

SCHEER: In your writing, you put a lot of emphasis on the Soviets' Communist ideology. Yet until quite recently, the Chinese ideology was, if anything, more extreme.

ROSTOW: I don't think the Chinese have the slightest interest in ideology. It's a culture without a religion—they are the most pragmatic people on earth. Sure they're Communist—the leading group is a Communist group—but I think they use it [the ideology] and when you talk to them about it, they just laugh.

SCHEER: Is this a recent perception of yours, or is this something you've felt all along?

ROSTOW: I've felt it all along.

SCHEER: Why did the Chinese go into Korea?

ROSTOW: They wanted Japan. In relation to Japan and the Soviet Union, Korea is a very important place.

SCHEER: But what were they responding to, if not ideology?

ROSTOW: No, it was the threat, to move north—

SCHEER: You mean that we provoked the Chinese to move into Korea?

ROSTOW: That's what they all said. That's what the Indians told us . . . I've never read over the whole hearings and reached a conclusion about it, but that seems to me a very plausible hypothesis. And they were bidding for leadership of the Communist movement. The Soviets had had enough and wanted out. The Soviets pulled back and [the Chinese] took over for a while.

SCHEER: So, in retrospect, U.S. policy in Korea was in error, and it forced the Chinese into intervening?

ROSTOW: I haven't come to a fixed conclusion about it. I haven't studied it carefully enough, but I'd certainly be inclined to that view.

SCHEER: China is a country that said nuclear war with Russia is inevitable. And the Soviets haven't been able to do anything about the Chinese. And they weren't able to do anything about the defection of Albania, and they weren't able to do very much about Romania or Yugoslavia.

ROSTOW: Well, Albania and Yugoslavia, yes. Romania is still in the embrace, more or less. No, I think that's right. But the question is, you see, these hesitations only reflect their [the Soviets'] analysis of the possibility of an American intervention. If America were hopelessly impotent, both at the nuclear level and at the conventional level, then that would not have to enter into their calculations.

SCHEER: But that isn't close to happening. We're not talking about unilateral disarmament, we're talking about whether—

ROSTOW: Well, we are talking about unilateral disarmament in the Carter period. That's exactly what we're talking about. And it really began before, we went through the seventies without . . . The United States had to wake up and rearm.

McNamara Interview

Robert McNamara was Secretary of Defense from 1961 to 1968 serving under Presidents Kennedy and Johnson and has been judged one of the most influential individuals to occupy that position. Before joining the government he was president of the Ford Motor Company. From 1968 to mid-1981 McNamara was president of the World Bank. I interviewed McNamara in his Washington office in the spring of 1982. This edited version of the interview was approved by McNamara and appeared in the *Los Angeles Times* on April 4, 1982.

SCHEER: What about the geopolitical balance? We hear how the Soviets have gotten stronger and how they've made gains all over the world.

McNAMARA: I, myself, believe they've gotten weaker. That may sound naïve when one says it in the face of what has clearly been an increase in the number of their nuclear weapons and an increase in their conventional forces—not nearly as great, by the way, as many say, but still an increase. But I think they've gotten weaker because, economically and politically, there have been some very serious failures. In my opinion, they are in a weaker position today than they were fourteen to fifteen years ago.

SCHEER: When you said that the increase in Soviet conventional forces is not as great as many say—

McNAMARA: I'll expand that to make two points: Soviet conventional strength is not as great as many state it to be, and the NATO [North Atlantic Treaty Organization] conventional weakness is not as great as it is frequently said to be. Therefore, the conventional balance is not as favorable to the Soviets as is often assumed.

The Soviet advantage in tanks is frequently used to illustrate the strength of the Soviets and the weakness of the West. I believe the Warsaw Pact countries have three times as many tanks as the NATO countries. But our response to the Soviet tanks should not necessarily be a one-to-one expansion of our tank force, but rather an expansion of our antitank weapons. And that is exactly the way NATO has responded. So the fact that the Soviets have three times as many tanks as NATO is not necessarily an indication of Soviet strength and NATO weakness. One could argue whether NATO has adequate antitank forces, but they certainly have very strong antitank forces. I simply use that as an illustration of the point I'm making.

In this country we commonly exaggerate the imbalance of Warsaw Pact and NATO conventional forces. In my opinion, NATO conventional forces are very strong indeed. They are not as strong as I would like to see them, not as strong as they ought to be, not as strong as they can be by applying modern technology within realistic budget constraints. But, still, they are a much greater deterrent to Soviet aggression than we commonly recognize.

SCHEER: One of the arguments that is made by the Administration is that the Soviets are engaged in—I forget the exact words—the most unrelenting, massive military buildup, in both conventional and strategic weapons, and that we now have to counter that.

McNAMARA: I don't want to get in an argument with the Administration; I just want to state what I believe is a fact, which is that we overstate the Soviets' force and we understate ours, and we therefore greatly overstate the imbalance. This is not something that is new; it has been going on for years.

SCHEER: Did it go on while you were Secretary of Defense?

McNAMARA: Of course it did. I tried to correct it; I frequently made statements correcting it, but because it appears to serve the interests of some to consciously or unconsciously overstate the Soviet strength and understate ours, that frequently occurs.

SCHEER: Who are the "some"?

McNAMARA: Well, particular elements of our society that feel their programs are benefited by that. The missile gap of 1960 was a function

215 / McNamara Interview

of forces within the Defense Department that, perhaps unconsciously, were trying to support their particular program—in that case, an expansion of U.S. missile production—by overstating the Soviet force. I don't want to state that they were consciously misstating the facts, but there is an unconscious bias in all of us. In any case, it was a total misreading of the information, and by early 1961 all who had examined the evidence concluded that there was no missile gap, despite the fact that in the latter part of 1960 it was a rather common belief.

SCHEER: Is there a military-industrial complex?

McNAMARA: I don't think there is a military-industrial complex that consciously advances its own financial interests regardless of the cost to the nation. But I do believe that one has to look beyond the military and its industrial supporters for an evaluation of what is in our national interest with respect to security. There are other participants in the security debate that need to be heard from who may have different interests, different views or different knowledge of how to achieve our common goal.

SCHEER: Going back to the missile crisis and the showdown over the missiles in Cuba, do you feel that we compelled or encouraged the Russians to engage in this buildup?

McNAMARA: No. I have never understood why [former Soviet Premier Nikita S.] Khrushchev sent those missiles into Cuba, but I don't think it was our action that caused him to do so.

SCHEER: But that is when you date the start of their buildup. Up until that time they seemed relatively indifferent to developing these missiles.

McNAMARA: No . . . I think they had under way—that was October 1962—by 1962 they had under way a plan to substantially build up their nuclear forces. One possible explanation of their action, and I don't put it forward as the only explanation, is that they were moved to rapidly expand their forces because they thought we were trying to achieve a first-strike capability, that is to say, a large enough numerical superiority to give us the power to launch against their nuclear weapons and destroy so many that the remainder would be inadequate to carry out a second strike against us. That was never our intention. It was not only not our intention, but we didn't believe we could possibly achieve such a capability. But they, looking at our force and the substantial numerical superiority of that force, might have believed that we either had that capability or were trying to achieve it. And they might have looked upon the movement of the weapons into Cuba as a means of reducing that capability.

SCHEER: On the first-strike question, was there a shift? You are always associated with the "mutually assured destruction" deterrence notion. Yet some people have argued that within the period in which you were in charge, there was a shift in the targeting scenario, and that was when the beginning of the notion of limited nuclear war actually started.

McNAMARA: No, no, we moved from Dulles's strategy of massive retaliation to what was called "flexible response." That was, I think, a major advance because it substantially reduced the risk of nuclear war. And the level at which nuclear weapons might be used under flexible response was raised so high that it was, in effect, the equivalent of mutual assured destruction.

The point on the Soviet concern about our first strike is an important one [lifts a document]. This is a highly classified memorandum from me to President Kennedy, dated November 21, 1962. In the memorandum I state, "It has become clear to me the Air Force proposals are based on the objective of achieving a first-strike capability. In the words of an Air Force report to me, 'The Air Force has rather supported the development of forces which provide the United States a first-strike capability.'" This is my memo to the President and that is a proper quote from the Air Force. The Soviets didn't have the document, at least I hope they didn't. But they may have heard talk that we were trying to achieve a first-strike capability and, in any case, they saw the size force we had.

I was absolutely amazed—a man [author Fred Kaplan] brought this document in to me the other day and he asked me about some things that happened in 1961. He quoted from this memo. I said, "For God's sake, where did you get it?" And he said it was declassified under the Freedom of Information Act. So I called the Defense Department and said I wanted the same memos he had and they gave me four of them. This is one.

The issue of first-strike capability is absolutely fundamental. And I have no doubt but that the Soviets thought we were trying to achieve a first-strike capability. We were not. We did not have it; we could not attain it; we didn't have any thought of attaining it. But they probably thought we did.

SCHEER: Well, also, the argument that is made here now is based on finding Soviet defense manuals. If the Soviets did have access to this or some other document, that is a lot stronger than what arms control negotiator Paul Nitze or National Security Council Soviet expert Richard Pipes or these people come up with about Soviet intentions. All we can point to on the argument of Minuteman vulnerability is that they have a civil defense program, why are they piling on the missiles. . . . As far as I know, we don't have any statement by them. . . .

McNAMARA: No, absolutely not. But if I had been the Soviet secretary of defense, I'd have been worried as hell about the imbalance of force. And I would have been concerned that the United States was trying to build a first-strike capability. I would have been concerned simply because I would have had knowledge of what the nuclear strength was of the United States and I would have heard the rumors that the Air Force was recommending achievement of such a capability. You put those two things together: a known force disadvantage that is large enough in itself to at least appear to support the view that the United States was planning a first-strike capability and, secondly, talk among U.S. personnel that that was the objective—it would have just scared the hell out of me! That memo is dated November, '62. It's by coincidence a month after the Cuban missile crisis.

That, I think, lends some support to the point I'm making.

However, I want to reemphasize these points: Number one, I didn't believe, and President Kennedy didn't believe, we had a first-strike capability, number two, we didn't have any intention of trying to attain a first-strike capability. Number three, if we had had any such intention, there is no way we could have done it, in my opinion.

SCHEER: If you couldn't have done it then, how could one make the claim that the Soviets could do it now?

McNAMARA: They no more have a first-strike capability today than we had then. No one has demonstrated to me that the Soviets have a capability of destroying our Minutemen. But even if they could destroy our Minutemen, that doesn't give them a first-strike capability, not when they are facing our Polaris submarines and our bombers. The other two legs of the triad are still there.

SCHEER: The argument that is made is that they would destroy enough of ours that they could come back—

McNAMARA: The argument is without foundation. It's absurd. To try to destroy the 1,054 Minutemen, the Soviets would have to plan to ground-burst two nuclear warheads of one megaton each on each site. That is 2,000 megatons, roughly 160,000 times the megatonnage of the Hiroshima bomb. What condition do you think our country would be in when 2,000 one-megaton bombs ground-burst? The idea that, in such a situation, we would sit here and say, "Well, we don't want to launch against them because they might come back and hurt us," is inconceivable! And the idea that the Soviets are today sitting in Moscow and thinking, "We've got the U.S. over a barrel because we're capable of putting 2000 megatons of ground-burst on them and in such a situation we know they will be scared to death and fearful of retaliation; therefore we are free to conduct political blackmail," is too incredible to warrant serious debate.

SCHEER: Those in the United States who put forward such a Soviet view stress that the argument is one of nerve and perception, and that the Soviets will perceive us as being weak and take advantage.

McNAMARA: The world isn't run that way. Political leaders, responsible political leaders, don't behave that way. The first responsibility of a political leader is to preserve the safety of his people. No political leader I know of—including the Soviet political leaders—would run that kind of a risk.

SCHEER: Their argument is that an American President—and you've been close to this kind of decision-making—an American President would not order a Polaris to fire once our Minutemen were destroyed because that would just invite greater retaliation from the Russians.

McNAMARA: But when they say that, they fail to take account of the fact that the Soviets know that he might—and I am convinced he would. No Soviet leader would wish to accept that risk. The Soviets know what is going to happen here when those 2,000 megatons ground-burst. They know what would happen in this country. In many respects, it would be hard to distinguish between "the counterforce strike" and a general nuclear strike. Almost certainly, communications would be destroyed. And there is a distinct probability that there would not be an American President alive because the initial Soviet strike would undoubtedly target command and control facilities. There is an established safeguard against the nation being defenseless under those circumstances, and the Soviets know it. If the President was not available to fire the weapons, there are appropriate safeguards to assure that the nation would not be defenseless.

SCHEER: Let's return to the issue of the buildup of nuclear forces. How did it occur?

McNAMARA: Go back to 1960 when many in the U.S. believed there was a missile gap favoring the Soviets. With hindsight it became clear there wasn't any missile gap. But Kennedy had been told there was. What actually happened was this: In the summer of 1960, there were two elements in the U.S. intelligence community disagreeing on the relative levels of the U.S. and Soviet strategic nuclear forces. It's a little like the conventional force situation I discussed earlier. One element greatly overstated the level of the Soviet nuclear force vis-à-vis the other element. The first element had data which they believed justified their interpretation. When one looked over it, it became clear the data didn't justify the conclusion. And within two years of that time, the advantage in the U.S. warhead inventory was so great vis-à-vis the Soviets that the Air Force was saying that they felt we had a first-strike capability and could, and should, continue to have one. If the Air Force thought that, imagine what the Soviets thought. And assuming they thought that, how would you expect them to react?

The way they reacted was by substantially expanding their strategic nuclear weapons program. Now, when they did that, we sat back here and saw the way they were moving—and we always had to take account of their capability more than their intentions, because we weren't sure of their intentions—we looked at their capability and they were building submarines, missiles and planes, and experimenting with new warheads, at such a rate that we had to respond. We probably overresponded because it is likely that their capability, which we observed, exceeded their intentions. So you have an action-reaction phenomenon. And the result is that during the last twenty-five years, and particularly during the last fifteen, there has been a huge buildup, much more than people realize, in the nuclear strength of these two forces. That has changed the nature of the problem and increased the risk greatly. I have read that the total inventory of warheads in the two arsenals is on the order of 50,000. And I saw a week or two ago in the *New York Times* that our present plan is to build 17,000 additional warheads, some for replacement, in the next few years.

SCHEER: What is so scary about this, and it's not just from you, I've interviewed hundreds of people who end up using words like, "They are crazy!" or "Madmen!" But how did this happen?

McNAMARA: Because the potential victims have not been brought into the debate yet, and it's about time we brought them in. I mean the average person. The average intelligent person knows practically nothing about nuclear war—the danger of it, the risk of it, the potential effect of it, the changes in the factors affecting the risk.

SCHEER: I interviewed Hans Bethe, the famous nuclear physicist, and he said, "I was very scared in 1945, 1947, and I thought the world would only last two years. Then I stopped being scared because I realized that the leaders, certainly in our country and hopefully on the other side, would recognize the danger. Now I'm scared again because—"

McNAMARA: He is scared again because there are some people talking about nuclear bombs being no different than rifle shells or artillery shells. And some people [are] talking about fighting and winning nuclear wars and preparing for a six-month nuclear war. The problem is, there is no counter to that. Before, when that happened, there was . . . Today there is not an effective counter. There should be. And I think there is going to be; one is beginning to bubble up.

I didn't plan the timing of my recent statement recommending a complete reversal of U.S. and NATO nuclear strategy on the belief that there would today be a favorable environment for it. In a sense I was trying to trigger a change in the environment. But there couldn't be a better time for a statement on nuclear strategy to come forward, because the public is becoming sensitive to it, both here and in Europe. So I think a year from now, two years from now, you are going to see quite a different public attitude.

There has always been a nuclear hard-line group; you saw it reflected in that quote from the Air Force. That was 1962. There has always been a hard-line nuclear group, and there is today. But in the past, it didn't have the influence that it does today.

SCHEER: Have we been drifting in the direction? When you have weapons, you want to use them. . . .

McNAMARA: I don't really put it that way. I think, though, that as you vastly increase the number of weapons and as you try to develop characteristics that in some people's minds bring them closer to conventional weapons, such as a neutron bomb, you increase the risk of use of those weapons.

SCHEER: But hasn't our declaratory policy begun to reflect that?

McNAMARA: Yes, you are right. More and more there are suggestions that we should be prepared to fight and win a nuclear war—that we can recover from a full strategic exchange in from two to four years. And while others are not prepared to go that far, they say we should be equipped, and perhaps are equipped, to fight and win a limited nuclear war.

SCHEER: Well, you know when you push people, even in the Reagan Administration, they'll say, "Well, we don't welcome this, but we think that is what the Russians are aiming at, otherwise how do you explain their continuous buildup of—"

McNAMARA: The way you explain it—and you must understand that I am not justifying it—the way you explain it is by putting yourself in their shoes. When I've done that on several occasions, I must say I would do some things that were very similar to what they did. I'm talking about the action they took to build up their force. Read again my memo to President Kennedy. It scares me today to even read the damn thing: "The Air Force has rather supported the development of forces which provide the United States a first-strike capability credible to the Soviet Union by virtue of our ability to limit damage to the United States and our allies to levels acceptable in light of the circumstances and the alternatives available."

What that means is, the Air Force supported the development of U.S. forces sufficiently large to destroy so much of the Soviet nuclear force, by a first strike, that there would not be enough left to cause us any concern if they shot it at us. My God, if the Soviets thought that was our objective, how would you expect them to react? I think that explains—I thought at the time it explained—a lot of their actions. I gave a speech in San Francisco, I can't remember when, though I think it was in mid-'67, in which I said that "action and reaction," the internal dynamics of the nuclear race, explained a lot of what the Soviets were doing. Whether it explains it all is another issue. But it explains a lot.

SCHEER: When I interviewed Ronald Reagan as a candidate, he said that the problem with that whole calculation—and he mentioned your name and MAD [Mutual Assured Destruction] and everything—is that the Russians are monsters, they don't have the same respect for human life that we do, therefore they could take the 20 million, 30 million or 40 million casualties.

McNAMARA: The Russians are people that I would not trust to act in other than their own narrow national interest, so I am not naïve. But they are not mad. They are not mad. They have suffered casualties, and their government feels responsible to their people to avoid those situations in the future. They are more sensitive to the impact of casualties on their people than we appear to be in some of our statements and analyses of fighting and winning nuclear wars which would extend over a period of months.

So they are not mad. They are aggressive; they are ideological; they need to be restrained and contained by the existence of our defensive forces. But they are not mad, and I see no evidence that they would accept the risks associated with a first strike against the United States.

Vance Interview

Cyrus R. Vance, who served as Secretary of State during the Carter Administration from 1977 through April 1980, presently is a partner in the New York Law firm of Simpson, Thacher, and Bartlett. Mr. Vance was a member of the Independent Commission on Disarmament and Security Issues chaired by Olof Palme. The Commission, made up of international government officials, recently published a report of its recommendations entitled *Common Security*. I interviewed Mr. Vance in New York City in March 1982. Excerpts from that interview are included below.

SCHEER: What do you think of the Reagan Administration's plans to attain what they call a nuclear-war-fighting capability?

VANCE: I happen to be one of those who believe it is madness to talk about trying to fight a continuing nuclear war as though it were like fighting a conventional war, and that one could control the outcome with the kinds of precision that is sometimes possible in a conventional war situation. It is a totally different world, a world that is hard for any of us to conceive, because none of us knows what a nuclear war is like. But by extrapolation, we can have some idea of the incredible devastation that would come from it and the almost unimaginable consequences that would flow from it. I think it is sound and proper to have a command and control which could hopefully survive a nuclear attack.

However, to take the next leap, that it is important to have a command and control that is survivable so that you can fight a nuclear war, is a wholly different situation.

SCHEER: But didn't the Carter Administration attempt the same sort of thing with its Presidential Directive 59?

VANCE: What PD 59 was talking about was providing a range of options to the President so he had some element of choice and making sure that the only response need not be a total spasmodic launching of everything we've got. And that has been developing over a period of years. By "that" I mean providing a range of options to the President. Taking that step did not mean, in my judgment, that anybody believed you could fight a sustained nuclear war along the lines that some of the people in the new Administration are talking about. That again is, as I've said, fallacious, and totally unrealistic.

SCHEER: Isn't their argument that this is how the Russians think and to have a credible deterrence we must think in similar terms?

VANCE: You can find all kinds of theories on the use of nuclear weapons contained in writings by Russian military authors on the use of nuclear weapons, as you can in the United States. There are articles and papers that have been written about the fighting of a sustained nuclear war in the Soviet bibliographies. But that does not mean that that is the political doctrine of the Soviet Union. The Soviets deny that that is their political doctrine. They draw the distinction between strategy and tactics. So the fact that there are such writings does not mean that that is the policy of the Soviet Union.

SCHEER: What about the charge that America was disarmed unilaterally in the 1970s?

VANCE: Baloney. That is simply not true.

SCHEER: Do you want to elaborate?

VANCE: It simply is not true. There was a period of time when the United States clearly had nuclear superiority. It was inevitable that the Soviet Union would develop a capacity which would be roughly equal to our capacity. This indeed did happen, and the Soviets and the United States reached rough parity. In my judgment that continues to be the situation in the nuclear field. We are ahead in some aspects in the possession of nuclear weapons, they are ahead in others. We have more warheads, they have greater throw-weight. But when you take a look at the equation, you see that there is equivalence, or rough parity, between the two countries and neither country is going to let the other get ahead of him. Either is going to insist that this rough parity be maintained. I think anybody is foolish to think anything other than that. Certainly that has been the policy of all the Administrations since the 1960s, and at least up until now remains the policy of the United States.

SCHEER: You say up until now—has the Reagan Administration broken with the previous, bipartisan, strategic policy?

VANCE: I am not clear what the policy of the Reagan Administration is on this issue. At the outset of the Administration, and in some of the campaign rhetoric prior to the election, there were some suggestions that the United States embark upon a course of becoming superior in terms of nuclear capability. As I now understand the position of the Administration, they no longer take that position. They have become more realistic and are saying that what is possible is to have rough equality among the two countries, and that is what they intend to do.

SCHEER: But the Administration claims they cannot accept a freeze because the Soviets have nuclear superiority.

VANCE: I have not suggested that we should not modernize our nuclear forces. I think a certain amount of modernization is necessary. I have taken that position during the last several years. Where I have a difference with the Reagan Administration is as to how much is required to continue to maintain rough parity. I do not think that they have superiority.

For example, I think they are making a serious mistake in going ahead with the B-1 bomber. They are spending vast sums of money to buy an aircraft which is obsolescent, and may be virtually obsolete by the time it comes into the inventory. The same job can be done by the B-52s armed with air-launched cruise missiles, during the period of time when the advanced-technology bomber will come into the inventory. That will be a real step forward, I think we should go forward and develop that. But to me it is a waste of money to spend it on an obsolescent or perhaps obsolete weapon for use during this interim period of time.

SCHEER: Do you find anything new or interesting in the Soviet proposals, for example, the latest one about freezing the deployment of the SS-20s?

VANCE: No, merely the fact that the proposal was made. I don't see anything new in it. Let me come back to what I really think can be done at this point. I think there are three very important steps that can be taken at this point. One, if SALT II or START negotiations were resumed or begun, depending on which term you want to use, right now, that it would be possible to make real progress rapidly in negotiating an agreement. There are indications which lead me to believe there is a substantial chance that the Soviets would accept the reservations and understandings contained in the Senate Foreign Relations Committee's report on SALT. Secondly, I believe that the Soviets would be prepared to accept further cuts beyond the cuts provided for in the SALT II agreement. There might be, in addition to that, some cosmetic changes that might be able to be worked out as well. That, then, would leave you with one tough problem to resolve, and that is, what do you do now that the protocol of the treaty has expired and the related issue of the cruise missile. I do not think it is beyond the power of the negotiators on both sides to find a way of resolving that problem. What I am saying in short is that if people seriously begin to negotiate the central systems issues by getting going with the START negotiations that real progress could be made and made soon.

Secondly, I think it is important at the same time, in parallel, to pursue the Theater Force negotiations. Again, it is my judgment that even though there is a substantial difference between the two sides, progress can be made.

Thirdly, I think there is a possibility that new life could be breathed into the negotiations with respect to the reduction of conventional weapons in Central Europe, leading to agreement on equality of conventional forces. If my assumption is correct, that would be a major breakthrough because it would then permit you to go back to the situation that existed at the time that the decision was made to put battlefield nuclear weapons in Europe. The reason battlefield nuclear weapons were put into Europe was because of the lack of parity between the conventional forces of the two sides. At that time it was impossible to reach any agreement about equality of conventional forces in Europe. If you could reach agreement on that, that would change radically the whole situation, and it would remove one of the most dangerous aspects of the nuclear problem. There are battlefield weapons up near the front lines. It is conceivable that in a battle of conventional forces that those weapons could be overrun or threatened, and as a result of that there is the danger of possible early use of nuclear weapons. If you could reach agreement on equality of conventional forces, it would no longer be necessary to have nuclear weapons up near the front lines. They could be withdrawn to the back of the battle zone and perhaps even be removed. So this would really change the picture very substantially. That is something that should be attacked now, and should be attacked vigorously.

SCHEER: Why the optimism now?

VANCE: There have been signs and indications that there has been a change of mind on the other side.

SCHEER: Do you see signs and indications that our side would be receptive?

VANCE: I don't know.

SCHEER: In terms of the failure to ratify SALT, would you attribute much of the difficulty to the Cuban brigade issue? Was that a real issue?

VANCE: I think it's a tragedy that it became such a public issue, and I think it clearly hurt the ratification process, without any doubt. There was an erosion of the support for SALT prior to the Cuban brigade issue, but clearly it was a real blow that set us back substantially.

SCHEER: Secretary McNamara told me that they had discovered the same brigade when he was in office, and that the Administration had disposed of the controversy by saying, it's just a training brigade and we're not going to get agitated about it.

VANCE: The intelligence when this first turned up again led the intelligence community to state that this was not a training brigade, that this was a different kind of brigade, and that it was a new brigade. It was on the basis of that information and that interpretation that we reported to Congress that the situation had changed and that a new brigade had appeared. Subsequently that interpretation of the intelligence information turned out to be incorrect. Unfortunately by that time, some members of the Congress had gone public with it, and the fat was on the fire.

SCHEER: How did such a thing happen? Was it a mistake in interpretation of the photographs or—

VANCE: Well, information is sparse, it's difficult to get, some of it is human intelligence which is hard to evaluate and this is the evaluation that the intelligence people came to.

SCHEER: How important was the Team B reevaluation in changing our thinking about the Russians?

VANCE: Do you mean, how important was it to the current Administration?

SCHEER: Yeah. As a student of foreign policy rather than as former Secretary of State.

VANCE: It obviously had an impact on some people. I think it was grossly exaggerated. I think the analysis is flawed. The impact, however, was substantial on some people. I don't think the facts support the conclusion that the Soviets were moving toward a first strike. I don't think they were any more than we were.

SCHEER: That was a rather important error for us to have made if that is true. The whole thinking of the country changed.

VANCE: I don't attribute it to that alone. That was a factor.

SCHEER: Well, certain things came to be accepted as fact: that the Soviets had the most unrelenting buildup in the world, they were aiming toward superiority—

VANCE: There is no question that they continued to increase their forces. No doubt about that. But that doesn't mean that they were going towards first strike.

SCHEER: But that was the hook. The argument was that they were gaining first-strike capability.

VANCE: The whole purpose of Vladivostok and SALT was to put a cap and then to start reducing the number of weapons. This was negotiated.

SCHEER: There's been a thrust to American foreign policy in the postwar period, there's been an Establishment, a center, a consensus. It seemed that détente enjoyed that kind of support, and suddenly it broke.

VANCE: One of the problems with détente is that détente was over-sold as a panacea. It obviously could not be the panacea that people said it was, and this led to disillusionment.

SCHEER: You put the emphasis on détente being oversold as opposed to the Soviets having betrayed it?

VANCE: I think there were both, but it was not just the Soviets having betrayed it.

SCHEER: Do you think in retrospect that we might have exaggerated the Soviet betrayal as far as Afghanistan is concerned? The President called it the gravest crisis since World War II, the attempt to link it with Iran and the emotional feeling about Iran.

VANCE: I don't think it was the gravest crisis since World War II. I think it was a very important and a very serious step backwards, which clearly poisoned the relationships between our country and the Soviet Union. It was a very brutal act on the part of the Soviets, which I see no justification for. Having said that, I don't agree that it was the gravest crisis since World War II.

SCHEER: The issue is, was it the sort of act that would warrant shifting one's thinking from the position that we have an inordinate fear of Communism, which was the President's position at one point, to the point of view that is implied if not in PD 59 then certainly in the stance of the Administration at the end, that the Soviets are on the move, that their geopolitical power is growing—

VANCE: I have not accepted that. You are talking to the wrong person about this.

SCHEER: But there was a shift in the Carter Administration's thinking.

VANCE: Some people in the Administration shifted their views somewhat. But to say that what you just stated reflected the view of the Administration I think is an exaggeration. There *was* a toughening of the U.S. position with respect to the Soviet Union at the end. But it didn't go as far as you have suggested.

SCHEER: But it seems to have created the groundwork for the current Administration's position. If Afghanistan, in the eyes of the President, represented the gravest crisis since World War II, then Ronald Reagan was able to campaign on the idea that the Soviets now were up to something.

VANCE: Let's talk about what the realities were. The Soviets had, and have now, grave economic problems. They also have serious problems in terms of their manpower resources. They have very difficult problems in their agricultural production. They face a succession period in the months and perhaps years ahead, which will be of major dimensions. Politically they face a host of problems, whether you look at what is happening on their Western front, on their Eastern front, to the south of them or in other parts of the world. I don't have to say much about the problems they face in Eastern Europe—from Poland to Romania and Yugoslavia—major problems which are really graver than anything the Soviets have faced in many, many years. On their Eastern front they face a China which is growing stronger. They face an industrialized Japan which is growing ever stronger and more resilient. Looking at it from the standpoint of Moscow, they must see some real problems there, particularly in view of our close relationship with Japan and improving relationships with China. As they look to the South and the Middle East, it certainly can give them no cause for comfort. In Africa, they face a situation where they have been thrown out of Egypt, Sudan, Somalia; their influence is waning in Guinea and in many other countries in Africa. I think that generally as a result of what they did in Afghanistan their position and image in the Third World had been deteriorating so that the idea that the Soviets are strong and getting stronger or that they are ten feet tall, simply doesn't have a factual base. One of the difficulties and sadnesses of the past several years has been this growing feeling that the Soviets are a country which is ten feet tall, and that we therefore have to take a position of second place or be in fear of them. Unfortunately I think many people believe that and I think that has eroded the self-confidence of many in the United States, which I think has been bad for us and for how we are perceived in the world.

SCHEER: If that view is correct, it's directly at odds with the view of the Administration which is of a growing Soviet strength.

VANCE: I honestly don't know what the position of the new Administration is, as I've said on a number of occasions. I know what their rhetoric is. Their rhetoric is very strongly anti-Soviet. It implies that the source of most problems that arise around the world is Moscow, and that therefore that problem presents a basic confrontation between East and West. I think that's a vast oversimplification and is incorrect and will lead us into making erroneous decisions. The world is much more complex than that. It is a world of great change. It is a world where problems which have local roots—economic, political and social —have produced local conflicts which can only be resolved by dealing with the grassroots causes, and not by trying to make it into an East-West confrontation. And if we don't realize that and we don't attack those problems in a way that gets at the root causes, we are going to get ourselves into situations where we will make great mistakes and perhaps get hurt. We should, in my judgment, be more willing to let people in the various regions, such as Central America, take a leadership role in trying to resolve some of those problems by finding political solutions to these local problems, and we shouldn't feel that we have to be out in front making the decision as to what should be done all the time. Sometimes, where others will not take the lead, we may have to take the lead. But when they—countries like Mexico, Venezuela, Colombia, Costa Rica—are willing to take a leading position, we have to welcome that and work with them and try and help them find political solutions to these problems.

SCHEER: Have we had a breakdown in consensus in our foreign policy?

VANCE: I believe that if you take a look at the history of our foreign policy since World War II, you will see that the foreign policy of that period up to the beginning of the Carter Administration was one of a centrist policy, basically developed by a centrist coalition, and that by and large that coalition was bipartisan. And as long as we stayed in the center of the stream, we had a foreign policy which had the support of the country behind us and that it was basically successful, or at least acceptable to the majority of people in the outside world. From time to time during that period, we drifted to the right or the left on certain issues, and when we did, we got ourselves in trouble, as during the McCarthy period. We drifted off to the right, and once we got out of the center of the stream, we were in trouble. When we came into office, we decided that we were basically going to try to continue in the center of the stream.

I am worried now that we may be drifting to the right again when I listen to this rhetoric. And if we do, I think we may end up facing the same problems and paying the price for it, that has happened when we got out of the center of the stream in the past.

SCHEER: The analogy being with the McCarthy period?

VANCE: Too early to say yet. I hope not.

SCHEER: How scary do you think the current moment is?

VANCE: I think it's a very troubling moment. If you look around the world today and you see the danger of a real explosion in Lebanon, which I think is a serious danger at this point. You face a very difficult problem in the Middle East. If you take a look at what might happen in Iran following the passing from the scene of [Ayatollah Ruhollah] Khomeini, and the internal conflict that might follow from that, again you have a potentially very dangerous situation. If you have a continuation of a failure to get back on the track and start making serious progress in negotiating the issues of nuclear weapons and nuclear war, again that, I think, presents very serious problems and obviously has to give all of us a great deal of concern. There are serious and very troubling problems on the horizon. I hope that we will be able to avoid these potential explosions but it's going to take care and skill and patience and perseverance to do it.

SCHEER: What about these freeze initiatives, of the kind we have in California, or that Senator Kennedy and Hatfield have—

VANCE: Again, I think that they are primarily political initiatives expressing the concern of people, rather than suggestions that somehow practically this can be done.

SCHEER: But I gather you're not unsympathetic?

VANCE: Politically, I think they are making a point. I, myself, would like to see us concentrate not on talking about a freeze but on the practical ways that, I think, one could really reduce the number of weapons and reduce the threat of nuclear war. The three things that I mentioned to you earlier are examples of the kind of practical things that I think can be done and could be done now.

Reagan Interview

I interviewed Ronald Reagan over a period of several days during the 1980 Republican primary election campaign. The interview covered a wide range of topics. Excerpts from that exchange concerning foreign affairs are included below.

Boston–Atlanta

SCHEER: During the Saturday night debate you discussed a report about the number of bombers that would get through United States defense in the case of a Soviet attack.

REAGAN: Yes, depending on the route they took, it would range from 87 percent to 96 percent of them would get through. I don't feel free to reveal my source because he was still on active duty and a very high-ranking—extremely high-ranking—Air Force Officer.

SCHEER: Is this based on a study that the Air Force has conducted, or is this his judgment?

REAGAN: This is based on what they know at NORAD, you know, we can track the missiles if they were fired, we can track them all the way from firing to know their time of arrival and their targets, and we couldn't do anything to stop the missiles. NORAD is an amazing place —that's out in Colorado, you know, under the mountain there. They actually are tracking several thousand objects in space, meaning satellites of ours and everyone else's, even down to the point that they are tracking a glove lost by an astronaut that is still circling the earth up there. I think the thing that struck me was the irony that here, with this great technology of ours, we can do all of this yet we cannot stop any of the weapons that are coming at us. I don't think there's been a time in history when there wasn't a defense against some kind of thrust, even back in the old-fashioned days when we had coast artillery that would stop invading ships if they came.

SCHEER: Do they have a defense against our attacking them?

REAGAN: Yes, they have gone very largely into a great civil defense program, providing shelters, some of their industry is underground, and all of it hardened to the point of being able to withstand a nuclear blast.

SCHEER: So you think we should do that?

REAGAN: I think we're going to have to start a civil defense program. I think—see, they violated and we kept to the promise that McNamara, in the original getting together and what resulted in our doing away with our antiballistic missile system, at a time when we were ahead of them in technology on that. The idea was the Mutual Assured Destruction plan—MAD, the MAD policy, it was called—and what this policy said was that if neither country defended its citizenry, then neither country could afford to push the button, because they would know that in an exchange of weapons, both countries' populations would be decimated. And they didn't hold to that—and for several years this was a failure of the interpretation of our intelligence, the analysis of the intelligence material we were getting. We paid no attention to the fact that the Soviet Union had put a high-ranking general, who was on the Politburo, in a high command, in charge of civil defense. And they had come to the conclusion that there could be a nuclear war and it could be winnable—by them. And so, in addition to their great military buildup, they have practiced this, they have practiced evacuation, when we finally began to learn the facts, we learned that in one summer alone, they took over 20 million young people out of the cities into the country to give them training in just living off the countryside.

SCHEER: Do you think we should be doing this sort of thing—I mean, building underground shelters, putting our industry underground, taking the young outside?

REAGAN: I don't know whether we should be doing the same things of that kind but I do think that it is time to turn the expertise that we have in that field—I'm not one—but to turn it loose on what do we need in the line of defense against their weaponry and defend our population, because we can't be sitting here—this could become the vulnerable point for us in the event of an ultimatum.

SCHEER: But specifically, do you think we should do the things we did in the fifties, like the underground air-raid shelters, and building things in the back yard, and all that sort of thing?

REAGAN: I don't know about the back-yard shelters with today's technology or not, but as I say, one of the first things I would do would be to turn to those who are knowledgeable in military affairs, knowledgeable in the weaponry that would be coming at us, and so forth, to find out what we could do. Now it could well be that maybe there is another defense, maybe there is a defense through having superior offensive ability to keep them from doing this. See, what they have built their nuclear strength to is based on being able to knock out our missiles in their silos, and then to still have enough nuclear power left that if we, with say some remaining submarines or something, attack their cities, that they could wipe out our population, our industry, and our cities.

SCHEER: But they can't touch our submarines and our bombers and all that stuff, can they?

REAGAN: Yes, they can. The only bombers that we have are the aging B-52s and . . .

SCHEER: What about the nuclear subs, and all that?

REAGAN: All right, we have some but we can't match them in number, speed, diving depth, or range of missiles.

SCHEER: So what is the vision here, that you would vastly increase the—what—the civil defense, the military spending, and . . .

REAGAN: We have to improve our defensive capability. It's . . .

SCHEER: Everybody says they want to do that. You would just do a lot more of that sort of thing?

REAGAN: Well, I know that one of them . . . during the campaign, even Carter is saying it, and he's the man that stopped the military buildup, so I question his sincerity and whether he's talking, I would like to see some deeds, he talks in terms of, well, we're going to increase the military budget by 3 or 5 percent. That isn't the way you talk. What you say is, we are going to begin a buildup program of this, this, this, this, and you take—one of the first lines of defense that must be built up, and that he cut in half, the building program of the Navy. The Soviet navy now has a blue-ocean navy for the first time in their history and it's far more than a two-ocean navy. It is aimed at intercepting the some sixteen choke points in the world—choke points being those narrow passes ranging from the canals to the Straits of Gibraltar to the Malacca Straits and so forth, and the Sea of Japan, where world commerce and trade can be cut off. Our Navy was once aimed at keeping those sea lanes open, that was its task.

SCHEER: Well, was Carter able to do this just for three years or wasn't this also the Ford policy, Kissinger, they favored détente, they favored SALT I, they got into all this.

REAGAN: But under the Ford Administration, we had started to build up with the B-1, the neutron warhead, the cruise missile was going forward, and this was where the Russians were desperately propagandizing against that, because we were ahead of them in technology in cruise missiles then, we aren't anymore. And we have adopted a ship-building program that was aimed at, I believe, seventeen ships a year, and all of this was cut in half, including the fact that we reduced our replacement of aircraft. We are losing through obsolescence and accident more airplanes each year than we're building. Our Air Force is getting—our air might is getting smaller. And it's true that Congress, the Democratic Congress over the years, every time it's wanted money for some social reform, it has cut the defense budget to get it. But, before he left, the Ford Administration had started . . .

SCHEER: Well, would you change that priority? Do you think we've overemphasized these social reforms and, you know, this is an election time—somebody's got to say what they really believe. Would you be for building up the military and cutting back some of these social programs?

REAGAN: Well, I think some of the social reforms have proven to be colossal failures.

SCHEER: Which ones?

REAGAN: There are so many. We're talking about more than 400 programs.

SCHEER: . . . You mentioned an Air Force report on the number of Soviet bombers that would get through U.S. defenses. Is this a report that the rest of us can see? Is this a secret report?

REAGAN: No, this wasn't a report at all.

SCHEER: Was this the judgment of someone who has seen secret information?

REAGAN: It was a high-ranking officer who told me squarely what the situation was.

SCHEER: Was he revealing secret information that a reporter or a citizen couldn't get?

REAGAN: I'm quite sure that this is available to anyone but—look, the media just doesn't pay attention to that sort of thing. Just recently I was reading where some group that devotes itself to this, a national group here, has checked for the last two years on one of the major networks and found that in their newscasts, over a two-year period, they had devoted a total of two minutes in two years to the Soviet buildup of their armaments.

SCHEER: But he wasn't releasing any secret information? This was just something the Russians would know, we would know?

REAGAN: Sure they know . . .

SCHEER: In your campaigning, you keep stressing this godless Communism we're faced with. Do you feel that applies to Iran, where the Ayatollah, at least, claims to be a very religious Muslim?

REAGAN: No, I'm not—I used godless Communist tyranny with regard to Afghanistan, I think, in my speech, but that was with reference to the invasion there.

SCHEER: So is Iran a case of a god-fearing tyranny?

REAGAN: As a matter of fact, it is ruled by the Shi'ite sect of the Muslim religion which is a very minority sect, only about 9 or 10,000 . . .

SCHEER: They claim to be very religious . . .

REAGAN: And they are extremely conservative or rigid in their doctrine, much more so than the majority of Muslims. They are the ones who actually will go to the point of not believing that women should be educated. Well, recently, the execution of an eighteen-year-old girl who was pregnant—she was executed and the man who'd gotten her pregnant only received 100 lashes.

SCHEER: So you can have a tyanny that's god-fearing? That's the only thing I wanted to establish because you're always stressing the godless element of Communism. You said in the Saturday debate we should never again fight in a war that we did not win. Was the Korean War an example—should we have defeated the Chinese Communists in Korea?

REAGAN: Yes, MacArthur was absolutely right, and a funny, funny thing that few people have ever noticed about MacArthur—I never realized what a great student of Asia he was until—and I didn't know it at the time—until I looked back and found that when he voiced his resistance to the no-win war, he said, "We will have to do this again," and he specified, he said, "in Vietnam." Now at that time I didn't even know what the word, Vietnam, meant. I had heard of French Indo-China. I didn't even know any place called Vietnam.

SCHEER: Are we weaker because we didn't defeat them?

REAGAN: Well, the thing about the defeat and what would it have meant, particularly after you have asked that many young men to die in that cause and it wasn't even for our country—remember, we fought that war under the United Nations flag. But, when you have a no-win war, and there is no punishment for aggression, as there wasn't in that case, and you finally settle the war, right back with a divided Korea, and right back at where the temporary—the 17th parallel was actually the dividing point for the Soviet occupation of Japanese-run Korea, and we occupied the southern part. Now they've made it two nations.

SCHEER: But now the North Koreans are very anti-Russian, they've broken with them, the Chinese have broken with the Russians, so maybe it was all right that we lost, and these people have turned out to be very anti-Russian.

REAGAN: I think it would have been far better if we'd won the war and there had been a united Korea, a democratic Korea, with the people all of one race and ethnic group that would have been united in one country.

Detroit–New Hampshire

SCHEER: In your speech of last night, your press conference, you said the Shah of Iran was one of our great friends, that you would testify on his behalf at a tribunal, and you based this upon your observations in Iran. How long were you in Iran?

REAGAN: We were there several days.

SCHEER: That was two years ago?

REAGAN: About a year and a half ago. Wait a minute, let's put something else in context, because I've read the paper item about that too. A reporter asked, would I testify? I specified that I did not think anything I had to say would be such that I would be called to testify. Now, when he persisted and said, "But if you were called, what are you going to say? 'No, I would refuse a subpoena'?" So I said, "Yes." What would I testify to? I'd testify to what I saw, which is all I could do, and my other knowledge about the Shah. When I speak of him as an ally of the United States—

SCHEER: When you said you'd testify about the housing he's built for the poor, the farms for the poor, the reforesting, would you testify, did you see any of the secret police, SAVAK?

REAGAN: No, and I'm quite sure that there were violations of what we would consider human rights and things of that kind, but I'm quite sure that they are nothing as severe as what goes on in Russia and countries like that where we want to maintain a détente. I think this Administration is completely hypocritical. It talks human rights, but it has never found anyone guilty of violating them except a friend.

SCHEER: Yeah, but it doesn't satisfy the Ayatollah or the people in Iran to talk about Russia. They have their own criticism of Russia. What they're saying is, that in their country we trained the SAVAK, there was this secret police, and that the American media and government ignored it. I was just curious on the basis of your trip there, that you didn't see any signs of that?

REAGAN: No, I didn't. But I wasn't in any jails either. But on the other hand, who is the Ayatollah to talk? He has just had executed an eighteen-year-old pregnant girl for prostitution. The man who made her pregnant just received a flogging.

SCHEER: We're aware of the crimes of the Ayatollah, the media has been alerted to that and the government. What has been suggested is that when the Shah was in power we ignored his problems and that one of the reasons this ended up being a problem for us, is that in effect that is why he was overthrown. If he was as popular as visitors like yourself thought, if he had done as much, then he wouldn't have been overthrown as easily.

REAGAN: He was overthrown for a number of reasons that I don't think had anything to do with public demand. And part of his being overthrown was inspired by a radio station inside the Russian border that was broadcasting in Farsi, the language of the country, constantly against the United States and against this whole union with that country. But—

SCHEER: You don't think there was a generalized revulsion against the Shah in Iran?

REAGAN: No, not really. But part of it could have been this. His land reform. The first land that was given up to be divided up among the peasants was the Shah's own personal land holdings. The second great land holdings were in the hands of the mullahs, the ayatollahs, the priests of the religions. And he took that land. Could it be that's why they're so angry at him? Remember also—

SCHEER: But your feeling basically was that the Shah was a popular and remained a popular figure in Iran?

REAGAN: Well, I would say that those young women I saw who were learning to be doctors and lawyers in the university would adopt Western ways, and now are told they are denied an education because under the precepts of this present reign that takes them back to the fifteenth century, women are not to be allowed—

SCHEER: But you're the one who always, you give speeches against godless Communism, and you talk about religion. Now these people think they are practicing their religion. Are you saying it's in some way inferior to Christianity?

REAGAN: Well. There have always been in religions, extremists. And some of the great crimes have been committed under the name of religion, but—

SCHEER: In their religion women definitely have a different and inferior role. They claim it isn't. They say it's inscribed in their religion. Are you saying they shouldn't practice it?

REAGAN: This is only one sect of the Muslim religion, and a minor sect of about 9 percent—

SCHEER: But it happens to be the one that predominates in that country and are we saying we're going to tell them what kind of god to follow?

REAGAN: People seemed to like it. The majority of people were driving automobiles, going to motion-picture theaters, and the Shah also did something else that we consider human rights also. And they didn't like. He gave them religious freedom. He protected the minority religions in that country.

SCHEER: That's a valid point. In terms of the Shah, one last question. You opposed the Panama Canal give-away. Were you surprised that Panama, this country you thought was a potential enemy, was willing to bail us out and give sanctuary to the Shah?

REAGAN: Well, I don't think they did this to bail us out, and I hope the Shah is safe there. But I don't have very much faith in the authoritarian government of Panama. It has proven boldly that it is far closer to Castro's Cuba in line. It has allowed itself to be used by the Sandinistas and the other rebels of Central America, and I think we're going to live to regret the day we gave them the canal.

SCHEER: Were you surprised they were willing to give sanctuary when Mexico wasn't and certainly Cuba—to this man you said was a great ally and friend of the United States?

REAGAN: No, I wasn't surprised about that. He was a very wealthy man, and whatever their reasons were, but I would not want to have my life depending on their continued good favor.

Birmingham–Orlando

SCHEER: The last time I talked to you, you said no President of the United States should rule out the possibility of a preemptive nuclear strike . . . Now in serving notice on a confrontation down the road—would that include the possibility of a preemptive nuclear strike by the United States?

REAGAN: What I'm saying is that the United States should never put itself in a position, as it has many times, of guaranteeing to an enemy or a potential enemy what it won't do. For example . . .

SCHEER: Including a preemptive nuclear strike . . .

REAGAN: For example, when President Johnson, in the Vietnam War, kept over and over again insisting, oh no, no, no, we'll never use nuclear weapons in Vietnam, I don't think nuclear weapons should have been used in Vietnam, I don't think they were needed; but when somebody's out there killing your young men, you should never free the enemy of the concern he might have for what you might do. So you may feel that way in your heart, but don't say it out loud to him.

SCHEER: But isn't there something useful about developing a sense of . . . in the world that we never use nuclear weapons and that no nation should ever feel under any circumstance that it can use it . . .

REAGAN: I agree that no nation should but you're not getting a ban on all nations . . .

SCHEER: But if our President leaves open the option that we may use nuclear weapons, doesn't that leave open the possibility for another nation to justify its preemptive use of a nuclear strike? Isn't there something unthinkable about nuclear weapons and that they should be ruled out in any case?

REAGAN: I think there is, and Dwight Eisenhower offered to the world to turn to—to internationalize them, turn them over to the United Nations and no one had nuclear weapons, and who turned it down, the Soviet Union.

SCHEER: Unquestionably. What I'm asking you as a President, don't you leave the door open for another nation's using nuclear weapons—and many nations will have nuclear weapons in the future—don't you leave the door open for another nation using it on a preemptive basis if you refuse to rule it out categorically?

REAGAN: Don't you open up the possibility of being hit by a surprise nuclear attack far more if you assure the rest of the world that under no circumstances would you ever be the first to fire those bombs?

SCHEER: No, we were talking about a preemptive strike. Obviously, there would be a retaliation . . .

REAGAN: Suppose you're the President, and suppose you have on unassailable authority that as of a certain hour the enemy is going to launch those missiles at your country, you mean to tell me that a President should sit there and let that happen without saying to the other country, I've found out what you're planning to do and I'm going to . . .

SCHEER: That would be in the category of a retaliatory strike. One last question on that—do you think there is such a thing as surviving a nuclear war, do you think there is survivability?

REAGAN: The Soviet Union thinks there is.

SCHEER: But do you think so?

REAGAN: There evidently is for them on the basis in which they're willing to do it.

SCHEER: You mean because they have fallout shelters. We once had fallout shelters—does that mean we thought it was survivable?

REAGAN: They have, they have a very sophisticated civil defense plan.

SCHEER: But do you believe that we could survive a nuclear war?

REAGAN: No, because we have let [the Russians] get so strong and we have let them violate the agreement.

SCHEER: But let's say we get stronger than them again. Do you think we could survive a nuclear war? With the right underground shelter systems, with the right defense systems, could we survive one?

REAGAN: It would be a survival of some of your people and some of your facilities that you could start again. It would not be anything that I think in our society you would consider acceptable but then we have a different regard for human life than those monsters do.

SCHEER: You call them monsters and you used to call the Chinese, the Red Chinese, the . . . monsters, they were in Korea against us, they were behind the Vietnamese at one point. Now we have more normal relations, or we're developing normal relations with the Chinese. We're talking about them as a bulwark against Russia. Have they stopped being monsters—the Chinese Communists?

REAGAN: I don't know that I ever called them monsters or not, but I think it was monstrous, if you want me to say it, to slaughter as many millions of people as they slaughtered in order to impose that tyranny on their people.

SCHEER: You mean back in the fifties or sixties you thought the Chinese Communists were less monstrous than the Russians—during the time of the Korean War?

REAGAN: No, they were allies, and the only argument that caused their split was an argument over how best to destroy us. That was not one that reassured me that when they split, that we should immediately rush over there and trust them. And even now, though I think it's fine now that we are attempting to establish a contact, it should be done with our eyes open, it should be done with a cautious holding of one foot back because . . .

SCHEER: But how did they stop being monsters? I mean they were on a par, at least, with the Russians in treachery and monstrous deeds, they are supposed to have killed 20 million of their people . . .

REAGAN: 50 million.

SCHEER: 50 million, so then—I don't think the Russians have killed 50 million of their own people—when did they stop being monsters?

REAGAN: I don't know that they have.

SCHEER: And yet we're talking about having an alliance with them.

REAGAN: Because we're hoping that through time and through their animus and fear of the Soviet Union, that maybe they'll become more like us. Now there is indication—people who have gone there say there is indication—that they're trying to improve the situation and that they allow more human rights for their people. At the moment, I don't think they come anyplace close to meeting . . .

SCHEER: The Chinese who fought us in Korea and who were described in very strong and hostile terms in the past could change in such a relatively short time—why do you think that the Russians couldn't change and that there isn't a future in détente, in negotiations with them, and so forth, that they could stop being monsters in as short a time as the Chinese Communists?

REAGAN: Well, you've got an entirely different situation. The Soviet Union has used détente to build the biggest military force the world has ever seen.

SCHEER: I'm talking about the nature of their Communism, the nature of their system. Is it fundamentally different than the Chinese Communism, and why couldn't the Soviet Union change in the same way as the Chinese have?

REAGAN: Have the Chinese changed? I don't know. The Chinese people are still the victims of tyranny. Have you read Solzhenitsyn's article in *Time* magazine, about both countries, and the fact that he says, don't talk about the Russians, talk about the Soviets, because the Russians don't like the Soviet at all.

SCHEER: Well, then, if that's true, and the Chinese are still in the same bag, how come you justify normalization of relations with them, or even a two-China policy which you favor, how can you say that it's all right that we now take tentative steps toward some kind of alliance, which you have said—

REAGAN: I think it is in our practical best interest, for the simple reason that if this hostility is real between them and the Soviet Union, the Soviet Union has a further deterrent to go adventuring against us, because they've got a great big back border there with the hostile Chinese. Now, I don't see anything wrong with that. We're not doing anything to hurt the Chinese people in this alliance that we have, and if it is going to keep them at odds with the Soviet Union, we have made the free world safer.

SCHEER: But you would even entrust them with sophisticated weapons at some point?

REAGAN: No, because just like the Soviets broke their agreement—or Hitler broke their agreement with the Soviets, they could turn right around and the day after tomorrow discover that they and the Soviets have more in common than they have with us.

SCHEER: Talking about geopolitical power, back in the forties and fifties, we were told that when we lost China to Russia, we lost power. Now we've gained China back and, at the same time, we were told that Russia is stronger than ever. How come that hasn't entered into the geopolitical thing? The other connected question with that is—you were against the Panama Canal treaty. Your argument was that Panama represented a subversive threat to us. Now we have a situation where Panama, another country, turns out not to have been lost to us but in fact they gave refuge to the Shah, they seem to be a pretty good ally.

REAGAN: No, I said that giving up the Panama Canal was a mistake in turning it over to a dictatorial country, a dictator who was never elected, a dictator who has shown . . .

SCHEER: The Shah was never elected and was a dictator and you said he's one of our best allies.

REAGAN: But this particular ally seems to have shown a greater affinity for association with Castro in Cuba.

SCHEER: But this particular ally gave refuge to the Shah and you said that was a good thing.

REAGAN: I want to see what the outcome of that is going to be. I don't know what it is you're trying to get at here, with what I am trying to point out. I am also the fellow who said that I thought it might be worthwhile to sit down with all of the Latin American states, with all the American states who use that canal and are dependent on it, and talk about maybe internationalizing it. What I was objecting to was the giving away under threat of violence from a pipsqueak dictator who hasn't got as much gross national product as Cincinnati, Ohio, giving away what was clearly ours, which was not the result of imperialism, which has been the biggest asset those people ever had, and has given them the highest standard of living of any Central American country, that giving it away under duress and threat, from the minute that their dictator down there told us that we had to give up the canal or there was going to be trouble—he was going to make trouble for us—that's when we should have said to him, "Look, buster, you withdraw that threat or there's no more negotiation or sitting at a table with you because we're not, in the eyes of the world, going to give this up in answer to a threat of violence."

SCHEER: What I was getting at is, are there any surprises? The world situation has changed, I never would have predicted that Panama would have given refuge to the Shah, I never would have predicted that China and Russia would be at odds now. I'm not claiming any great prophetic ability here, and I'm not holding you at fault for lacking one. I just wonder how we all react to a changing world situation, and I just thought you might have been surprised at what happened in Panama. I was. It is not an attack . . .

REAGAN: Maybe it had something to do with the wealth of the Shah, because I happen to think there's a pretty money-hungry bunch down there in Panama, and many of them, since they hold government positions, have gotten far wealthier than their salaries would indicate they should have had.

Detroit–New Hampshire

SCHEER: . . . In a *Los Angeles Times* interview with Carl Greenberg in 1967 you said, speaking of the Sino-Soviet dispute, "As for the contest between Russia and Red China, that is over what's the best way to destroy us." Do you still feel that way about China—that they're out to destroy us and Russia?

REAGAN: No, I think there's been a change, but at the time I said

245 / Reagan Interview

that, that was the great argument between Russia and China. If you remember, it was the Chinese calling the Soviets revisionists because they would not join in and say let's go after the capitalist world and defeat it. So at that time I was absolutely, I think, on the nose. Now, there have been several changes in personnel at the leadership level in mainland China. I think that the opening up of China as Richard Nixon did was a calculated effort to hopefully widen the gulf between those two countries and hope that some day the Red Chinese might review their ideology and find that they are not that close to the original Marxism, to Communism, but in the meantime I will say this, I think that we should be realistic and kind of keep one foot back until we are definitely sure as to the direction they're going.

SCHEER: Is there any danger in our selling sophisticated equipment to the Red Chinese?

REAGAN: I would think right now, yes. I don't know as much as I would like to know about mainland China and the kind of information that probably you would only have access to if you were President, but I would be very hesitant about that. I think a policy of not doing that is correct at this time.

SCHEER: Do you believe the Soviet Union and the geopolitical balance in the world has shifted toward the Soviet Union, that the Soviet Union is now in a stronger position vis-à-vis the United States?

REAGAN: Oh, for heaven's sake, you only have to look at a map to know that. You only have to look at the fact that they have 4,800,000 men in uniform in the military, we have 775,000. But also in weaponry, the Soviet Union has done something that we had not counted on at all—they have surpassed us in many instances in military technology which we thought they certainly could not do in the foreseeable future. They're still way behind us in consumer-good technology, in civilian-type technology, but they, I think, are embarked on a course that is widening the difference between us and I think if we instantly reverse our own course and set out to rebuild, reinstitute the program of building that we had before Carter became President, in which he cancelled virtually every weapon system that we were developing, I think that it's possible to keep the Soviets from getting the kind of edge that would lead them to go adventuring against us.

SCHEER: You say you only have to look at a map to see that the Soviets have gotten stronger, but looking at the map—one big area, the one we just referred to, China—with a massive army, a massive manpower, a billion people—has been lost to the Soviets and, if anything, seem to be moving over to our side. Egypt is another case in point where the Soviets had enormous influence and have now lost it, and you could look at other—Ghana, Guinea in Africa, in Latin America they've been checked in Cuba, so—where have they gained in the world?

REAGAN: Where have they been checked in Cuba? There are nuclear-capable fighter-bombers stationed in Cuba, there are nuclear submarines there of the Soviet Union, we now know there's a combat brigade there with first-line weaponry for that brigade which has led to the statement that I made recently of the possible connection with the further advance over in the Persian Gulf. If this is a training brigade, as they say it is, isn't it a strange coincidence that exactly the duplicate of the equipment being used in Cuba by that training brigade is now stockpiled in South Yemen? And you have forgotten, even though the Russians did not do it directly but through their proxies, there is Ethiopia, there is South Yemen, there is Angola, there is Mozambique, they have moved and advanced their positions and all of them in areas—and in the Caribbean we are seeing by way of Cuba and the export of revolution to the point that our sea lanes for the essential things we must have, particularly in minerals and energy, are much endangered right now if the Soviets should decide to adopt that course.

SCHEER: But what about the places where they've lost out, I mean in the late forties and early fifties, Republicans attacked the Democrats for having lost China. You yourself attacked the United Nations as well as the Democrats for not having backed Chiang Kai-shek. Now it turns out, twenty years later, that we have won China and they have lost China and yet you don't enter that into your balance-of-power equation.

REAGAN: Well, because we don't know how far this alliance with us —whether it is an alliance or not—they have never retreated one step from their Marxist philosophy and therefore we could look back to World War II and see a time when the Soviet Union had an alliance with Hitler's Germany and when you have authoritarian powers, we saw what they could do. Hitler's Germany decided to break that agreement by crossing the frontier and did so at gunpoint. This is what I mean about keeping a foot back with Red China—that their expansion throughout the world—to say that they have lost ground in Latin America, I think, is to ignore reality there. Right now Colombia, Bogotá is having a great infiltration of the same kind of people that have brought the downfall of other countries there in Central America, the moving into Africa, Afghanistan, Iran—once the great bulwark between the Soviet Union and their advance southward to the Indian Ocean is shattered and gone.

SCHEER: Sticking to the China thing for a minute, I mean this was a big issue once in our history, about losing China. Is it possible that the leopard can change its spots—that you can have a Communist government that in fact can become an ally of the United States and fiercely anti-Russian?

REAGAN: Well, this is what I have been trying to say here, that when we lost China we did lose them. There was an outright Communist takeover of China and Communist China obviously had an ideological link with the Soviet Union. Then, as I say, the falling-out came not because of any apparent difference in their belief in Communism or Communism's mission to conquer the world, but the falling-out really came because the Chinese leaders of that day were impatient and thought that the Soviets were not moving fast enough. Now the cooling-off came over that issue, and Richard Nixon took advantage of that and I think we have to give him credit for that in going there to explore. Now we hope, yes, that we can persuade over a period of time the Chinese, to whether they totally give up even in name the doctrine of Communism, but if they give up that philosophy of eventual world domination, if they truly want to throw their lot in with the free world, that remains to be seen. In the meantime, I don't think we should be naïve and just say oh goody, look, we have a great big new friend.

SCHEER: But were you surprised at all, given your feelings about Red China in the past, that we would now end up being allies in a sense, and that the Chinese seem more hostile to the Russians than even we are. Does that surprise you at all?

REAGAN: Well, I think we've had a number of years to get used to it. I think we went—all of us, a lot of us went through a period of wondering if it was a part of a strategy of the two countries to lull the Western world. Now we have felt our way further and the only complaint I've had with what has happened now with us in our relations with mainland China is I don't believe that we had to betray a longtime friend and ally and throw Taiwan overboard as Carter did in order to have the relationship we have with mainland China. I think we could have had everything we presently have and had Taiwan—well, preserved our honor.

SCHEER: So you still think there's a chance there might be a trick, and that the Chinese—I mean after all, they still proclaim themselves Marxist-Leninist Communists—might be lulling us in, and if we give them strategic weapons, aren't we exposing ourselves . . .

REAGAN: That's it, we haven't yet given them strategic weaponry, and that I think is part of what I say, keeping one foot back and making very sure that we don't face the same thing we faced with the Soviet Union—multiple warheads on their nuclear missiles that they couldn't have had at least as early as they've had them, without giving them the technology and the sophisticated machinery for building them. We look to Afghanistan. The Soviet Union solemnly pledged us. We put over $350 million into that . . . truck plant for them. They couldn't have had it and they couldn't run it without our technology, our computers, and they solemnly pledged that the motors and the trucks there would not be used for military purposes. Well, that's what carried the Russian divisions into Afghanistan.

SCHEER: Going back to an earlier period, it was thought that Communism was monolithic, worldwide—now we see that these Communist regimes are at each other's throats. You yourself have advocated aid to Communist Yugoslavia. The Chinese seem a very strong bulwark against Russian expansionism and so forth. Does this breakup of Communism and the rise of a nationalist component surprise you?

REAGAN: I think that this has been something of a change in that the Soviet Union as it spread and as these other countries—human nature being what it is—you're going to have leaders in other countries that want a little more of the say-so and want to sit a little higher nearer the salt at the conference table. It is true that Communism was once monolithic with the Soviet Union the mother lode, the center. We know that even the American Communist party back in those days when they were trying to take over Hollywood, their first allegiance was to the Soviet Union. Now, I don't know where they stand now, they've been rather quiet of late, but they still—I haven't seen even Tito suggesting that if there were a war between the West and the Soviet Union that Yugoslavia would be on the side of the West. As a matter of fact, he has specifically stated otherwise. What we're worried about now, speaking on behalf of Communist Yugoslavia, is not because it's Communist but, that if the Soviet Union now—if Tito is strongman enough that his departure from the scene would lead the Soviets to move into that, I think it would be of great concern to the Western world.

SCHEER: But if Tito's Communism and Chinese Communism have

become nationalistic and anti-Soviet, or at least suspicious of it, isn't it possible then that, for instance, Cuba could be encouraged to take that road, that normalization of relations with Cuba would allow it to break away from the Soviet Union and they would find their interests different?

REAGAN: Yes, but don't you think that they have to make some signs first that they want that kind of independence, and they've made no such signs. You only have to read the transcript, Castro's remarks at the recent Third World conference in Havana, to realize that Castro is just about as handy a loyalist to the Soviet cause as they could hope for.

SCHEER: But as you point out, on the very eve of the Nixon visit to China, their rhetoric was very strong, and they were condemning the Russians for not being vigorous enough—and after all, we fought against the Chinese in the Korean War and now here even Korea has condemned—North Korea has condemned the Russians on Afghanistan. Isn't there a sign there that maybe these Communist regimes can be worked with as well as opposed?

REAGAN: Yes, and I think that's what all of us should try to do. But again, as I say, do it with our eyes open, be realistic enough to know that they may be nationalistic and there may be arguments within their own network of countries as to how much voice each one should have, but until they abandon some of the basic principles of Marxism, the one which has been reiterated by everyone who's a Communist, and that is the world revolution, that the world must become a Soviet state or a Communist state.

SCHEER: Do you think that would apply now to the Chinese as well?

REAGAN: Well, we haven't heard anything from them that differs, have we, so as I say, I think slow and easy is the way to go.

SCHEER: Do you think our Defense Secretary, Brown, who went there, was moving too fast and talking about satellite equipment and . . .

REAGAN: He talked, if I recall, he talked about some communications equipment, some purely defensive things such as radar, and then the support kind of equipment, trucks and so forth, he did not talk sophisticated weaponry.

SCHEER: You were very critical of the earlier, I mean—the following of the two-China policy and so forth—do you feel that we now . . .

REAGAN: I'm still critical of it—I think that we betrayed a longtime friend and ally unnecessarily and I think in doing so we alarmed all our other friends and allies in the world. In fact we gave the Soviet Union a great propaganda advantage in trying to woo some of our allies, such as some of our NATO allies, away from us by questioning our reliability so I think one of the—I would feel better with a different Administration than the one that is in Washington because I think—I've seen nothing about their foreign policy that makes me feel more comfortable or that even shows that there is a foreign policy of some coherence. I think we do as I say—we go forward hoping that we can win back the trust of our allies and our friends, and at the same time keep ourselves in a position to where the Soviet Union could not make the move against us.

SCHEER: If you were the head of the Soviet Union looking at the sudden loss—or the loss over a decade really—of China, she shares a very extensive border with you, and the official Chinese position is that war with the Soviet Union is inevitable, having these people suddenly on your border, wouldn't that make you insecure and wouldn't you think that Afghanistan with its relatively small population was a rather insignificant trade-off for the loss of China?

REAGAN: No, I think Afghanistan should be looked at with much more concern than that, because this is the first time outside their own circle of satellites that the Soviet Union has used its own military instead of proxy troops, and this bespeaks an arrogance and a confidence born of their military strength, that they made that move, and we have been sending the wrong signals. We've been sending the kind of signals that made that possible, and what we need to do is send them some signals that let them know that there is a point beyond which they cannot go in the world without risking a direct confrontation with us. Now I say that because I don't believe the Soviet Union at this time wants a direct confrontation with us. They're not—they don't want that until they have such an edge that they could realize their dream of perhaps taking us by telephone. That we would have no choice left except surrender or die.

SCHEER: Do you believe that in terms of confrontation with the Russians that we would have to think about a nuclear option?

REAGAN: About a nuclear option? No, I think we have thought of —we've still been following the Mutual Assured Destruction plan that was given birth by McNamara, and it was a ridiculous plan, and it was based on the idea that the two countries would hold each other's population hostage, that we would not protect or defend our people against a nuclear attack. They in turn would not do the same. Therefore if both of us knew that we could wipe each other out, neither one would dare push the button. The difficulty with that was that the Soviet Union decided some time ago that a nuclear war was possible and was winnable, and they have proceeded with an elaborate and extensive civil protection program. We do not have anything of that kind because we went along with what the policy was supposed to be.

SCHEER: Should we institute a program of that sort?

REAGAN: Well, I think that we have to take a look at this, and study with it again to see where this would come in the priorities of reestablishing our military strength. I would have to have access to more information than I presently have. But knowing that the Soviet Union is following that policy, the belief that such a war can—there can be such a war and that it can be won, we have to build up our deterrent capacity to the point that they never can see the point at which it could be won. In other words, that damage to themselves would not be unacceptable, and I think we're late in starting that building of our military.

SCHEER: You don't see any prospect at this time for any caps on expansion of strategic weapons—the SALT sort of agreement?

REAGAN: Oh, the fault with SALT is it's not a limitation agreement; how do we call something, an arms—a strategic arms limitation program—that begins by letting the Soviet Union add 3,000 more nuclear warheads, and then even permits us, if we can, to try to catch up—but we'll be about ten years behind them and that'll be a dangerous ten years. No, I would . . .

SCHEER: Isn't it also true that we have the cruise missile and that NATO stationed them right on Russia's border and that was consistent with the SALT agreement?

REAGAN: We slowed the cruise missile program down in the first year of the Carter Administration to such an extent, we did have an edge in that technology at the time. We've slowed it down to where, look at the recent tests, we're splashing them all over our own countryside trying to find one that'll work. Now, also, look at this so-called limitation treaty—our subsonic cruise missiles, low-yield missiles, are judged to be strategic weapons. The Soviet Union's multiple warhead nuclear rockets that they have targeted on the western European capitals, London and Paris and all the other cities, they are not included in the SALT treaty as strategic weapons. Now you asked me a moment ago . . .

SCHEER: That's true of the NATO cruise missiles that were put in also, that are aimed at the Soviet heartland?

REAGAN: But they are in SALT—they're limited as to range, as to numbers, as to deployment. There is no restriction, the nuclear rockets the Soviet Union is placing, the SS-20s, are not contained or considered, just as the backfire bomber is not considered a strategic weapon. Now when you asked a moment ago what would I feel about this or how do I feel about treaties of this kind, I criticized the SALT treaty. I would be willing to sit down with the Soviet Union any time and say, look, we'll sit at the table with you as long as it takes to work out a treaty that will legitimately reduce the nuclear weapons on both sides to where neither one of us can represent a threat to the other. That is arms limitation, not this kind of a chess game that's being played where they tell us a twenty-five-year-old subsonic bomber is a strategic weapon but their supersonic B-1—well, almost a B-1 type, their backfire bombers are not supersonic.

SCHEER: I just want to clear up this one thing—it was my understanding when NATO put in those hundreds of missiles just this last fall that that did not come under the SALT agreement.

REAGAN: Well, the cruise missiles are in there, I know that. As to our deployment of them—and of course the Soviet Union has used propaganda campaigns to stop us from putting a weapon that we—a great deterrent weapon—that we had developed and they didn't have —and an economical weapon—and that was the neutron warhead. They've got more than 20,000 tanks massed there opposite the NATO line. The neutron warhead could have neutralized those tanks but again we stopped it, we delayed that or just put it on the shelf.

SCHEER: Do you think a situation could arise in which we would have to use first-strike or limited nuclear warfare that countered their advantage in conventional arms?

REAGAN: I honestly don't know, but I would say this—I think there have been too many people, particularly in this Administration, and there were earlier Administrations, the Johnson Administration in Vietnam did the same thing, that we too often say the things we won't do. I think we ought to keep our mouths shut. Now I don't want to see a nuclear war. I would not like to think we would ever fire our nuclear weapons at an enemy. But we shouldn't go around saying we won't. If we keep saying to the other fellow, look, whatever you do, we're not going to fire first—that's like inviting them to fire first. Johnson in the Vietnam War, when he repeatedly went out of his way to say, oh no, we would never use them, well, I don't believe that nuclear weapons should have been used in the Vietnam War but I don't think there'd be anything wrong with letting Hanoi when our young men were dying over there—letting Hanoi go to bed every night thinking we might—and let me recall one point where this was made by a President named Eisenhower. Every bid for peace in the war we fought for the United Nations in Korea was rejected by the North Koreans until a new President came into office—Dwight Eisenhower —and he just publicly made the remark that he was going to study and review the weaponry that we were using in that war, and the implication was very clear, he made it very clear, that he, the former general, was going to review and see whether nuclear weapons should be considered and it was almost immediately that the North Koreans said let's sit down and have armistice talks and that was when Panmunjom started.

SCHEER: So you feel then that—just so I understand this—that it should not be ruled out categorically on a first-strike basis, our use of nuclear . . .

REAGAN: . . . yourself—you may have said we'll never do this thing, we're a civilized people, but I just don't think you go saying it to the other fellow.

SCHEER: Don't you think there's some value in creating a world climate in which nations would find it unthinkable to use them on a first-strike basis and in which there would be pressure in the world not to ever use them on a first-strike basis?

REAGAN: Has there ever been a time when the United States hasn't been taking the lead in that sort of thing? Remember, we were the ones when we were the only ones who had the bomb, we were the ones who offered to turn it over to the United Nations.

SCHEER: Didn't we also—we did drop the bomb.

REAGAN: Yes, and ended a great war—and probably saved, well, it's been estimated 2 million casualties, in what would have eventually been the invasion of Japan. To say nothing of what their casualties would have been. But then we did offer to internationalize this great power and offer it to the world in the interest of peace. I think the United States—it is so hypocritical—and that's the only word to use when you hear Gromyko sound off as he did in his talks in India the other night —and to hear him use the word imperialist with regard to us, remembering even that the Chinese referred to us for a long time as running imperial dogs, but our record with whatever mistakes we've made is so far superior and so much on the side of peace, we—at the end of World

War II, if people would let themselves imagine one thing—what if it had been the Soviet Union whose industrial plant was intact, their cities not bombed and destroyed, they had the great unscarred military machine that we had, and they had the bomb and no one else did, would the world be free today? I don't think so.

South Carolina–Florida

SCHEER: In the debate Saturday night, you once again attacked "godless Communism," and I'm curious about the use of the word "godless"—why is that an important element there?

REAGAN: Well, because this is one of the vital precepts of Communism, that we are accidents of nature.

SCHEER: But is it the godlessness that makes them more violent, more aggressive, more expansionist?

REAGAN: Well, it is one that gives them less regard for humanity or human beings.

SCHEER: But here we have the Ayatollah in Iran, who certainly is not godless, and he seems to be—

REAGAN: A fanatic and a zealot—

SCHEER: But he's not godless.

REAGAN: No, not in his sense—and we have had that all the way back through history. We can go back to the Inquisitions in Spain. So, there are people who, through their fanaticism, misuse religion. But the reason for the godlessness with regard to Communism—here is a direct teaching of the child from the beginning of its life that it is a human being whose only importance is its contribution to the state—that they are wards of the state—that they exist only for that purpose, and that there is no God, they are just an accident of nature. The result is, this is why they have no respect for human life, for the dignity of an individual. And I remember one night, a long time ago, in a rally in Los Angeles, 16,000 people in the auditorium, and this was at the time when the . . . Communists, the American Communist Party—and this is all well-documented—was actually trying, and had secured domination of several unions in the picture business and was trying to take over the motion-picture industry, and all of the rewriting of history today and the stories that we have seen and screenplays and television plays, and so forth, about the persecution for political belief . . . Hollywood, believe me, the persecutors were the Communists who had gotten into positions where they could destroy careers and did destroy them. There was no blacklist of Hollywood. The blacklist in Hollywood, if there was one, was provided by the Communists. There were blacklists by our customers and clients who said, to the motion-picture industry, "We won't go to see pictures that these people are involved in."

SCHEER: What about . . . Senator Joe McCarthy. Do you feel he got a bum deal in our reminiscence of that period?

REAGAN: Well, no, but let me just point out something about McCarthy. The whole Hollywood thing was all over before McCarthy even came on the scene. When CBS put on a documentary on the McCarthy era and showed Gary Cooper, and Bob Taylor, and some people as witnesses, sitting at a witness table, before the Committee, showed him appear at the Committee, never showed the two in the same shot, the reason they didn't was because Gary Cooper and Bob Taylor and those people were witnesses in 1947, at the House Committee on Un-American Activities and McCarthy's hearing didn't take place until 1952, five years later. And I know because I was at that House Un-American Activities Committee hearing, and for CBS to deliberately cut a film this way and imply that this was McCarthyism involved in the Hollywood episode was an outright lie, and they knew it had to be a lie because they edited the film.

SCHEER: But do you feel that looking back on it that McCarthy was himself given a bad deal by the media, and so forth?

REAGAN: No, McCarthy, unfortunately, was using a shotgun when he should have been using a rifle. In Hollywood, the Screen Actors Guild probably led the fight more than anyone else, to keep the Communists from winning. We never used the word "Communist" once. We never called anyone a Communist. We met them on the basis of what they were trying to do. Joe McCarthy was just—as I say, he went with a scatter gun and he lumped together fellow travelers, innocent dupes, and hard-core Communists.

SCHEER: Just to tie up this thing, though—on the godlessness. You say, the Inquisition, the Ayatollah, there are many examples where being very religious leads one to have contempt for human lives, as well —and we have—Yugoslavia is a Communist country; would you put them in the same category? China has become—we think—more reasonable, and they are still just as godless in their outlook. Do you really think that's the key word, the key thing to emphasize, whether they're godless or god-fearing?

REAGAN: Well, I think that it is important to point out this facet, because I think that the Communists are the menace to civilization in the world today. And I think that the more we know and understand about them, the better off we are.

SCHEER: Do you agree with the Chinese—

REAGAN: I don't think there's anything wrong with calling attention to the fact that the Communist party has substituted Karl Marx for God. And this is what they have done.

SCHEER: Can they change their spots? Will they always have contempt for human life as long as they are Communists and, if that's the case, is war inevitable with them—or is it inevitable that we live in a confrontation with them?

REAGAN: It is inevitable unless we, the leader of the free world, maintain the strength that will prevent them from ever daring to take the action which they would plan if they feel we're weak enough.

SCHEER: But you don't think a situation could evolve through diplomacy and changes in their thinking where, without giving up their godless Communism, that we could live in a reasonable, peaceful world the same way we do with Western Europe and so forth, and have disarmament? Do you think that's naïve?

REAGAN: It is naïve unless we maintain the strength to the point that they see that they can never accumulate enough superior strength to have their way.

Augusta–Manchester

SCHEER: What about fear—you know my fear of a Ronald Reagan presidency—I don't know about these guys—my fear is, are you going to push the button, are you going to get us blown up, are you going to get us into a nuclear war?

REAGAN: I've known four wars in my lifetime. There have been four, going back to my early youth, childhood, but four wars—I've only been in one, granted, no one shot at me or anything, through no fault of my own, I went where the orders put me—but no, I don't want it, but what I have seen in all of those wars is that we have gone into those wars, backed our way into them, through weakness. I have never seen us get into one through strength. Woodrow Wilson ran for his second term on the promise or the pledge that he kept us out of wars. His policy was called the "doctrine of Woodrow Wilson," it was watchful waiting. So he took insult after insult from the Germans, sinking of a ship, and so forth, and said, oh, no, no, let's not be precipitous, so finally the Germans declared open warfare on all shipping in the Atlantic Ocean, regardless of whether you were a neutral nation or not. And the *Lusitania* was sunk and, finally, we were in a war.

SCHEER: Woodrow Wilson was pretty good, in retrospect. Saber-rattling, demagogic talk, you used the words in relation to Connally, soft talk can also bring on a war that may not be necessary. You know, you yourself admit we once screwed the Chinese Communists, we once hated them, now they may even be our allies, things change. But we want the President as someone who can see change—I think we want, I don't know.

REAGAN: Now, wait, though. Woodrow Wilson, however, remember, the early campaign of his, remember there was a man named the Kaiser, and history now shows us the Kaiser got the idea from the watchful waiting policy that the United States was determined not to go to war. So he ignored that possibility in his attack on the western front of the allies. Now World War II, Franklin Delano Roosevelt ran for his third term, and ran on his own personal promise, "I will not send young Americans, your sons, to fight."

SCHEER: You can't just blame that on Roosevelt. General Motors had contracts with the Germans, Henry Ford said Hitler was a great man. Come on, we can't rewrite history. A lot of people in this country thought that Germany was a great bulwark against Bolshevism. Henry Ford was a close friend of . . .

REAGAN: Henry Ford wanted to take a ship over there and do what some other people have done—tried to do with the Soviets, wanted to try and talk them into being reasonable.

SCHEER: But, I mean, you can't just put it on Roosevelt. General Motors had a deal and they gave them equipment that they wouldn't even give our military. They gave them the Messerschmitt, they gave them other planes that they wouldn't even give our army.

REAGAN: Wait a minute. There were cartel agreements, sure, yes. We all know that. But in a government, when a President, running for his third term, makes this pledge, and when you've got an ambassador who is assuring von Ribbentrop that the United States wouldn't go to war, you now had a Hitler at this time said, we can count on it, the Germans won't go to war. Now, the Japanese attacked Pearl Harbor.

SCHEER: Wait a minute, Hitler did go to war against Russia.

REAGAN: I'm talking about the agreement that he had.

SCHEER: But he did go to war against Russia and Russia was left alone, fighting against Germany. I hate to bring this up.

REAGAN: No, Britain and France were in the war.

SCHEER: But first, Churchill/Chamberlain strategy was let Germany and Russia knock each other off, too esoteric, I know, for our interview here.

REAGAN: But Germany made a deal.

SCHEER: And then that was broken and they were fighting like crazy and we still held out.

REAGAN: Right—all right—why did he turn it in Russia? Because he thought that the allies would leave him alone if he did that—well, they didn't; they remained true to their agreement and they became allies with the Soviet Union. But what you're ignoring again is the other side of the impression that he gets that you won't fight under any circumstances. With the Japanese and the bombing of Pearl Harbor, when the war was over, our leading military figures, the men who could now talk to their counterparts in Japan, said to them, "Why Pearl Harbor?" The Japanese said, "Why not Pearl Harbor?" They said, "You held your largest military maneuvers in your history in Louisiana, the Louisiana maneuvers, your soldiers carried wooden guns and you used cardboard tanks to simulate armored warfare, armored forces." They said, "We didn't think you'd fight." Now, am I a warmonger or am I for peace when I say that after two wars and then there's Korea in which a Secretary of State gave a perimeter and said here is the line of our interest, perimeter of the Pacific, and let Korea outside that perimeter and we had 40,000 men occupying Korea at the time, almost driven into the ocean by the attack of the North Koreans without warning, when they crossed the line and attacked. Now there's three. Is a person really a warmonger for saying, "Look, the answer is to never let an enemy believe that you lack the will to defend, that there is a point beyond which you will not buy peace, you will not buy it at any price, and that is slavery or humiliation." I'm not a warmonger, I say that we are going into a war if a man like Carter continues giving the wrong signals, backing away from the Soviet Union. We will one day find ourselves pushed to the point where there is no retreat and we have no further choice.

SCHEER: But do we ever make mistakes? I mean, for instance, I would have thought fifty years ago, with the Red Chinese, the Chi Coms would be against the Russians. Do we make errors, do we make mistakes?

REAGAN: Well, I think we made a mistake in falling in with the Communists at that time, and undercutting Chiang Kai-shek in mainland China and making them flee to Taiwan.

SCHEER: But now those very same Communists are the most anti-Soviet people in the world.

REAGAN: Ah, and we're trying to promote and hope that they stay that way.

SCHEER: They're probably stronger against Russia than Chiang Kai-shek would have been . . . You don't think that any big errors have been made on the other side of the fence—I don't mean the Taiwan betrayal. I mean, do you think any errors have been made being too strong?

REAGAN: No, as a matter of fact, some of the errors that have been made on our side, there's a book called *Command Decision*, and I think everyone ought to read it, because it shows the number of times in which we overestimated the Germans and did not take the actions we could have taken. How many people know that—we had such an awe of the Wehrmacht, the great German military force, that it was invincible. How many people know that the Germans actually sent soldiers to the Russian front in summer uniforms, that they had a drive in Berlin asking women to contribute fur coats to send to the troops on the Russian front? How many people know many other times when the Germans had a very . . . Well, do you remember the Cold War? Not the Cold War that we talk about with the Russians—where the term was first used, the fake war when the Germans first made their great attack and then stopped and for about a year nothing happened on the western front. Do you know that if the French and the British had advanced at that point, they could have gone right to Berlin because the Germans had now, having done what they wanted to do, had now used kind of militia-type troops on that front and had a very thin line and were not able—and we didn't make that decision that should have been made. But all I'm trying to say is I don't know of any country that has gotten into war by being too strong, unless it was an aggressive nation that set out to be an aggressor, but a nation defending itself.

SCHEER: . . . Why do you want to be President?

REAGAN: . . . It isn't any easy question to answer, because I don't know about other people. There is a side of being President that I don't like at all. You give up, for the rest of your life, a privacy for yourself and your family—your whole family is sacrificed to that too. I certainly don't like it for the idea of living in the White House and any ideas of glory or being well-known or famous or anything of the kind, maybe because I've been in an occupation where you have something of that kind already. But I just happen to believe that circumstances, circumstances that I never anticipated, because I was dragged kicking and screaming into running for governor, I never really wanted ever to be in government office or political office.

SCHEER: But what's the mission?

REAGAN: Maybe those circumstances, the experience that I had, has made me believe that I can do what needs to be done.

SCHEER: Would you turn the clock back to the fifties?

REAGAN: It isn't a case of turning the clock back. Well, maybe in one sense, but then you have to go back beyond the fifties.

SCHEER: Where would you turn it back to—the thirties, the twenties?

REAGAN: One thing is that I believe the American people have the greatest capacity for great deeds of any people on earth. Pope Pius XII —and I'm a Protestant—Pope Pius XII, at the end of World War II, when the Soviet Union—when it looked as if the world might go into a thousand years of darkness—Pope Pius XII said, "The American people have a great genius and capacity for performing great and generous deeds. Into the hands of America, God has placed an afflicted mankind." I want to see—I want to help get us back to those fiercely independent Americans, those people that can do those great deeds, and I've seen them robbed of their independence, I've seen them become more and more dependent on government because of these great social reforms. And I believe in their greatness and I believe that this country has a destiny.

Bush Interview

I interviewed George Bush during December 1979 and January 1980 on his campaign plane when he was running for the Republican party presidential nomination. Excerpts from the interview, a longer version of which appeared in the *Los Angeles Times* on January 24, 1980, are included below.

SCHEER: What changes could one expect in a Bush budget?

BUSH: Generally speaking, President Carter was wrong to knock out of the [Gerald R.] Ford budget the main things he did, which were the MX [missile], the manned bomber and the naval improvement—many of which he wakes up three years later and feels he now must restore.

SCHEER: Don't you reach a point with these strategic weapons where we can wipe each other out so many times and no one wants to use them or be willing to use them, that it really doesn't matter whether you're 10 percent or 2 percent lower or higher?

BUSH: Yes, if you believe there is no such thing as a winner in a nuclear exchange, that argument makes a little sense. I don't believe that.

SCHEER: How do you win in a nuclear exchange?

BUSH: You have a survivability of command and control, survivability of industrial potential, protection of a percentage of your citizens, and you have a capability that inflicts more damage on the opposition than it can inflict upon you. That's the way you can have a winner, and the

Soviets' planning is based on the ugly concept of a winner in a nuclear exchange.

SCHEER: Do you mean 5 percent would survive? Two per cent?

BUSH: More than that—if everybody fired everything he had, you'd have more than that survive.

SCHEER: So have we made a mistake, then, in not thinking of nuclear war as a possible option that we could survive?

BUSH: Our strategic forces should be considered a deterrent, and that is the way I'd do it, and I think I would be able to—if we did what we needed to do to be sure the trend that set in doesn't continue, the trend that makes them superior—I think what I'd be able to do would be to push away, plug away and negotiate a reduction that can be verified.

SCHEER: What is the connection between the possession of an MX missile system and being able to do something about problems like Afghanistan or Iran?

BUSH: The direct linkage is rather remote, but in the overall linkage, as long as the United States is perceived to not be slipping behind the Soviets in strategic forces, the Soviets will be constrained from adventure.

SCHEER: They were weaker in '68 than they are now.

BUSH: Much weaker.

SCHEER: In '68 they invaded Czechoslovakia. That was adventurism.

BUSH: But it doesn't follow that therefore if we're weaker, that will constrain adventure. They're stronger today and they invaded Afghanistan.

SCHEER: Yes, but in the late forties, we were the only one who had nuclear weapons. Our superiority was total and awesome. It didn't stop the Soviets in Berlin, [or] from the Korean War. Aren't your ideas a throwback to the old massive retaliation position of John Foster Dulles?

BUSH: I'm going back to the fact that the United States should not be inferior to the Soviet Union in strategic balance.

SCHEER: Going back to the criticism of massive retaliation, perhaps a huge MX missile system costing $55 billion would have no effect whatsoever on one's ability to intervene.

BUSH: See, what the MX does is give you an ability to retaliate against hardened sites, and does not make the President have the choice of killing people. That is the key to an MX system, because without a platform of that nature you are not going to be able to retaliate against their hardened sites. And the President's choice would be at that time, if our retaliatory capacity were knocked out, his choice would be, "Sir, our retaliatory capabilities have been knocked out, but good news for you, we still have the Polaris boats, and you can destroy a third of Leningrad and a third of Moscow. Bad news, sir, is they can wipe out, because of their SS-18s, two thirds of Washington," etc. A President shouldn't be faced with only that kind of choice.

SCHEER: You were critical of the return of the canal to Panama.

BUSH: Yes, I was critical of it.

SCHEER: Do you still remain a critic?

BUSH: Yes, I think particularly at this time. I think one of our big problems is that our foreign policy is viewed as retreating and pulling back and unwilling to keep commitments. And my concern with the Panama solution was not the desire to make a change that would take care of the so-called colonial problem—that I can understand—but rather the overall view that as we did this, as we made the deal we did, that it added to the perception that the United States was going to pull back, unwilling to keep commitments.

SCHEER: But, in fact, since we've done this, the government of Panama has seemed to be a strong ally of ours, they've accepted the Shah, took him off our hands. Has it really weakened the United States?

BUSH: The jury is still out.

SCHEER: Right now it would be fair to say that, in fact, they've assisted us in a very major way by taking the Shah, haven't they? It got the Carter government off the hook on that one.

BUSH: It was a helpful step, yes.

SCHEER: One of the questions that was asked at the Iowa debate, was, was there anything politically that you would take back, and I thought the answers were quite weak.

BUSH: You're in a political campaign. Who wants to point out his weaknesses? I mean, I thought the question was quite dumb in terms of everybody making a confession to Mary McGrory about one's weaknesses. What kind of idiot is going to answer the question—"Wait a minute, these five things show that I've been wrong." Come on.

SCHEER: Could you summarize your differences with Carter on foreign policy?

BUSH: Well, I think Jimmy Carter sees the world as he wishes it were, not as it is, and thus when he came in and cut way back on many of the things that the Ford budgets had projected in terms of defense, he sent out a signal around the world that caused concern among some of our allies. I think he's—I can say this with the advantage of hindsight

—that we made a mistake when we sent out a signal that we were going to pull out our troops from Korea, and then some of our allies and others begin to worry, "What commitments will the United States keep?" I think when we normalize relations with China on their terms and their terms alone, we further enhance the image of a country that was really not prepared to keep its commitments. I think when we indicated that Cubans were in Africa as a stabilizing influence, people around the world must have looked at us like we were nuts in foreign policy. Eventually, that statement was not permitted to stand, but it stood too long in my view before it was slapped down by the President. I think if we let our human rights policy appear to override everything, including our strategic interests, that the policy is wrong. Our application has often been selective, hypocritically so, in my view: Slap around Argentina and Brazil and move closer to Castro. I remember Mrs. Carter going down and meeting with the dissidents in Brazil. What would we have thought if Brazil's president's wife had come up and met with the person who bombed the laboratory in Madison, Wisconsin? I don't think we'd like that.

SCHEER: Do you feel it's comparable?

BUSH: I do, I do feel it's comparable.

SCHEER: That dissidents in Brazil have the same avenues for peaceful protests as dissidents in the U.S.?

BUSH: No, I don't think they have.

SCHEER: How is it a comparable situation?

BUSH: One has violated the laws of the country and so have some of the others—I don't believe that you can go out there and take the law into your own hands as guerrillas in Brazil and Argentina . . . do they overreact? Yes, but I just wouldn't use that style of diplomacy.

SCHEER: I don't understand—you don't believe it's over . . .

BUSH: Print it the way I've said it and you'll understand it, read it.

SCHEER: Take Hungary, in 1956, the people resisted the Soviets, the freedom fighters—you would say they should not have been supported? They took the law into their own hands?

BUSH: That's not what I said—I told you what I said.

SCHEER: You don't think that's an example of people taking the law into their own hands?

BUSH: I think that was an effort to overthrow a totalitarian regime that had violated everything in human rights. Certainly the difference between me and some others is that I see areas of gray, I don't think everything is pure and impure, and I think we have been hypocritically selective in our indignation on human rights, and have diminished our strategic interests in the process. That's what I believe.

SCHEER: What is your Mideast plan?

BUSH: We should improve relations with the moderate Arab countries without diminishing our commitment to Israel. My view is it should not be thrown up for negotiation—in other words, we must never have the perception as a country of being willing to trade off an ally, which is a moral and strategic alliance, for a hoped-for economic gain.

SCHEER: Do you feel in your reading of the Camp David accords that there was a commitment to a Palestinian state?

BUSH: Solution to the Palestinian question, yes.

SCHEER: Do you have any criticisms whatsoever of either the Begin or the Sadat governments in this process?

BUSH: Yeah—I've been critical of the settlements—you know, the advance in moving forward, for example, in settlements by Begin's government and Sadat . . .

SCHEER: Could you be more explicit?

BUSH: No I couldn't. I've given you that and that's all I'll give you.

York Interview

In April 1982, I interviewed Herbert York in Los Angeles, California. Dr. York was director of Lawrence Livermore Laboratory from 1952 to 1958, and Ambassador to the Comprehensive Test Ban Negotiations in Geneva from 1979 to 1981. Dr. York is now the director of the program in science, technology and public affairs at the University of California, San Diego. Excerpts from the interview are included below.

SCHEER: Do you agree with the notion that the United States has unilaterally disarmed over the last decade?

YORK: I don't believe it is true that we unilaterally disarmed. We did practice some unilateral restraints but I believe the reasons for those restraints were essentially budgetary and not for some doctrinaire or ideological reasons. There are things we could have done and didn't do but as far as I know, in every case the reason for not doing them was a combination of budgetary reasons reinforced by the fact that there was no good reason for doing it.

Throughout this period, most of our Presidents have taken the attitude when they've become President and really seen what the situation is, that my God, this is awful, these forces are just simply beyond belief, beyond what is necessary; they haven't been able to cut them back for practical political reasons but they have held them constant.

SCHEER: Do you think that the Soviets betrayed the spirit of détente?

YORK: No, not any differently than we did. On both sides there has always been a tendency to look for loopholes, to skate close to the edge and fully exploit what is allowed. And in the case of the Soviets, SALT I gave them really a fairly generous deal. It was plausible but it also was generous, that is, it allowed them to finish everything they were building and that's what they did. One can argue that we were too generous, that the deal was too generous, but I don't think you can argue that they took an unfair advantage of it.

SCHEER: For the layman, what you've just said . . . is totally at odds with conventional wisdom.

YORK: It's at odds with the common wisdom as based on the claims of the Administration and the standard claims of some people who prepared the way for this demonstration, that is to say, the Committee on the Present Danger, which had some pretty propagandists.

SCHEER: Is this an area where it's possible for reasonable men to disagree, or has there been distortion—

YORK: . . . to some degree it is possible for reasonable men to disagree because the question of what you ought to count when you rate a balance—how much weight to put on megatons, how much weight to put on individual warheads—that has something to do with how you see the balance and there is a certain arbitrariness there, therefore, a certain room to disagree. But by and large it is a distortion and a distortion, in turn, is based partly on the fact that many of the so-called experts in this field simply do not know the history . . . it's in part faulty memory, in part bad history, and in part reliance on folk history instead of real history, and in part wishful thinking—it's all those sort of wishy-washy wrong things more than it is deliberate deception.

. . . The great majority of the strategic community get their pay from the military and not from somewhere else. Mostly they are either in think tanks or, if they're in universities, they're frequently senior consultants, or they're people hoping to get in on the next Administration or something. But most of the people you call strategic thinkers these days are actually employees of either think tanks or even defense industries whose livelihood does, indeed, depend on their good relations with the people in the Pentagon who, by and large, are hawks and who—whenever there is room for doubt—always come down with one particular kind of doubt. But if there's room to make some kind of judgment, the judgment they will make will be the one that favors doing something. And as these people, for whatever reason, have become more and more convinced there was a problem, they have tended to become more strident and to exaggerate their views in order to persuade the public there's a problem. And in doing so, they've even persuaded each other. Also, there are some underlying unpleasant truths. For example, it's a fact that in the sixties we had a huge advantage in all these—take any parameter to measure the strategic balance, we had a big advantage. Somewhere along in the seventies, we lost that advantage. That is not a good thing. It's better to have a balance in your favor than to have just a plain old everyday balance, so in part it's a reaction against the fact that the Russians have caught up and that, in turn, has produced a rhetoric designed to persuade the American people there's something bad that has to be fixed and the people believe their own rhetoric . . . Most of the people who work full time on arms control issues or nearly full time are also people paid by the defense establishment. The number of people who work on arms control issues and who are paid by sources which are entirely independent of the defense establishment are only a small minority of all the people who work on arms control issues.

What happened is that with the creation of ACDA and the institutionalization of a set of opportunities to work on arms control with government sponsorship, the other agencies of government—the Pentagon, the various sub-units of the Pentagon which service it, their major contractors, and then also the Department of Energy, which is where all the nuclear weapons are—all of those people began to work on arms control, mainly, though not entirely, in a defensive mode. I mean, they figured they'd better understand all this. Now, the reason they wanted to understand it is that they wanted to be able to talk back and win an argument with this strange new breed of people. So I can't give you a figure and I can't give you a solid basis for this; it really is sort of a general perception based on a lot of anecdotal observations, but the overwhelming majority of even the people who consider themselves as working primarily on arms control are paid by the defense side of the house, not some other way. These (defense-sponsored) arms control experts are mainly people whose predispositions range from barely tolerant to extremely hostile. If you take the general defense analysts, not just the arms control analysts, the situation is even more so. No one realizes how many people there are in the think tanks, either organizations which are overtly think tanks, but also the big companies have them—T. K. Jones, for example, comes from Boeing . . .

SCHEER: Among Establishment people like yourself and McNamara, there is a sense of alarm.

YORK: . . . The point is that when you get high enough in this sort of thing . . . and when you get to the point where you can, indeed, see the big picture, you discover that (and you get convinced that) the way we're going is wrong, it cannot lead to a good end . . . There are many people like that who, when they got in a situation where they could see everything and not just selected parts of it, and where they had full access to the intelligence instead of just what somebody wanted them to know, found that the picture is different from what they saw when they were middle-level experts. So it's no surprise to me that people like McNamara and Bundy, Harold Brown, myself and others, as well as a whole string of Presidents, with the possible exception of this one, come out with different view than they had when they went in.

It's amazing to actually be really briefed on the SIOP [Single Integrated Operational Plan] instead of just talk about it—go to Omaha and they tell you what it is, it's amazing. What the plan calls for is, not to exaggerate—the strip-mining of the Soviet Union.

SCHEER: You mean after their first strike?

YORK: Yeah, whatever.

SCHEER: What about the President's statement that the Soviet Union could absorb our retaliatory blow and hit us again?

YORK: Well, he himself doesn't know anything about it. It's what somebody told him, and I don't know who told him. There are a series of scenarios that artificially break down what would happen into first we do this, then they do that, then we do this. It's kind of an artificial sequence invented solely for the purpose of being able to make some calculations. There's no reason to believe that any of those things will happen that way.

What's going on right now is that the crazier analysts have risen to higher positions than is normally the case. They are able to carry their ideas further and higher because the people at the top are simply less well-informed than is normally the case. Neither the current President nor his immediate backers in the White House nor the current Secretary of Defense have any experience with these things, so when the ideologues come in with their fancy stories and with their selected intelligence data, the President and the Secretary of Defense believe the last glib person who talked to them.

SCHEER: From the right.

YORK: That's the only people they talk to. They don't have a basis for forming even a rudimentary judgment in which to place a new fact that Richard Perle or somebody else comes in with . . .

SCHEER: Most Americans have heard this thing about the Soviet buildup and about the window of vulnerability and so on.

YORK: It's a big exaggeration and it's a big rationalization. The people, for instance, who make up the Committee on the Present Danger are genuinely concerned about the fact that the Soviets have, in truth, caught up. That's bad enough. In addition, they feel that the American people should be responding to that more vigorously than they are. There's enough ambiguity so that it's easy to convince yourself that parity is not parity but superiority—marginal superiority perhaps, but nevertheless superiority on their side, and if your job is to convince the public of that to get proper support, to get people in the right mood, it's easy to justify a little bit of exaggeration, even beyond what you might otherwise believe. So there is an enormous amount of salesmanship going on here. But it's a mixture . . . Some people only know recent information. And there's been a certain amount of revisionist history on the right as well as the left. Revisionist historians are not always on the left.

SCHEER: Reagan has said repeatedly that we are weaker than the Russians.

YORK: He, of course, is talking about much more than just the strategic balance. He contends that we are weaker on the nuclear balance in Europe.

He probably believes that, but it's just another example of the fact that he simply doesn't know much about it and doesn't understand it. The basic situation in Europe is that there have been for a long time these SS-4s and -5s, the European capitals have, therefore, been nuclear targets for more than twenty years for very large bombs. The Russians, as a same kind of rational act of modernization that we talk about when we put in enhanced radiation weapons or when we talk about a new generation of Pershing, the Russians are modernizing that force and they're putting in the SS-20. The SS-20 is better in a number of ways and certainly is more modern . . . It's simply the language that has become customary—rather than just say buildup, it's always a "massive" buildup or an "unprecedented" buildup. Now, that's the Soviet side. There have always been these land missiles there for twenty years, they are adding some new ones. On our side, we do not have any land-based missile of corresponding range. But we have for years had at sea, in the form of so-called Polarises, long-range rockets devoted to use by NATO to hit targets in Poland and further inland, so that the targets that would be hit by the new Pershings and other things we're talking about putting in have been targeted by us for years. So all of the talk about zero options has a certain hollowness to it in that context. We frequently hear it said that we have nothing corresponding to the Soviet SS-4s, -5s and SS-20s. That's true only in the narrowest sense, that we don't have a land-based equivalent, but as I've said, we've had for a long time a sea-based equivalent to them, which is conveniently forgotten in all of these arguments . . .

SCHEER: So does the United States have to catch up with the Soviet Union or can we stop?

YORK: If you accept what I've been saying, there is no catching up to do. There is parity and, furthermore, there not only is parity, I would go further and say that if the ratio changed by a factor of two either way, there would still be parity. It isn't the kind of strategic situation —strategic nuclear balance does not depend on fine details. It only depends on fairly general questions and, right now, it is truly a good parity, a fairly accurate parity, but it could be way off and still be parity.

Bethe Interview

Nobel Prize–winning theoretical physicist Hans A. Bethe has been continuously involved with the U.S. nuclear weapons program since his participation in the Manhattan Project, which developed the first atomic bomb. Bethe, a refugee from Nazi Germany, was the chief of the Theoretical Physics Division of the Los Alamos Scientific Laboratory during the war years and later returned to the laboratory to work on the development of the hydrogen bomb. From 1959 to 1969 Bethe served as a member of the President's Science Advisory Committee. He continued as a consultant to the U.S. government on nuclear weapons during the Carter years. Bethe is now a professor at Cornell University. The following interview was published in the *Los Angeles Times* on April 11, 1982.

SCHEER: Do you agree with the Reagan Administration that we need more nuclear weapons to counter the Soviet threat?

BETHE: I would like to state that there is no deficiency in armaments in the United States, that we don't need to catch up to the Russians, that, if anything, the Russians have to catch up to us. The Russians have their forces mostly in ICBMs [intercontinental ballistic missiles], a type of weapon that is becoming more and more vulnerable. I think our military people know this, but they always talk about the vulnerability of our nuclear ICBMs, and never talk about those of the Soviets.

The Russians are much more exposed to a possible first strike from us than we are to one from them.

SCHEER: Do we have the means of deterring a Soviet first strike?

BETHE: I don't think that either country is going to make a first strike, because it is absolutely crazy to do so. But suppose there were a first strike from the Russians, and suppose they could destroy all our Minuteman missiles. It wouldn't make the slightest difference. Would we be defenseless? Not at all. We have the submarine force with an enormous striking power.

SCHEER: But the submarine-launched missiles are said to lack the necessary accuracy to retaliate effectively.

BETHE: The submarine-launched missiles, the new generation, are going to be extremely accurate. President Reagan himself has said the Trident II missile will be accurate enough to hit any hard target. This is one point where I would endorse the Administration's program: we should have the most accurate missile for our submarines. Also, we have a good bomber force.

SCHEER: Yet the President refers to the bomber force of B-52s as ancient and incapable of penetrating into the Soviet Union.

BETHE: They themselves cannot penetrate Russia, either today or tomorrow, but they are getting equipped with cruise missiles. Cruise missiles are probably the most accurate weapon that has yet been invented. The Russians don't have them, and I consider them most important, just as a penetration aid for our bomber force. Our bombers don't need to penetrate the Soviet Union. It would be an unnecessary exposure. Once they have cruise missiles on board, they launch them from outside the Soviet Union and to get, say, within 200 miles of the Soviet Union, they don't need to penetrate a screen of Russian air defenses. The cruise missiles, as you know, have devices to follow the terrain, and find their way by comparing with a map. And they are going on our bombers this year, perhaps even this month.

SCHEER: What about the general argument that the Carter Administration's policies left this country vulnerable to a Soviet attack?

BETHE: On the contrary, the most important progress in weapons in the last decade, I would say, was the cruise missile, which was developed under Carter. Now, in case of an all-out Soviet attack, of course, some of our bombers would probably be destroyed on airfields. However, a long time ago we dispersed our bombers over many, many smaller airfields so that, on warning, a lot of them will take off. And, of course, you take off those which are armed with cruise missiles before any others. I don't see that there is any cause for us to be alarmed by the possibility of a major Soviet attack.

SCHEER: So what is this emphasis on U.S. weakness all about?

BETHE: I believe we are repeating the mistake of 1960 when people talked about the missile gap. The missile gap did, in fact, exist, but it was the other way around. We had lots of missiles and the Russians didn't. It took the Russians a decade before they caught up with us, and even then their missiles were not as good as ours because they largely used liquid missile propellant, whereas we went to solid propellant in the 1960s. I believe we have repeated the missile gap story once more, and it is just as wrong today as it was in 1960.

SCHEER: But what about these statements that President Reagan and others make that the Soviets have just undertaken the "most unrelenting military buildup in the history of the world"?

BETHE: That is true, they have kept building missiles, constantly, and in tremendous number, and in much larger numbers than makes any sense. Why? Chiefly, they wanted to catch up with us. Now they have more missiles than we, but in general the numbers are very comparable in the Soviet arsenal and in ours. Both are close to the ceiling permitted by SALT II [Strategic Arms Limitation Treaty]. The only way to ensure that they don't surpass us is to have an arms control agreement.

Actually, ours is a much better arsenal because our forces are better distributed. Less than half our missiles are ICBMs, a weapon, as I said before, which is getting vulnerable; we have 1050, they have 1400. In submarines, while the numbers are about the same, we have more serviceable ones. Then we have the bombers which, together with the cruise missiles, are a formidable force, while they have not paid any attention to their bombers at all. Most of their bombers are propeller-driven, totally obsolete, and without penetration aids; you can write them off. Yes, the Russians have built, unrelentingly, more and more missiles. There is no question—but it is irrelevant.

One more point on that. The SALT agreements are very much to our advantage because they limit the number, on which the Russians are very good, and they don't limit the technology, on which we are very good. So we can put the most sophisticated technology into the given number of missiles, which is what we have done in the case of the cruise missile, for instance.

SCHEER: One justification of the arms race is that the Soviets are aiming at gaining the capability to win a nuclear war.

BETHE: I quite believe that we could win an arms race. But it is, of course, absolutely crazy to think of winning a nuclear war. You cannot win a nuclear war, neither they nor we, even if some fraction of the population might survive. The Russians are very cautious, so they will not risk starting a nuclear war. They have publicly stated that they want arms control, and probably we could get arms control more easily from them now than ever before. I don't think we were doing badly before. I think SALT I was excellent, and SALT II was good, though not excellent. In my opinion, we could get a lot of agreements from them, but our negotiators have to be willing to negotiate, which means to make concessions. There was the Russian proposal of a two-thirds cutback [in Europe]; instead of rejecting it out of hand, I think what we should have done is to say, "This is a possible negotiating position, now let's talk. Just how do we specify that cutback? What do we do about missiles, what do we do about your SS-20, what do we do about planes carrying nuclear weapons? Could we agree, perhaps, that this be a first step, and that further steps are to follow which would make us free of missiles in Europe?" But instead of accepting it as a basis for negotiations, we said, "No, that's impossible." I think that way you don't get an agreement.

SCHEER: What do you make of the decision to build the MX missile?

BETHE: The MX is a first-strike weapon. It makes no sense in any other way. The MX has extremely good accuracy. I want to give President Reagan credit for abolishing that completely crazy shell game which Carter and [former Secretary of Defense Harold] Brown had proposed. I think that was out of this world. Instead, Reagan proposes, "Let's develop the MX and, in the meantime, let the Pentagon think where to deploy it. They will probably find some way to do it." It would have been politically impossible to say immediately, "Let's not develop the MX at all." Maybe in three years the Pentagon will not have come up with any good method of deployment, and then they can say, "All right, we give it up."

One other point concerning arms control. I think it is just paradoxical to build up your weapons and then have arms control. Any weapons buildup on our part is only an incentive to the Russians to do the same. So if we want reduction in armaments, let's reduce from our present position. But negotiations are always a lengthy affair. Perhaps a challenge would be a quicker way to get results. Professor [Robert F.] Bacher of Caltech and George Kennan of Princeton have, therefore, proposed a series of small steps: We reduce the number of our weapons by, let us say, 5 percent, and challenge the Russians to do likewise. If they don't we go no further. If they do, we continue and perhaps a new spirit grows.

SCHEER: We talked before about how you cannot win or survive a nuclear war. What do you make of the view of, say, Edward Teller, who believes that you can? Do you meet with Teller?

BETHE: I meet Teller from time to time. I agree with Teller on the matter of nuclear electric power generation, which is a totally different subject from nuclear weapons. One of the things I wish you would emphasize from time to time in your writings is that the two things have very little to do with each other. They have less to do with each other than dynamite for mining purposes and explosives in conventional bombs. So Teller and I agree on the need for energy, including nuclear energy, but we don't talk about military matters. I did, at one time—it must have been two years ago; I listened to him about some of the specific military equipment that he advocated, just in order to learn not to argue and when it comes to matters like surviving a nuclear war, we agree not to discuss it.

SCHEER: How is it that there is a disagreement about the presumably objective scientific question of whether or not we can survive a nuclear war?

BETHE: I think there are many different ways you can understand the word "survival." Surely, if the attack were limited to ICBMs even though fallout spread across the country, without an attack on cities the country would survive, there is no question about that. There would be lots of casualties, but recovery would be entirely possible, and might even be fairly quick. But if you talk about an all-out nuclear war, with attacks on industry and attacks on cities and so on, then I would think that, while there will be survivors, the United States as a functioning society would not survive. Such an attack, it has been estimated by the Defense Department, could mean 100 million casualties, but that doesn't fully describe it. The important thing is the aftereffect.

For instance, there would almost certainly be a total breakdown of transportation. Everything in the country depends on transportation. Once many highways and railroad beds are made into rubble and the remaining highways are so radioactive that no truck driver will go on them, you cannot bring food to the cities. Nor can you bring fertilizer to the farms, nor energy to either place. I simply cannot understand how anybody can believe that we can recover from that in any short order.

One of the great mistakes that most people make when they talk against nuclear war is that they put the emphasis on radioactivity. That isn't the worst part. It may be the most widely spread effect, but it is not the worst part. The worst part is the death of people by third-degree burns, and that there is no possible medical help for them. We must expect that many of the explosions would be set off in the air, not on the ground. Heat radiation from the fireball, that is infrared rays and even visible light, is enormous. It increases faster than the area of destruction by blast, so most of the death would come from this source. Many people would be burned directly. Many people would get third-degree burns, and you cannot save a person like that if you don't bring medical help immediately. There will be no medical help because hospitals will be destroyed along with other buildings.

However, that is not the end of it. The thermal radiation sets newspapers on fire, even stacked newspaper. It sets wooden buildings on fire. So even if people are inside the normal kind of houses that we have in this country, which are mainly built of wood, they will burn up inside the house. If they go outside the house, they will burn up directly. The next thing, of course, is buildings collapsing by blast and burying people. If you talk about a large city with office buildings, people can go into shelters in the cellar but, in the meantime, the building above them will collapse or, at least, there will be yard-deep layers of shattered glass. How will they ever get out? Even if they get out, the heat radiation will cause fires all over the place, and many secondary fires, because blast will destroy gas lines and the gas will begin to burn. It is not certain but there is a high possibility that these fires will cause a so-called fire storm, which means the fire consumes all oxygen, and the people down in the shelter will not get any oxygen. So I think that protection of the city population by shelters is totally futile if you have a direct attack on the city. Let me add here that I do not think that even an all-out nuclear war would destroy all life on earth.

SCHEER: How do you feel, I mean you've been with this issue, with this bomb, for such a long time, and then one day you pick up the newspaper and some person says we can recover from general nuclear war in two to four years. What are your thoughts?

BETHE: Anyone who says we can recover from nuclear war in two to four years is crazy.

SCHEER: What about the clock on the cover of the *Bulletin of the Atomic Scientists* showing how close we are to midnight? Are we now in a more dangerous moment? What has happened to our thinking?

BETHE: The main increase of danger, in my opinion, is psychological.

People are scared when the Reagan government says we are in mortal danger and need to increase our armaments. But I am scared when he claims that more arms, especially nuclear ones, can protect us. It creates a war psychology. Human beings who are very scared don't act rationally. My greatest fear is that it will make the American people less rational, and then anything can happen. Many of the wars in history have happened because of fear. If there comes an all-out nuclear war, I think it will come because of fear. I believe that in this respect Franklin Roosevelt is right again: we have nothing to fear but fear itself. In my opinion, we have nothing to fear from the Russians, nor the Russians from us, but fear itself, namely the fear that each country creates about the other.

SCHEER: Did you think at the time of the atomic bomb's discovery that we would be here now?

BETHE: No. I was very much afraid in 1946. My wife and I discussed this matter and concluded that probably within ten years there would be a nuclear war. That has not happened and it is a ray of hope. It has not happened because the statesmen, both in this country and in the Soviet Union, have clearly recognized that nuclear war is unthinkable. It is impossible, it would make such destruction that we have to use every means to avoid it. This realization seems to have escaped the present government. I think the real danger lies in this loss of understanding. Until the end of the Carter Administration, whether the President was Republican or Democrat, it was a generally recognized principle: Nuclear war must be avoided by all means. We are now told that this is not so. So here is a psychological difference. I think it is traditional, and therefore perfectly legitimate, if you want to win an election, to play up the relative armaments of the United States and the Soviet Union; that is good election propaganda. But once you are the government, you must not make this primitive approach the basis of your military and foreign policy. That is very dangerous.

SCHEER: We've all read about [Dr. J. Robert] Oppenheimer and his feelings of guilt. What can you add to that? You've been intimately connected with this for much of your life.

BETHE: Having worked on the weapon does not give me a monopoly on deciding. All I can do is to try to tell people what I think about nuclear weapons, and I will continue to do so as long as they let me. The decision has to be made by the government . . .

A single missile will destroy a city without having any soldier putting his life on the line. We have some 9,000 strategic weapons. Every one of them is bigger than the Hiroshima bomb. The Russians have a similar force. After hitting military targets, if you direct the remaining weapons against cities, you can destroy at least 5,000 cities of over 100,000—there are maybe 200 of those in each country. Why would you need more than 200 weapons?

Warfare has become totally different because the destructive power is greater than the totality of the things you can destroy. That has never happened before . . . The destruction can happen in an hour or two, instead of in five years. If it happens over five years, you can recover in part, again and again, you can adjust to it, you can bring help to the city which has been hit. If in two hours all our cities are destroyed, no help can be brought. That is not a difference in size but a difference in kind. Against missiles there is no defense. This is a subject on which I worked quite carefully and industriously for many years before '68, looking at many ways how to tell decoys from missiles, and so on. Whatever you did, the offense could always fool the defense and could do it better. So antiballistic missiles for city defense are technically nonsense.

Let me come back to the question of survival once more. If there is an all-out attack on the Soviet Union and the United States, there will afterwards be no United States nor a Soviet Union.

Index

About the Author

ROBERT SCHEER was born in the Bronx, New York, on April 4, 1936. He attended City College in New York and did graduate work in economics and Chinese studies at the University of California at Berkeley, where he was a fellow at the Center for Chinese Studies. Scheer has taught at City College, Antioch, and Berkeley. He was managing editor and later editor-in-chief of *Ramparts* (1964–1969); he was also an editor of *New Times*. Scheer has written extensively for *Playboy* and *Esquire* magazines. In 1975 and 1976 he appeared regularly on *Good Morning, America*. He has been a national correspondent for the *Los Angeles Times* since 1976. In 1980 he was a Pointer Fellow in Journalism at Yale.